PROCESSIVE REVELATION

ALSO BY BENJAMIN A. REIST

A Reading of Calvin's Institutes

PROCESSIVE
REVELATION

BENJAMIN A. REIST

WESTMINSTER/JOHN KNOX PRESS
LOUISVILLE, KENTUCKY

Book design by Kevin Raquepaw

First edition

Published by Westminster/John Knox Press
Louisville, Kentucky

This book is printed on acid-free paper that meets the American National Standards Institute Z39.48 standard.

PRINTED IN THE UNITED STATES OF AMERICA
9 8 7 6 5 4 3 2 1

Library of Congress Cataloging-in-Publication Data

Reist, Benjamin A.
    Processive revelation / Benjamin A. Reist. — 1st ed.
        p.   cm.
    Includes bibliographical references and index.
    ISBN 0-664-21955-1 (alk. paper)

    1. Theology—Methodology.   2. Revelation.   3. Christianity and culture.   4. Process theology.   5. Theology, Doctrinal.   I. Title.
BR118.R44 1992
230'.046—dc20   91-38570

To

PAUL LEHMANN

Teacher, Mentor, Friend

CONTENTS

CONTENTS

PREFACE

Early in 1973 I came across Ian Barbour's *Science and Religion: New Perspectives on the Dialogue* (1968). This encounter was soon coupled with a close reading of Joseph Sittler's *Essays on Nature and Grace* (1972). These two works had a tremendous impact on my reflections. This marked the beginnings of the expansion of my long-standing concern for theology under the influence of theological ethics to an inclusion of all that has been happening in the development of what is now known as postmodern science. Somewhere early in that process I became convinced that the developments on the front of the contextualization of theology, particularly as we know them now in the theologies of liberation and the emergence of a new era in the relationship between theology and the natural sciences, must be understood together. The present study is the result of that deepening and expanding concern.

Some of my thinking along the way has been published in the preliminary form of journal articles. In 1986, my colleagues in the Graduate Theological Union (GTU) honored me with the invitation to deliver the annual GTU faculty lecture that year. This lecture, "Dogmatics in Process," epitomized the book that was then taking shape and now reaches its present form. The third section of Chapter 1, "The Expansion of Contextual Theology: Theology and Postmodern Science," is an adaptation of a discussion of "New Theological Horizons in the Light of Postmodern Science" (1985). Two articles, "Faith and the Natural Sciences: Focus on the Thought of Michael Polanyi" (1983) and "Ricoeur for Preachers" (1983), plus an unpublished paper delivered to the Pacific Coast Theological Society in April 1985, "Theology and Philosophy in the Thought of Paul Ricoeur," form the background out of which the second and third parts of Chapter 4 ("Discovery and Interpretation," "Heuristic Theology") have emerged. The first section of that same chapter, "Theology and Biology," is a slightly adapted form of a paper under that title prepared for a consultation of the Presbyterian Church (U.S.A.) in 1987 on "The Church and Contemporary Cosmology," the proceedings of which are published under that title.

The integration of these lines of reflection has been under way in my GTU seminar, "Theology in Process Modes of Thought." Prolonged attention to the thought of Alfred North Whitehead has played a major role in that seminar, and this work informs the perspective in operation here. I am increasingly aware, however, that Troeltsch, Bonhoeffer, and Lehmann play equally significant roles in my attempt to come to terms with this way of thinking, and that Polanyi and Ricoeur, as I read them, are as decisive as Whitehead for my emerging, tentative conclusions. Even more significant are the indelible marks on my theological work resulting from the fact that my apprenticeship in teaching included courses on the Old Testament and the Synoptic Gospels during my years as an instructor at Wellesley College. I did not know that becoming so imbued with the relational thought of the Bible was making a process thinker of me even before I knew and used these terms.

The discussion of Calvin, in the first part of Chapter 2 ("Calvin's Shift"), is adapted from my commentary A Reading of Calvin's "Institutes" (1991). The line from Calvin to Barth on the doctrine of election has been for several years the central focus of my GTU seminar on Calvin and Barth and reaches completely written form for the first time here.

I have received much encouragement and insight from my colleague in the Graduate Theological Union, Professor Charles McCoy, of the Pacific School of Religion. Twice we taught together a seminar on the thought of Michael Polanyi, and in the fall of 1988 he joined me in an adaptation of my process seminar, which we entitled "Theology and Ethics in Process." Many of the points I develop in this discussion first emerged in conversation with McCoy, and I am sure that the present state of my reflections owes much to his resonating lines of thought. In the work of putting this book in its final form, I have been singularly blessed in having the invaluable and expert help of Harold Twiss, my editor at Westminster/John Knox Press.

As will become clear, we are now confronted with the task of developing a *theology of theologies*—a sort of meta-contextual understanding of the theologies of the contexts now converging. This will force us to see that contextual statements of theology are always also statements about statements of theology. The further we go along this route, the more we will recognize that the processive character of revelation is rooted in the processive nature of God. Given the gospel, perhaps we should have realized this long ago. And yet it is equally possible that we could not have known it until now, because both God and reflection about God only now proceed to this frontier and beyond it. That God's revelation is processive deepens the long-standing insight that serious theological reflection defies closure. All are welcome to the continuing and adventuresome tasks of moving intentionally into these realms and to discoveries yet to be made in interpreting the unfinishable gospel it is ours to proclaim.

ACKNOWLEDGMENTS

Grateful acknowledgment is made for permission to reprint the following copyrighted material:

Karl Barth, *Church Dogmatics*, II/2, ed. G. W. Bromiley and T. F. Torrance (Edinburgh: T. & T. Clark, 1957). Used by permission of T. & T. Clark.

Charles Birch, "Can Evolution Be Accounted for Solely in Terms of Mechanical Causation?" in *Mind and Nature*, ed. John B. Cobb, Jr., and David Ray Griffin (Washington, D.C.: University Press of America, 1977). Used by permission of the author.

Charles Birch, "What Does God Do in the World?" in *Union Seminary Quarterly Review* 30, nos. 2–4 (Winter–Summer 1975). Used by permission of Union Seminary Quarterly Review.

Delwin Brown, *To Set at Liberty: Christian Faith and Human Freedom* (Maryknoll, N.Y.: Orbis Books, 1981). Used by permission of the author.

Sallie McFague, "Models of God for an Ecological, Evolutionary Era: God as Mother of the Universe," in *Physics, Philosophy, and Theology: A Common Quest for Understanding*, ed. Robert John Russell; William R. Stoeger, S.J.; and George V. Coyne, S.J. (Vatican City State: Vatican Observatory, 1988), 249–271. Copyright © 1988 by Vatican Observatory. Reprinted by permission of University of Notre Dame Press.

John T. McNeill, ed., and Ford Lewis Battles, trans., *John Calvin: Institutes of the Christian Religion*, vols. 20 and 21 of the Library of Christian Classics (Philadelphia: Westminster Press, 1960). Copyright © 1960 W. L. Jenkins. Used by permission of Westminster/John Knox Press, Louisville, Ky.

Heinz R. Pagels, *The Cosmic Code: Quantum Physics as the Language of Nature* (New York: Simon & Schuster, 1982). Copyright © 1982 by Heinz R. Pagels. Reprinted by permission of Simon & Schuster, Inc., and John Brockman, Associates.

Michael Polyani, *Personal Knowledge: Towards a Post-Critical Philosophy* (Chicago: University of Chicago Press, 1962). Used by permission of University of Chicago Press. © Copyright 1958, 1962 by Michael Polyani.

Benjamin Reist, "Faith and the Natural Sciences: Focus on the Thought of Michael Polyani," in *Pacific Theological Review* 16, no. 3 (Spring 1983); and "New Theological Horizons in the Light of Post-Modern Science," in *Pacific Theological Review* 18, no. 3 (Spring 1985). Used by permission of *Pacific Theological Review*.

Benjamin Reist, "'Ricoeur for Preachers," in *Homiletic* 8, no. 2 (1983). Used by permission of the journal.

Benjamin Reist, "Theology and Biology," reprinted from *The Church and Contemporary Cosmology*, edited by James B. Miller and Kenneth E. McCall, Carnegie Mellon University Press, 1990.

Paul Ricoeur, *The Conflict of Interpretations: Essays in Hermeneutics*, ed. Don Ihde (Evanston, Ill.: Northwestern University Press, 1974). Used by permission of Northwestern University Press. Copyright © 1974 by Northwestern University Press.

Paul Ricoeur, "Listening to the Parables of Jesus," in *The Philosophy of Paul Ricoeur: An Anthology of His Work*, ed. Charles E. Reagan and David Stewart (Boston: Beacon Press, 1978), 239–245. Copyright © 1978 Charles E. Reagan and David Stewart. Used by permission of Beacon Press.

ACKNOWLEDGMENTS

Juan Luis Segundo, *The Liberation of Theology*, trans. John Drury (Maryknoll, N.Y.: Orbis Books, 1976). Used by permission of Orbis Books; Gill and Macmillan Ltd. (Dublin); and Ediciones Carlos Lohle (Buenos Aires).

1

THE DYNAMICS OF

CONTEXTUAL THEOLOGY

What is the meaning of revelation? This is the question H. Richard Niebuhr posed at the outset of his most important book, one of the truly significant theological treatises from the middle decades of our century, *The Meaning of Revelation* (1941).[1] The question will always be with us. It nagged at the immensely creative Ernst Troeltsch, and under his influence Niebuhr wrestled with it too. The nature of the theological creativity of any generation will be disclosed in the manner in which it works with the issue at hand. Both Troeltsch and Niebuhr found it necessary to speak of *progressive* revelation.[2] In so doing, though neither particularly liked the term, they sought to deal with the fact that revelation is *continuous*, and thus never finished.

But there is more involved. Even Niebuhr's question will no longer suffice. How are we to understand revelation? The depths of the fascinating and awesome relationship between God and humanity can be reached only when we see that God's self-disclosure, in the midst of use, is *processive*, not progressive, in character. The issue is not simply the continuing unfolding of the implications of God's self-disclosure. Rather, it is that of coming to terms with the moving presence of *the Ultimate One's own becoming*. And it has to do with the nature of the God who knows us, and whom we know, in Jesus Christ—the God, that is, who summons our becoming in Jesus of Nazareth confessed to be the Christ, under the guidance of the Holy Spirit and witnessed in scripture.

THE RISE OF CONTEXTUAL THEOLOGY

A summons to the contextualization of theology confronts all theological reflection today. It comes from many quarters and confronts theology in all its myriad forms, in each of its traditional configurations. To suggest that this summons is being received with open arms would be misleading. The so-called theological establishment characteristically dismisses it as a fad. It is, however, a summons that cannot be evaded so easily, for this summons is too manifold in its origins and too robust in its manifestations to be deflected by such a defensive maneuver.

Liberation Theology

In the American scene—in both North and South America—this summons has taken shape in terms of the theologies of liberation. Note well that we immediately encounter the decisive fact that one must speak in the plural and refer to the theolog*ies* of liberation.

In the United States, the events generating the rise of the liberation theologies were those leading to the deepening of the civil rights movement into the full-scale black revolution of the late 1960s. Out of this deepening emerged the compelling and vigorous black theologies. Moreover, the revolution in question is not confined to the black community alone, for the black revolution generated equally comprehensive deepenings into positively celebrated ethnic self-consciousness on the part of all the components comprising the mosaic that is humanity, ethnically perceived. This has opened the way for some members of the dominating white community to discover the possibility of their own new identity—entailing and demanding a liberation from the role of the oppressor by way of full participation as one element in the mosaic. These theologies of liberation have developed in terms of the focus of oppression caught up in the struggle against *racism*.[3]

Closely attending these developments, and in some ways caused by them, has been a quantum shift in the long-standing women's movement. The black revolution paved the way for the emergence of what we now know as women's liberation. In the midst of this nexus, too, theological voices compel attention. These have set in motion the effort of breaking new paths into hitherto unrecognized terrain. They have done this so significantly that no responsible theologian, male or female, can ignore these efforts. Thus, alongside theologies of liberation forged on the anvil of the struggle against racism are those that have emerged from the crucible of *sexism*.

A third focus of the theologies of liberation is immediately apparent when one ponders the origins of the phraseology with which we began. In its current usage, the summons to the contextualization of theology epitomizes the manner in which the theologians of the oppressed throughout Central and South America—Roman Catholic and Protestant alike—confront the theological establishment of North America. The years that saw the rise of the civil rights movement and its deepening into the black revolution also saw the first successful challenging of the hegemony of the United States in the Western Hemisphere, and this occurred within one hundred miles of its own shore, in Cuba. Very significant lines of theological reflection have been part of the restive creativity that sweeps through the whole of Latin America on this side of that occurrence. One of the decisive components of this creativity has been a searching critique of the concept of development, yielding a consensus that no reduplication of the exploitative materialism of the United States can ever bring liberation to the peoples of Latin America. This critique has been informed by a robust Marxism that insists on going its own way in reckoning with colonialism and imperialism of any sort. Out of this has emerged a cluster of theologies of liberation taking shape in terms of the focus of oppression caught up in the words *classism/colonialism/imperialism*.

What is emerging from this complex dynamism is a set of theologies that intersect with each other but do not always coincide. The theologies of liberation related to each of the three foci I have noted take differing shapes and touch differing emphases. They know in common the struggle against oppression, but they do not employ identical points of departure, and they do not necessarily utilize identical methodologies. In fact, they may not even agree on the sine qua non of human liberation. What we behold, rather, are *patterns of affinity*.

The discerning of these patterns of affinity is by no means restricted to theology in the Americas. The whole world is involved in the contextualization of theology. In the midst of the vast complexities that are Africa and Asia, similar ferments of theological creativity are at hand. Some of these are clearly theologies of liberation. At the same time, some of these expressions touch other nerves, evoking a new radicalism on the front of Christianity and culture necessitating reflection in ways as yet untried. These forcefully expand the summons to the contextualization of theology by combining the motifs of the liberation theologies with the insistence on deliverance from "cultural captivity" into untried theological construction.

These developments can be expected to increase both in tempo and in productivity. The freedom that the gospel of Jesus the Christ brings cannot be forgotten once it is experienced. These new currents of reflection deny dismissal. They can only be engaged. However, the disciplining of this engagement is fraught with problems that may well have precedents but at the same time take a form that is genuinely new. These theologies are developing with explosive force *simultaneously*. Nothing less than the babel of a thousand voices will prevail unless we learn how to listen in new ways to voices that resonate with, but are not identical with, each other. We are confronted with theological creativities as perhaps has never been the case until now.

The fact is that the most dangerous enemy in reflecting on this widely varied panorama of theological effort is oversimplification. This is obvious enough in the case of those who would dismiss these voices as merely ephemeral disturbances. The real threat of oversimplification, however, lies much deeper. Pervading the entire spectrum of the theologies of liberation is the unmistakable element of confrontation. What is at stake is the wresting of the agenda of theological reflection from the hands of the establishment on the grounds that the continuation of theology in a business-as-usual mode leaves theology as the informer of oppression.

It is entirely possible to operate on the view that this process is recognizably akin to much that has transpired in the history of the Christian tradition under the banner of the search for relevance. The trouble is that to seek to reckon with what we are attempting to understand as simply a struggle for relevance assumes that the only real problem with theologies long regnant is that of their application to a seething situation. It assumes, that is, that the theologies already developed over centuries of effort are so reasonably intact that we may proceed to the question of applying their hoary insights to the varying dimensions delineating our times and places *without any alteration in the insights themselves*. On close inspection—in a manner that is now absolutely necessary, and, as we shall see, one that has been insisted upon before, though the insistence did not receive wide acceptance—this attitude manifests a fatal flaw. It is the fallacy of assuming that the contexts that yielded theologies supposedly intact are easily related to the contexts that have generated a new problematic. This is why the issues involved in any attempt to contextualize theology lie deeper than is immediately apparent. The problem is not simply that of confrontation. Nor is it simply that of relevance. The problem is the formulation of the agenda of theological reflection on utterly new bases, an effort that in a given instance may or may not find precedent in the long unfolding of the Christian tradition. For to say that theology must be contextual is to say that the relationship to the context is normative, in some way, for the theological enterprise as a whole, and that involvement in the context itself is the threshold across which one must move in order to dwell in the locus of new creativity.

Here we must insist on a sharp differentiation of terms. The contextualization of theology does not simply entail the effort to think and move with integrity when faced with the vicissitudes of the situation. "Context" and "situation" are different terms. The trouble with the word "situation"—witness the controversies around "situation ethics"—is that it points to a singular fluidity, that of the problematic itself. Contextualizing theology has to do with more than that. It has to do with the fact that more than simply the situation is at stake in the fluidities of our time. The whole of theology shifts with the reordering of the agenda of reflection. It must shift drastically—indeed it is already doing so—with reference to the issues now at hand. For racism, sexism, and classism/colonialism/imperialism point to demonic dimensions pervading the whole of the present, and they defy treatment as peripheral questions calling simply for rearrangements of prior clarities. Moreover, faith seeking understanding in terms of cultures that were not intertwined with the unfolding of medieval Christendom in the West will need far more than even radical extensions of earlier conclusions. Nothing short of new creativity will suffice.

How, then, do we proceed constructively on the task of understanding what this new creativity entails? Our initial move must be that of coming to terms with the historic dimension of this effort. Depending on the origins of one's own theological journey, one may have known already that the whole of theology shifts with the reordering of the agenda of its reflection. St. Augustine, St. Anselm, St. Thomas, the Reformers, Friedrich Schleiermacher, Karl Barth, Paul Tillich, Dietrich Bonhoeffer—an inexhaustible list of pivotal figures comes to mind when one ponders the role of the shifting of the agenda of reflection in the long history of faith seeking understanding. The question is not whether our attempt has a historic dimension. The question is, rather, How is this historic dimension to be understood and appropriated? How is it that these figures, and others that could be named, relate to our present effort? If a simple line of development from their efforts to our own is not possible, how then do we draw strength and insight from the committed labors of preceding figures as we attempt to be authentic in the midst of the contexts in which we have been placed?

Troeltsch and the Essence of Christianity

These questions, knowing a new urgency at the levels at which we encounter them now, lead us into an immense terrain that we are not the first to traverse. The decisive problem is this: What constitutes the *essence* of Christianity? The most incisive treatment of this problem was worked out in the opening decades of our century by Ernst Troeltsch (1865–1923), the pioneer figure in the attempt to relate theology and the rising social sciences.

Troeltsch's line of reflection on the question of the essence of Christianity was pushed into its deepest levels by a brilliant set of lectures given by his friend, and later his colleague, Adolf von Harnack (1851–1930), to students of all faculties at the University of Berlin in 1900. Harnack, the most celebrated historian of doctrine of his time and still king of that mountain for some, deliberately chose Schleiermacher's and Feuerbach's phrase *das Wesen des Christentums* (the essence of Christianity) as the title of his lectures. (Unfortunately, this is obscured for the English-speaking world by the fact that the title of the translation is *What Is Christianity?*)[4] The publication of the stenographic transcript of these lectures evoked an extremely wide response.

For Troeltsch, Harnack's attempt to delineate the essence of Christianity raised more problems than it solved—problems of both a methodological and a substantive kind. The beginning of his response to Harnack occurred with the publication, in 1903, of a lengthy essay entitled "What does 'Essence of Christianity' Mean?"[5] Meticulously comprehensive though it was, this essay was indeed only the beginning of his refining of the problem at hand. As he wrote it, he was hard at work on his first massive book, *Die Soziallehren der christlichen Kirchen und Gruppen* (1912) (English translation: *The Social Teaching of the Christian Churches* [1931]).[6] In this work he elaborated on the broad scale an understanding of the history of Christianity informed by a radically different conception of essential Christianity as over against Harnack's celebrated discussion.

Despite the close friendship between them, which never faltered, and without ever diminishing his high regard for Harnack's scholarship, to which he always felt indebted, Troeltsch nevertheless was profoundly bothered by Harnack's understanding of the essence of Christianity. For him, this was too narrow and confined, too restricted to ideas, and, most of all, too unmindful of the social contexts within which the great insights of the Christian tradition received formulation. In *The Social Teaching* Troeltsch in fact was treating more than he may have realized. He was not just elaborating the history of Christian social thought; he was spelling out the social history of *all* Christian reflection. In a word, he was unfolding the history of Christian thought *contextually*.

To be sure, this was controversial; it still is. For example, countering the well-nigh canonized, received Protestant polemic, Troeltsch insisted that medieval Catholicism did not represent a deterioration of the gospel, but rather an expression of it that made sense in its time. Again, challenging his own theological birthright so vigorously that many would never forgive him, he demonstrated that it was with the Reformed, and not the Lutheran, tradition that Protestantism developed its own far-reaching system of Christian social thought. Moreover, he contended that the Reformation was as thoroughly medieval as the Catholicism against which it struggled, that the modern world began not with it, but with the Enlightenment, in such a way that both it and Catholicism would have to face the radically open-ended question— Whither Christianity in the modern world?—without any self-evident answers.

Shortly after completing *The Social Teaching* in 1912, Troeltsch wrote an article entitled "The Dogmatics of the '*religionsgeschichtliche Schule*'" (1913).[7] Here he stated unequivocally a basic conclusion he would never desert:

> The "essence" can only be understood as the productive new interpretations and new adaptations of the historical Christian power, corresponding to any total situation at any given time. The essence is different for each epoch, resulting from the totality of its influence.
>
> (Reist 1966, 185)

In this light we must put the matter sharply: Because the essence of Christianity differs for each epoch, no given formulation may ever be regarded as final; and because what is involved is a productive power, only terms delineating this dynamism in operation may be used in discussing it. To put it succinctly, given Troeltsch's insight, the essence of

Christianity cannot be defined; it can only be described. Because it is always under way, it is intrinsically incapable of that kind of closure a definition requires.

The case for this contention was, and remains, inductive. No doubt, this was one of the reasons why it was, and remains, controversial. Though the terms are ours, not Troeltsch's, we may focus the matter this way: His insight was the yield of his development and use of a sociologically shaped hermeneutic for the contextual reading of the history of Christian thought. Its implications for our present inquiry are as follows.

First, Troeltsch did not claim that there is no such thing as essential Christianity. His claim was that essential Christianity is a historically productive power. Christianity, being historic, unfolds, develops, proceeds, and it does so by means of a creativity that always bears the marks of the contexts within which it comes into play. One may never reduce the essence of Christianity to any one of the insights its creativity has yielded, for that would confine this creativity to one instance, or one set of instances, of its operation. Our propensity is to define the essence of Christianity so that this creativity can be controlled. The better the definition, the more any subsequent effort is foreclosed—restricted, that is, to the endless task of commentary on a fixed set of insights. If, on the other hand, one runs the risk of describing the essence of Christianity in terms of its historically productive power—the only option for a contextual reading of the history of Christian thought—then one knows at least the possibility of authenticity, the possibility of stimulating subsequent effort to new ventures in the long journey of faith seeking understanding. One could say that this is much ado about nothing, that history happens this way whether we like it or not. But this will not suffice. Contextualizing theology explicitly entails the task of deliberately contributing to tomorrow's effort. Only so can it participate in the processive development of essential Christianity.

Second, to join Troeltsch in the insistence that the essence of Christianity differs in each epoch as the result of the influence of context is to force into the open an inherent weakness that theology has always had, and that we cannot deny now. This is the weakness of its strength. It is the weakness of a false certainty. The trouble is that the better we perform our labor, the more comprehensive are the claims we make for the clarities we forge. We confuse our efforts with God's. What God has done in Jesus the Christ has been done once and for all. But this does not yield, nor does it demand a once-and-for-all statement of the meaning of that act, good in all times and places, in all circumstances, in all epochs. To borrow one of Alfred North Whitehead's great phrases, we always seem to be caught in the trap of "misplaced concreteness" (Whitehead 1925, 55). We focus on finished conclusions rather than on the continuum whence they spring and which they serve.

Now the way out of this trap is not to experiment with indecisiveness, but it is to undergo the *discipline of tentativeness*. In saying this, one is not advocating the absolutizing of the fragmentary character of serious reflection about ultimacy. To be sure, we think in pieces, but we must do so with a passion for comprehensiveness. The point is that the comprehensiveness of our effort must always be that of the tentative formulation. We must become far more adroit in looking around the corners of our clarities. We must become far more adept in utilizing the perspectives we have labored to perfect *for the purpose of discerning what we have not yet seen*. Only so can the genuinely new come before the scrutiny of rigorous reflection. The discipline of tentativeness offers rich rewards. For one thing, it unlocks the past. The fact that other understandings of the essence of Christianity unfolded in contexts other than our own becomes an asset, not a liability. We need not deny our own context in order to grasp what was forged in another. For exactly the same reasons, this provides the possibility of an entrée into an ongoing conversation in which the similarity of contexts compels attention. Again, an asset, not a liability, is at hand. The fact that others in their struggles grasp the significance of the gospel differently than we do can only nourish our own efforts to understand the presence of ultimacy where we are.

In all this we are extending Troeltsch's insight, placing upon it a construction that was at best implicit in his own day. We have some things going for us that he did not. We are on this side of the development of theological perspectives, Protestant and Catholic alike, that were far beyond the horizons of his own purview. More than that, we live in a time when the intensity of his insight has, if anything, increased. Surely we have come to be sensitive to the fact that simply transplanting theological systems from one frame of reference to another does not work. It never yields new clarities; it at best generates cultural imperialism. This is why the entire missionary enterprise has always been vulnerable to assault in the name of the cultures confronted. What we behold now, in many quarters, is an increasing vigor of that challenge at the hands of the sons and daughters of the converted. We must, therefore, understand that if the essence of Christianity is stated in once-and-for-all terms, cultural imperialism is the inexorable result of the proclamation of the gospel. If, on the other hand, the essence of Christianity is understood as a historically productive power always capable of new formulations and configurations, then the intransigence of cultural imperialism will always be the clue to the idolatry of a prior clarity.

Third, to say that the task of contextualizing theology knows from within the *discipline* of tentativeness is to insist that it does have norms, that it is not a matter of caprice. Now this cannot be settled on the grounds of Troeltsch's thought alone. But before we move beyond him, there is one further construction we must place upon his insistence that the essence of Christianity is a historically productive power. His understanding of the historical character of Christianity was so radical that for him the only thing normative for theological reflection is the continuum of ideas in context. Whatever else we do in disciplining the contextualization of theology, this radical note must be included, for it offers the only responsible way of coming to terms with the historic dimension of our task. Now this is hard enough to accomplish when one thinks one is dealing with a simple linear progression, and it must be conceded that for a long time Troeltsch thought that this was what he was doing. But the fascinating tale of his own struggle into the depths of wrestling with a simultaneity of creativities is too convoluted to recount here. What we must be clear on is this: When a simultaneity of new efforts beyond old certainties confronts us, the issue at hand is infinitely compounded. It is precisely thus that we now find ourselves confronted. In the emergence of the ecumenical era it cannot be reversed, and with the rise of the theolog*ies* of liberation, the complexity is intensified. We must move into the depths of the ancient saying of our Lord: "The Kingdom of God is in the midst of you" (Luke 17:21b). For we know, and know that we know, that it is only in terms of *many* expressions that the gospel can be heard now.

Ours is hardly the first attempt to wrestle with the fact that theological reflection has at least two foci—the received faith and the new demands. Accordingly, ours is hardly the first line of inquiry to assert that if only that which is received is dominant, then new contexts will be denied their vitality and reality, and if only new demands are regnant, then innovation is king and history is dead. More than this, however, is before us in saying that the essence of Christianity is a historically productive power. For to say that the continuum of ideas in context plays a normative role for the discipline of tentativeness is to call relentless attention to the open-ended character of the enterprise. This raises what, in some quarters, is an unheard-of claim; namely, that theological reflection, like any other human reflection worth its salt, is faced with unknowns. It is the open-endedness of the continuum, with the urgency of exploring beyond fixed outposts, that inspires the attempt at the contextualization of theology. The disciplining of this effort has to do with the faithfulness whereby it seeks to pass on to other contexts that which meaningfully signals ultimacy in its own. Thus, at least this much is clear on the grounds of Troeltsch's insistence alone: The normative dimension has been relocated from a prior clarity to a present involvement, one that is conditioned and nourished by the past but knows integrity only in terms of its own effort. Moreover, this is the only kind of normative concern Troeltsch's historical understanding of the theological process can countenance. To work *systematically* at the theological task with this perspective in control is to do theology *historically*. This is what historical theology is all about. For too long the phrase "historical theology" has been restricted to theologically informed investigations of the history of Christian thought. What is now at hand does not deny the significance of these efforts, for obviously it is dependent on them. But what we must now be about is at the other end of the spectrum. We must do theology with frank acknowledgment of the historically conditioned character of both our efforts and our conclusions. What looks like relativism to some is the only road ahead. The only valid theology is a historically relativized one.

We may borrow again a celebrated phrase from Whitehead: "The many become one and increase by one" (Whitehead 1929, 21). There must pass through our attempt to grasp it the whole of the tradition as we know it. In our very grasping we will add to it. All that is before us will become unified in the struggle to understand; and from the vantage point of those who follow, we will become one of the many they must grasp and pass on. This processive, relational normativeness of involvement forces us to see that to become a Christian is not to adhere to a static entity; it is to join a moving history. This involvement in a moving history is possible only for those who will pay the price of adding to it. The ancient biblical command looms up before us: "Work out your own salvation with fear and trembling" (Phil. 2:12).

Bonhoeffer and Lehmann:
The Primacy of the Ethical Component

The question all this generates is as follows: What characterizes a theological creativity that is capable of functioning with norms that are processive, relational, and contextually involved? To deal seriously with this question is to encounter the primacy of the ethical component in the task of contextualizing theology. Contact with the context is always initially ethical in character. A contextual theology, then, will invariably find itself ordering its comprehensive reflection in such a way that theological-ethical considerations play a formative role. For the process of contextualizing theology, concrete reality and direct involvement in it rule and direct all its reflection. As we shall see, this is not to suggest that such an effort may be reduced to theological ethics. But it is to insist that the effort to think theologically about ethics marks indelibly the broader theological reflection it both presupposes and induces. Those theologies of liberation that will have a lasting significance are, in each instance, exemplifications of this, but they are neither the first nor the only instances in which it is to be observed. Before the advent of these efforts, two key figures were hard at work on this front, Dietrich Bonhoeffer and Paul Lehmann. The intersection of the lives and work of these two figures demands more attention than it has received, and it is of critical significance for our effort to respond to the summons to the contextualization of theology as we hear it now.

Precisely the same age, Bonhoeffer and Lehmann first met at Union Theological Seminary in New York in 1931. Lehmann had just finished his B.D. there and was commencing his doctoral studies. Bonhoeffer, with his Lic.Theol. in hand, was spending the year there in preparation for the duties he would assume as Privat-Dozent at the University of Berlin the following year. Their rapport was immediate. In Lehmann, Bonhoeffer found his closest "kindred spirit in America."[8] Their theological comradeship deepened when Lehmann studied in Europe in 1932–33 (doing a semester with Barth at Bonn, and one with Brunner at Zürich). Later, Lehmann played *the* indispensable role in finding the means and supplying the encouragement that enabled Eberhard Bethge, Bonhoeffer's close friend, to place at the disposal of the theological world, with meticulous precision, Bonhoeffer's life and work.[9]

The works of these two figures are crucial for our present inquiry, for in the labors of each of them we see both the operation of the *constructive* role of context in theological reflection and explicit indications of how this is to be understood and disciplined. Although this pervades Bonhoeffer's writings as a whole, it is most notably evident in *The Cost of Discipleship* (Bonhoeffer 1963) and in the posthumously published fragments we know as *Ethics* (Bonhoeffer 1965) and the *Letters and*

Papers from Prison (Bonhoeffer 1967). The fruition of Lehmann's contribution came later, particularly with the publication in 1953 of an extremely influential essay entitled "The Foundation and Pattern of Christian Behaviour" (Lehmann 1953). What was succinctly stated there has been explored at length and extended in his two major works, *Ethics in a Christian Context* (Lehmann 1963) and *The Transfiguration of Politics* (Lehmann 1975).

Both Bonhoeffer and Lehmann were profoundly influenced by Karl Barth. Accordingly, for them, as for him, Christology is central for all theological construction. With Bonhoeffer and Lehmann, however, a point is lifted up that, although present, is not all-encompassing in Barth's thought. This has to do with the fact that Christology makes sense only in terms of ethics. Now Barth's own breakthrough on this front is a marvel to behold, and anyone who has worked through his interrelating of *election* and *command* in *Church Dogmatics*, II/2, surely knows this. The fact is, though, that most of what we have from Bonhoeffer's hand was written before Barth developed this argument. This suggests the real difference between them. Bonhoeffer was always beginning, so to say, where Barth's discussions culminated. Bethge tells us that II/2 (published in 1942) was the last volume of the *Church Dogmatics* Bonhoeffer saw. It was one of the works he read in the prison cell at Tegel (Bethge 1967, 1102–1104). But by then he had already developed his incisive discussion of the relationship between *belief* and *obedience* (in *The Cost of Discipleship*) and his understanding of *reality* (in *Ethics*). And we will never know whether the argument of II/2 had any relationship at all to the pivotal fragment, "What Does 'Telling the Truth' Mean?"—published as the final piece in *Ethics* but written in the Tegel prison cell. In each of these instances he was already moving beyond even Barth's bold thrusts, and each of them was so intimately tied to the understanding of the uniqueness and significance of Jesus the Christ that we can say, from our vantage point, that ethics was at the heart of his Christology, and thus the point of departure for the whole of his reflection.[10]

How else are we to understand one of the most suggestive of all the fragments from his hand, the "Outline for a Book," one of the very last pieces in the *Letters and Papers from Prison*? Here he speaks of Jesus as "the man for others" (Bonhoeffer 1967, 202). Bethge calls attention to the fact that for Bonhoeffer this was "a new Christological title" (Bethge 1968, 56–57). This is of choice significance because it forces us to see that one can never deal with the ultimacy of Jesus the Christ without asking, Who are the others he is for? The contextual character of any real attempt to deal with this question demonstrates the fact that for Bonhoeffer, at least, the relationship between Christology and ethics is reversible. That is to say, to insist that we must always move *from* theology *to* ethics, along with Barth, is to discover that we must also be able to move *from* ethics *to* the broader reaches of theology.

It will probably always be debatable to argue that this is the central thrust of Bonhoeffer's thought, and that debate will never know any final resolution because we can never be certain as to how he would have worked things out had he lived. In the case of Lehmann's thought, however, the matter is beyond dispute. What receives fragmentary demonstration in the case of Bonhoeffer receives comprehensive, systematic expression in the case of Lehmann—namely, that any serious attempt to deal theologically with ethics results in the profoundly ethical coloration of theology at large.

In Paul Lehmann's thought, ethics and theology are so deeply intertwined that they can never be separated. He has devoted his life to the expansion of the intersection between them. This will immediately qualify the use of the terms "systematic" and "comprehensive" with reference to his productivity as compared with Bonhoeffer's. A restless, probing, faithful mind is at work in each case. Bonhoeffer's labors yielded truncated conclusions—Lehmann's, extended forays into difficult, often unknown, terrain. The difference between them has to do with the fact that Bonhoeffer was summoned to martyrdom, whereas Lehmann has been assigned a lifelong task. In Lehmann's thought one sees in operation that kind of expanding coherence that exemplifies what we have called the discipline of tentativeness. Sharp conclusions, rigorously pressed, punctuate his reflections, but always in a proleptic way, inchoately disclosing the urgency of new questions.

Almost invariably the word "context" will be present in Lehmann's most penetrating formulations. It is always present in his central lines of reflection. In 1972, at a high moment in his life, he prepared a lead editorial for the issue of *Theology Today* devoted to essays in his honor. In this succinct discussion, simply entitled "Contextual Theology," he characterized the criteria of such a theology with three terms— *confessional, dialogical,* and *catalytic* (see Lehmann 1972, 6–7). It is the genius of his thought that all three of these criteria are simultaneously operating in everything he writes.

This was clearly in evidence in the 1953 essay "The Foundation and Pattern of Christian Behaviour." There he argued that the running task of Christian ethics has to do with figuring out "how to live constructively in the gap between the will of God, theologically understood, and the concrete human situation, pragmatically understood." Building explicitly on Bonhoeffer's "What does 'telling the truth' mean?" Lehmann contended that this can be accomplished only in terms of an understanding of ethics that is (1) concrete and contextual rather than absolutistic, (2) indicative rather than imperative, and (3) social rather than individualistic (see Lehmann 1953, 101, 104–110). This is the nexus of insights he explored at length, a decade later, in his first major work, *Ethics in a Christian Context*. In the midst of this discussion he arrived at a crucial clarification:

> Perhaps the most enduring fruit of the higher criticism of the Scriptures will be the liberation of biblical images. Biblical investigation from Wellhausen to Bultmann may be credited, among its many achievements, with having set the biblical images free—free from their confinement by the text, free for the literary and historical context in which biblical imagination could give pointed expression to what God is doing in the world.
>
> (Lehmann 1963, 90)

How far-reaching is this freedom? How radically may a biblically shaped imagination forge ahead toward new frontiers? In the 1972 editorial for *Theology Today*, Lehmann insisted that a theology that is confessional, dialectical, and catalytic must be able "to express and to explicate the Christian referent to which it is committed, in an openness to and confrontation with other perspectives and referents" (Lehmann 1972, 7). A theology that succeeds in accomplishing this, however, runs the risk of what he calls "creative iconoclasm." This points back to the ancient word "prophetic," but it also points forward to the jeopardy of contextual involvement, for "a creative iconoclasm in the doing of theology is always prepared for the collapse of its own idols as it exhibits the idolatry in other perspectives" (Lehmann 1972, 7–8). Thus prophetic confrontation is a double-edged sword. The changes it demands are internal as well as external. This explains both why and how Lehmann's theology is always in process. The vigorous conclusions with which his writings abound are tentative, not in the sense of indecisiveness, but in the sense of open-endedness.

In Lehmann's second major work, *The Transfiguration of Politics*, a choice and illuminating example of this character of his thought is in operation. Well into the discussion he develops a "typology of current revolutions" (Lehmann 1975, 103). He is working on the grand scale indeed. He deals in turn with sections entitled "From Marx to Mao and Ho Chi Minh," "From Fidel and Che Guevara to Camilo Torres and Nestor Paz Zamora," and "From Frantz Fanon to Martin Luther King, Jr., Malcolm X, and the Black Panther Party" (Lehmann 1975, 110ff., 138ff., 162ff.). From his own theologically informed vantage point, Lehmann insists that the crucial issue in this panorama is *revolution*, not Marxism. Given this, the capstone of his analysis is fitted into place by means of a twofold maneuver. First, he contends:

> Neither Mao Tse-tung nor Fidel Castro became revolutionaries because they were Marxists. They became Marxists because they were revolutionaries. Marxism, particularly in its Leninist version, provided an ideology of power that illuminated the experienced realities of the power struggle and tended to be confirmed by them.
>
> (Lehmann 1975, 165)

What strikes Lehmann is that things were not exactly the same with the American black revolution. He finds his own way of beholding what many others have pondered at length—namely, that in the American black revolution the Marxist-Leninist dimension plays no significant role at all. Thus he contends further: "What Marx and Lenin had done for Mao, Ho, Fidel, and Che, Christianity had done for King, and Islam for Malcolm X" (Lehmann 1975, 165).

This juxtaposition carries Lehmann's reflection onto the concrete barriers and forces us to think, along with him, about a disturbing set of questions: How is it that Christian faith informs revolutions? Does it do so better than other options? Can either of these questions be answered without considering an even deeper one; namely, how does Christian faith inform the critique of *any* political system? These questions drive us to the central insight of the book. The heart of Lehmann's argument is an incisive demonstration of the fact that Romans 13 and the Fourth Gospel's account of Jesus' trial before Pilate (John 18:33ff.) must be understood together. Lehmann's understanding of that trial is epitomized in these words:

> At the moment of truth the power that shows itself as strength is overcome by the power that shows itself as weakness. The weakness of power is that when power is con-

fronted by the authority of truth, it is no match for the power
of weakness that bears the marks of truth.

(Lehmann 1975, 59)

So it is that in the case of Lehmann the freeing of the biblical
images operates. He will go this far—and the only way beyond him is
along this route—in the effort to help faith understand that with Jesus
the Christ the crucial problem in any revolution, indeed, in any politics,
is "whether or not the reality of power points beyond itself to a source
whose purposes shape the exercise of power" (Lehmann 1975, 52).
That all this evokes critical response is the real mark of its integrity.
There is an intensity of debate that always animates the conversation
between Lehmann and those who sense an affinity with the open-
endedness of his theological agenda. Confessional, dialectical, and catalytic his theology always is. The running question for anyone is whether
in Lehmann's case, or one's own, these three criteria operate in perfect
balance. Both Bonhoeffer, in fragmentary form, and Lehmann, more
systematically, more comprehensively, demonstrate with compelling
coherence what will always be discernible in the task of the contextualization of theology. The creativity of a contextualizing theology emerges
when its ethic outruns its clarities and forces it beyond compassion to
the probing of the latent depths of its own central symbols.

Involvement evokes more than the exhortation to new deeds. It
brings the summons to the new thought that must accompany them.
Troeltsch, at midpoint in his career, used a phrase in concluding *The
Social Teaching* that is far more radical than it may sound. If we are to
deal with what we are up against now, he was insisting, then "thoughts
will be necessary which have not yet been thought" (Troeltsch 1912,
1012). This is precisely the possibility both envisioned and demanded
by the summons to the contextualization of theology. The disciplining
of the effort is intrinsic to the proclamation of the gospel in our times
and in our places. And if the gospel is to be *heard* in our times, the
liberation of creativity is an absolute necessity.

THE CREATIVITY
OF CONTEXTUAL THEOLOGY

One of the decisive contrasts at the heart of the theological exchanges
dominating twentieth-century theology has been the contrast between

the creativities of Karl Barth and Paul Tillich. Barth's break with nineteenth-century Protestant theology focused on his insistence that the sole subject matter of authentic theological reflection is God's self-disclosure in Jesus Christ. He emerges as *the* kerygmatic theologian of our time. Tillich, on the other hand, championed "apologetic theology," which he understood to have the task of answering the questions men and women ask. In the light of the rise of contextual theology, this distinction is no longer as clear-cut as it was in the days when Barth and Tillich were on center stage. The gospel itself must be understood in terms of the contexts within which it is heard. An unapologetic theology simply absolutizes its own context. An apologetic theology that ignores the gospel has nothing to say. We must now move beyond this impasse. We will start from the kerygmatic end of the spectrum, but in such a way that the passion for apologetic clarity is given its due.

The shortest route into this terrain unfolds by way of revising Barth's understanding of the theological task. One of the most succinct expressions of his understanding of this task is the delineation of dogmatics at the outset of his *Dogmatics in Outline:*

> Dogmatics is the science in which the Church, in accordance with the state of its knowledge at different times, takes account of the content of its proclamation critically, that is, by the standard of Holy Scripture and under the guidance of its confessions.
>
> (Barth 1949, 9)

Bearing in mind the fact that the German word *Wissenschaft*, rendered "science" in the translation quoted, refers to any ordered or disciplined inquiry and not just to the natural sciences, we see that for Barth there are three normative components in the work of dogmatics: the biblical base, the confessional tradition, and "the state of [the Church's] knowledge at different times." Despite the sequence in the passage just noted, this is the only order in which Barth would have these components considered, for the Bible and the Confessions entail the standard to be dealt with in accordance with what is known at a given time, and his greatest fear was that preoccupation with the latter would undermine the priority of the former. It is precisely here that wrestling with the task of contextual theology comes into view. For such a set of concerns, the sequence in which Barth would have us move must be rethought. The questions of the oppressed do not occupy the third priority in a list of three considerations—at least not for the oppressed themselves. At the outset, however, there are two strong emphases in Barth's concern that must be noted carefully. The first is the insistence that dogmatics is a function of the church. It has to do with faith seeking understanding, as he never wearied of saying; accordingly, whereas the church at any given time must render account of its proclamation intelligibly, it must do so in a way that carries forward the confessional tradition from which it draws both the gospel and the incentive to proclaim it ever anew.

But though the church is so bound, it is also responsible to what it knows to be the case at a given time, and this is the second strong emphasis in his understanding that must be highlighted. This aspect is often overlooked, by Barth's friends as well as by his detractors. He, too, was concerned with doing justice to the demands of the contexts within which dogmatics functions. That these demands are always approached with theological insight, and never generate these insights independently, is the hallmark of Barth's contribution.

What we must now recognize is that to be faithful to Barth's intentionality is to face the necessity of moving beyond just this certainty lying at the heart of his lifelong reflections and pervading the massive *Church Dogmatics*. We may no longer leave the task of theology where he left it. The fact is that the relationships between the three components of his delineation are far more fluid than he ever was willing to concede. One may not deal with any one of them without touching the other two, and one may begin the discussion with any one of them as long as the other two are taken into account. The fact is that the relationship between these three components is synergistic, rather than linear. A set, not a sequence, of factors is involved. In the mathematical sense of the term, the relationship between the three factors is *commutative*. That is to say, there is a sense in which the end product of the combination will be the same wherever one begins the process of interrelating them.

The point that has just surfaced must be handled with great care, for only an analogy from the realm of mathematics is involved. Multiplication is commutative. What this means is that

$$5 \times 3 \times 2 = 2 \times 3 \times 5 = 3 \times 2 \times 5$$

so that the order in which the factors are dealt with has nothing to do with the result. The "factors" of dogmatics are similarly related. But the end products are not literally identical. Thus, valuable though the mathematical analogy is, like all analogies it is transcended by reality.

Its decisive usefulness, however, sets in precisely here. Systems of faithful reflection that interrelate these components synergistically manifest intersecting patterns of resonance. Resonance, not identity, discloses the intersections. There are countless instances of these patterns in the overlapping theologies of liberation. And this is a clue to an even deeper fact. Whenever and wherever the gospel of Jesus Christ is a living reality, there it will manifest the marks of authentic relationship to the contexts within which it is heard.

To contend that the components of dogmatics are synergistically related runs risks that Barth was not willing to entertain, for nothing less than giving context its due is at stake. Barth could never allow a normative significance to the context within which dogmatics is attempted. We must do so. The risks involved must be run because they are intrinsic to creativity. Unexpected novelty will be the result. This is the case whenever and wherever the Spirit speaks.

So to understand the task of dogmatics is to encounter a possibility utterly unimaginable for Barth. What is involved is nothing less than placing the genius of Barth's delineation in close proximity to the kind of apologetic discussion that Tillich attempted—not for the purpose of fulfilling the apologetic task on its own terms, *but for the purpose of keeping it kerygmatically honest.* This focuses the sense in which the relation between dogmatics and apologetics is always dialectical and therefore reversible. Moreover, this dialectical relationship between kerygmatic and apologetic theology is intrinsic to the central issue at the heart of this entire discussion, namely, the normative character of contextual involvement in theological construction. We have now encountered not only a horizon beyond Barth, but one beyond Troeltsch as well. We not only know that thoughts not yet thought must preoccupy our reflection; we also know something of how they take shape.

The test case for verifying the claims here at hand lies in the interrelationship between theology and preaching. In Barth's terms, the point to dogmatics is the development of a critical account of the content of the church's proclamation. That is, it is the mustering of the church's treasury of insight for the purposes of the preaching of the gospel of Jesus the Christ. Only a synergistic relationship between three elements—the study of the scriptures; the mastering of, and addition to, the confessional tradition, and genuine involvement in the contexts of living faith—is alive enough and flexible enough to make good the most pivotal risk of the Reformation itself.

That risk was the replacing of the Eucharist with the effort to reword the Word of God as the center of the liturgy. That no preaching can ever treat this challenge lightly is clear. That much preaching does not merit even minimal consideration in this connection is terrifying. That the risks of the faithful are but an echo of the risks of the living God is astonishing. The fact remains that the pulpit is the nexus of theological creativity; for when, by God's grace, the Word of God is heard anew, there unexpected latencies in the central symbols of the faith emerge before the wonder, and the labor, of reason being redeemed for hearing and speaking what has not yet been spoken and heard.

Moreover, this "speaking" and "hearing" must not be literalistically restrained. Much, if not most, of the proclamation of the gospel of Jesus the Christ can be grasped only if it is acted out. The rise of the theologies of liberation is but the most recent indication of this. The history of Christian thought is replete with demonstrations of it. Social action—or even more deeply, given the labors of Troeltsch, Christian social theory—is intrinsically part of the vocabulary of proclamation. The hungry can hear the gospel only as it is preached and acted out by those who struggle not only to feed them but also to remove the causes of their hunger. The oppressed can behold the cogency of the parables of the kingdom of God only when the kingdom takes shape in structures that replace the mechanisms of oppression. The invisible *marginales* can only be actively rendered visible in the recognition of the languages and the histories that include them. Otherwise, the adducing of preaching and theology as the test case of a processive dogmatic is negated from the outset by the stricture of Jeremiah, for it is guilty of crying "Peace! Peace!" where there is no peace.

We have already noted Paul Lehmann's pioneering labor in clarifying the contextual character of theological reflection. Recall again his insistence that a contextual theology is necessarily "confessional, dialectical, and catalytic" in character, so that it is able "to express and to explicate the Christian referent to which it is committed, in an openness to and confrontation with other perspectives and referents" (Lehmann 1972, 7). Here too is a set of factors that can be understood only in terms of the synergistic character of their relationships. The "creative iconoclasm" Lehmann espouses will indeed be creative only if catalytic and dialectical functions are both rooted in, and yet normative for, the confessional commitment giving rise to them. "A creative iconoclasm in the doing of theology is always prepared for the collapse of its own idols as it exhibits the idolatry in other perspectives" (Lehmann 1972, 7–8).

Lehmann's insight is as indispensable as it is incisive, but it can be maintained only if it serves a larger purpose, because it is only in this way that iconoclasm can be *creative*. More than the collapse of idols is at stake. New construction is its reason for becoming. Such construction can build on only what the context gives it; and such an attempt is nourished by the conviction that the continuum of effort, not the final product, is the locus of the presence of ultimacy in the midst of its limited forays into an unfolding future. This is why the relationship between theology and preaching is its real test case. Barth's understanding of the task of dogmatics pivots on the contention that theology is done for the sake of proclamation. If this discipline is maintained, then the relationship is more than a test case; it is the locus of new theological creativity.

Theological reflection that takes its lead from the intrinsic relationship between theology and preaching entails recapitulating, extending, and then extrapolating the legacy of reflection from the past with an eye toward the creativity demanded by the present. Such reflection both enables and demands that the second, and above all, the third, of these responsibilities receive explicit attention for reasons that must be delineated carefully. The first of these steps, *recapitulation*, involves a rigorous elaboration of the dogmatic legacy, and here the confessional tradition is in control of the effort. To a lesser extent, the second step, *extension*, is also dominated by this legacy, because the moves beyond the confines of recapitulating the insights of the past are at least proleptically implicit if the effort is undertaken with the meticulous discipline that it needs and deserves. However, the third step, *extrapolation*, is the real locus of the creative risk, as any preacher worth her or his salt knows, because now reflection must unfold in terms of direct involvement in the demands of the context.

These demands are both "internal," in the sense that they function *within* the Christian *oecumene* (as is clearly the case, for example, with the liberation theologies as we know them), and "external," in the sense that the conversation between Christianity and the world religions, of which it is one, can no longer be either ignored or denied. Particularly, given the character of this *external referent*, it will become clear that the confessional and dogmatic tradition simply does not contain the lines of reflection now demanded. This, in turn, will force into the open an issue that struggles for expression in the current theological scene. The fact is that the *internal referent* at hand also demands more than has been thought out so far. The most forceful indication of this now before us is the sense in which we may not leave the phrase "God the Father" where the tradition has left it, for to do so is to leave half of humanity under the oppression of invisibility.

In the light of all these factors, whatever apparatus is employed for the purpose of theological construction must do justice, on the one hand, to the sweep of the tradition up to this point; but, on the other hand, it must succeed in pointing beyond itself to the broader, and more urgent, considerations now confronting any attempt at constructive theological reflection. The disciplining of contextual theology thus discovers its rigorous norms. Flexibility and adroitness must attend the synergistic relationship between scripture, the tradition, and the state of our knowledge at this our given time, for if the gospel is truly heard, we are listening to the voice of the Spirit in the midst of us.

THE EXPANSION OF CONTEXTUAL THEOLOGY: THEOLOGY AND POSTMODERN SCIENCE

Once one begins to move along the route from contextual ethics to the contextualization of theology, there is no restraining the process. Utterly unexpected in Troeltsch's day, unadmitted in Barth's, and perhaps unwelcome in Lehmann's (we can never be certain on the issue as regards Bonhoeffer despite several tantalizing clues) has been the emergence of the problem of *the theology of the natural*. This has taken shape, on this side of the development of postmodern science, but it has done so in a drastically challenging fashion. The probing of an issue initially seen in its ethical manifestations has evoked genuinely and radically new reflection across the full range of theological concerns.

One of the first to delineate with precision the emergence of this new problematic was Joseph Sittler, whose remarkable little volume *Essays on Nature and Grace* (Sittler 1972) called an end to solving all theological problems by updating the doctrine of justification by grace through faith alone. Sittler did this by arguing that the terrors now unleashed with the rising intensity of the ecological problem defy a simplistically ethical analysis. That is to say, *the crises indicated are not susceptible to solution by ethical exhortation alone.* Thus the most accepted style of Protestant reflection is called into question, and it is a choice move of the providential Spirit that it was one of the truly significant Lutheran theologians of our time who called attention to this with such relentless cogency.

New conceptualizations are necessary for any adequate coping with the new issues at hand. This is the basic reason why Troeltsch's now prophetic insight that "thoughts will be necessary that have not yet been thought" evokes a sense of fear and trembling. For to wrestle with the implications of Sittler's insights is to encounter the necessity of a new day in theological responsibility and construction.

A complex set of developments lies behind Sittler's contention that the ecological problematic cannot be addressed significantly on ethical bases alone, and they are still under way. A decisive shift in the understanding of nature now rules reflection in the scientific arena, one that differs sharply from the view regnant in the perspective of Descartes and Newton, and all influenced by them, notably Immanuel Kant. At least four great turnings are intrinsic to this shift, and each of these may be typified by a single word and a celebrated figure:

1. Evolution (Darwin)
2. Relativity (Einstein)
3. Uncertainty (Heisenberg)
4. Incompleteness (Gödel)

The scientific conversation under each of these headings is by no means completed, and, of course, wide-ranging conversations concerning the theological implications of these developments have long been under way.

Complicated though the first two on the list are, extended discussion is hardly needed, for they have become part of the presupposed frame of reference of present self-understanding. In many ways, the development of postmodern science has its beginnings with the work of Charles Darwin and the theories of evolution that have been the subject of prolonged consideration, and reconsideration, since the publication, in 1859, of his breakthrough study, *On the Origin of Species by Means of Natural Selection.* That humanity is linked with the whole web of nature can hardly be denied seriously now, and even more significant for theological reflection at large is the vast expansion of the notion of time attending these assumptions. Beyond that whole set of issues and implications lies the fact that the mere mention of the term "relativity" automatically brings to mind the work of Albert Einstein. Consider only the implications of his *special theory of relativity,* which pivots on the contention that "absolute rest is not observable."[11] Now time is the function of the observer, so the following dialogue is not gibberish:

"What time is it?"
"Who is asking? Where?"

On this side of Einstein's work we know, and know that we know, that space and time are inseparably intertwined (see Reist 1985, 5–7).

Uncertainty

All this is so much a part of the present that it may simply be stipulated as assumed. The same may not be said, however, with reference to items 3 and 4 on our list. The name of Werner Heisenberg is not quite yet instantly recognizable; and whereas theology has long been wrestling with how to come to terms with Darwin, and then Einstein, the same is certainly not the case with the yield of Heisenberg's reflections.

Werner Heisenberg (1901–1976) worked out the basic theory of quantum mechanics in 1925. Intrinsic to this line of inquiry was the development of the *uncertainty principle* that, as much as anything else, differentiates the physics of postmodern science from that which received its classic formulation in the work of Descartes and Newton.

Heinz Pagels, author of an illuminating volume entitled *The Cosmic Code: Quantum Physics as the Language of Nature*, offers indispensable help to the lay mind for grasping what Heisenberg's principle entails:

> Heisenberg was interested in Greek philosophy, especially Plato and the atomists, who thought of atoms conceptually, not as things with parts. Most physicists tried to make physical pictures of atoms, but Heisenberg, like the Greeks, felt it was necessary to dispense with all pictures of atoms, of electrons circulating about the nucleus with definite radii like little solar systems. He did not think about what atoms were but what they did—their energy transitions. Proceeding mathematically, he described the energy transitions of an atom as an array of numbers. Applying his remarkable mathematical resourcefulness, he found rules that these arrays of numbers obeyed and used these rules to calculate atomic processes.
>
> (Pagels 1983, 58)

Heisenberg and those intrigued by his insight came to regard these "arrays of numbers" as *matrices*, and the "matrix algebra" involved in working with these arrays of numbers informs the uncertainty principle. The fact is that matrices do not follow the multiplication rules that simple numbers do, and in thinking about the realm of particle physics, this makes all the difference:

> In classical physics the physical variables that describe the motion of a particle are simple numbers. For example, the position (q) of a particle from a fixed point might be 5 feet (q = 5); its momentum (p = mass of the particle times its velocity) might be designated by 3 (p = 3). Simple numbers like 5 and 3 obey the commutative law of multiplication: that is, $3 \times 5 = 5 \times 3 = 15$—the order of multiplication does not matter. Likewise for the position and momentum of a particle in classical physics; these variables, since they were always simple numbers, obeyed the commutative law, $p \times q = q \times p$.
>
> The main idea of the new matrix mechanics is that physical variables like the position q and the momentum p of a particle were no longer simple numbers but *matrices*. Matrices do not necessarily obey the commutative law of multiplication—$p \times q$ does not have to equal $q \times p$.
>
> (Pagels 1983, 58–59)

If $p \times q$ does not have to equal $q \times p$, we have left the world of the kind of certainty the lay mind always associates with mathematics, for we have entered the world of probability. We must emphasize that the mathematics of probability is not an exercise in caprice; one is indeed thinking with rigorous precision. But one is doing that thinking within the locatable limits of a range of possibilities, and within those limits predictions and possibilities rule. In this connection, Harold Schilling offers an incisive observation that clarifies the issue at hand:

> Because of this discovery that uncertainty, or indeterminacy, is a basic feature of the world, it has been necessary to revise our conception of the so-called "laws of nature" and of "causation." Since it is possible to predict probabilities only, the laws by means of which predicting is done must be probability laws, and the term "cause" must refer to a causing of probabilities.
>
> (Schilling 1973, 85)

This does not rule out certainty of any kind, but it does redirect the meaning of the term. Thus Schilling continues:

> This does not mean that the idea of a causally determinate character of nature's events has been abandoned. For post-

> modern science the world is quite as "deterministic" as ever, though its determinateness is now known to lie in the realm of the predictable probability of events rather than of their predictable certainty. Neither does it mean that all claims of certainty have been renounced. For we can be certain of this, that whatever is caused to happen, and does become actual, represents in principle one of a predictable set of probabilities.
>
> (Schilling 1973, 85)

What Heisenberg led his, and all subsequent, generations of physicists to grasp is the fact that reality is statistical in character. Heisenberg himself records that this contention was the ground of a never-to-be-settled argument between Einstein and himself, for Einstein could not agree that we can know reality only in terms of the statistically ordered notion of matrices (see Heisenberg 1983, 30–31). This is what is at stake in Einstein's celebrated statement that God does not play dice with the universe. If Heisenberg was right, God does! And Pagels has a memorable way of insisting on this:

> The indeterminism of the quantum theory is an issue of principle, of what is knowable and unknowable, not experimental technique—that is what distressed Einstein. Even God can give you only the odds for some events to occur, not certainty. About this time Einstein started stating his objection to the new quantum theory with the remark that he didn't believe God plays dice.
>
> (Pagels 1983, 65)

Certainty about the limits, the range, within which uncertainty in the sense of probabilities obtains is the hallmark of the precision informing the irreversible breakthroughs in the physics of the immediate present. The decisive import of this for theological construction is embedded within this fact. The clue to this import is already before us in Pagels's interpretation of the root of Heisenberg's creativity—he stopped trying to picture the atom! Instead, he contemplated what atoms *do*. This is crucial for the epistemological shift that marks the transition from classical to postmodern science, and it forces into the open the radical significance of Heisenberg's uncertainty principle for theological reflection.

The decisive issue may be stated in terms of an unavoidable question: Is the uncertainty Heisenberg demonstrated ontological? That is, is it observable because nature *is* indeterminate in some sense? Here the house divides, and the debate is still under way. Ian Barbour has set this out with illuminating precision in his *Issues in Science and Religion* (Barbour 1966, 298ff.). Following his delineation, there are three basic options: (1) The uncertainty Heisenberg speaks of is related to human ignorance, in the sense that we do not know enough yet to resolve the problem at hand. One day, though, we will. This was the view Einstein maintained, and it is the view championed today by David Bohm (Bohm 1980). (2) The uncertainty Heisenberg observes is the result of our own experimental and conceptual limitations. This is the view championed by the celebrated Niels Bohr, and it leads to his conception of complementarity (concerning which I will have more to say later). (3) Uncertainty, in Heisenberg's sense, has to do with an intrinsic indeterminateness in nature itself. That is to say, Heisenberg's uncertainty has ontological status. This is the view Heisenberg himself maintained, and it is the view adopted by Barbour.

If Schilling's insistence on the precision involved in thinking of probabilities is properly grasped, Barbour's own comment on the issues at hand is striking indeed:

> The future is not simply unknown, it is "not decided"; but it is not completely "open," since the present determines the range of future possibilities. Reichenbach suggests that this requires modification of the traditional two-valued logic (in which a statement is actually always either true or false, though our knowledge of it may be uncertain), in favor of a three-valued logic, in which uncertain means "not decided" and hence neither true nor false.
>
> (Barbour 1966, 304–305)

We have to add one word to Barbour's formulation for the far-reaching significance of his point to emerge. Given Reichenbach's three-valued logic, "uncertain" means "not decided" and thus neither true nor false—*yet*. Ian Barbour is one of those remarkable persons who is genuinely competent in both theological and scientific disciplines. His theological training at Yale, following his Ph.D. in nuclear physics, lies behind the fact that at Carleton College (in Minnesota) he was both professor of physics and chair of the religion department. He knows what he is up to when he presses to the limit his contention, in concert with Heisenberg, that uncertainty is ontological in character. For what this does is liberate history, and the future, into the possibility of encountering the genuinely new:

> If indeterminacy is thus an attribute of nature, more than one
> alternative is open and there is some opportunity for unpre-
> dictable novelty. Time involves a unique historicity and un-
> repeatability; the world would not repeat its course if it were
> restored to a former state, for at each point a different event
> from among the potentialities might be actualized. Potential-
> ity is objective and not merely subjective.
>
> (Barbour 1966, 305)

What happens to theological reflection if, following Barbour's appraisal of Heisenberg, we concur that the future is indeed open to the
not-yet-decided? The Christian tradition, given its roots in the Hebraic
religious consciousness, together with the Jewish tradition, carrying that
consciousness forward in a way that is intrinsic to its birthright, has
always insisted that God is alive. We are now forced to wrestle with the
fact that our long-standing confessional convictions entail more than
we could have possibly dreamed earlier. The future is not yet decided
for the living God, as well as for us.

Incompleteness

If the name of Werner Heisenberg is less well known than those of
Charles Darwin and Albert Einstein, the name of Kurt Gödel is stranger
than all three. Gödel developed his *incompleteness theorem* in 1931 with
direct reference to the pivotal work published between 1910 and 1913
by Bertrand Russell and Alfred North Whitehead entitled *Principia
Mathematica*. In this treatise, Russell and Whitehead reached the apex of
the attempt to formalize, comprehensively and completely, logical
thought as this is exemplified in arithmetical reasoning. What Gödel
demonstrated in his 1931 paper was that their effort did not yield the
finality they sought. A key formulation from Michael Polanyi focuses
this as follows:

> The most important theorems limiting the formalization of
> logical thought are due to Gödel. They are based on the fact
> that within any deductive system which includes arithmetic
> (such as for example the system of the *Principia Mathematica*)
> it is possible to construct formulae—i.e., sentences—which
> are demonstrably undecidable within that system, and that
> such a sentence—the famous Gödelian sentence—may say
> of itself that it is undecidable within the system.
>
> (Polanyi 1962, 259)

This demonstration led to a key conclusion, cited in the best technically developed discussion of Gödel's argument available for the lay mind, that by Ernest Nagel and James R. Newman: "If arithmetic is consistent, then it is incomplete" (Nagel and Newman 1956, 1694).

Douglas R. Hofstadter's *Gödel, Escher, Bach: An Eternal Golden Braid* (1980) is an illuminating though complicated study, one that sharply focuses Gödel's ingenious accomplishment. The work won a Pulitzer Prize. It was probably not within the purview of those responsible for making the decision leading to this award that one of the principal beneficiaries of Hofstadter's work would be the theological community. Likewise, given the author's own predilections to see implications of his writings in connection with Zen Buddhism, it probably was not uppermost in his mind that the Christian theological community would be well advised to read him carefully, though his understanding of Bach's fugues could be regarded as tending in this direction. However, his work truly is indispensable for coming to terms with the correct appraisal we have just cited from the writings of Michael Polanyi. The reason for this is that Hofstadter succeeds in making clear that the heart of the significance of Gödel's paper for all serious reflection on ultimacy resides in the notion of *self-referential systems*—systems, that is, that point beyond themselves in strange and fascinating, almost mesmerizing, ways.

Hofstadter writes as a computer scientist who has an impressive breadth of cultural and philosophical literacy. Thus, at the very outset of his discussion of Gödel's work, he sounds the philosophical chords needed to appraise its significance:

> In its absolutely barest form, Gödel's discovery involves the translation of an ancient paradox in philosophy into mathematical terms. That paradox is the so-called *Epimenides paradox*, or *liar paradox*. Epimenides was a Cretan who made one immortal statement: "All Cretans are liars." A sharper version of the statement is simply "I am lying"; or, "This statement is false."
>
> (Hofstadter 1980, 17)

The "liar paradox" defies a simple resolution because it cannot be settled within the limits of the statement itself. That is what it means to say that the intrinsic issue is that of a self-referential system; one must step outside it, so to say, in order to discern what's going on. Hofstadter notes that this is a little more clear if one expands the paradox itself into two sentences:

The following sentence is false.
The preceding sentence is true.
(Hofstadter 1980, 21)

He comments: "Taken together, these sentences have the same effect as the original Epimenides paradox: yet separately, they are harmless and even potentially useful sentences" (Hofstadter 1980, 21). This is precisely the point. When they are taken together, one must step away from them in order to discern that taken together they point beyond themselves.

We can only pause to note that it is this dimension of "pointing beyond" that Hofstadter finds to be the common element in the reflections and creativities of the mathematician (Gödel), the graphic artist (Escher), and the musician (Bach) with which his book is concerned. But we must do more than pause over the central insight informing his discussion, one that he formulates very late in the book, where he speaks of "the Gödelian-ness" of all our thought:

> People have said to me on occasion, "This stuff with self-reference and so on is very amusing and enjoyable, but do you think there is anything *serious* to it?" I certainly do. I think it will eventually turn out to be at the core of AI [Artificial Intelligence], and the focus of all attempts to understand how human minds work.
> (Hofstadter, 1980, 714)

The formulation, of course, indicates something of the urgency of the issue at hand as seen by a computer scientist, and it should be noted that Hofstadter's discussion plays a very significant role in the ongoing debate about the possibility of so-called artificial intelligence. However that debate unfolds, no discussion of the nature of human intelligence that seeks to include an understanding of "how human minds work" can now be what it was before Gödel's paper was published.

Hofstadter insists that it is one thing to understand what Gödel's incompleteness theorem states, and quite another to understand how it makes the statement. The latter aspect of this complexity cannot be avoided, because it turns on the ingenious idea at the heart of Gödel's demonstration, namely, the notion that one "can use mathematical reasoning in exploring mathematical reasoning itself" (Hofstadter 1980, 17). In a quite striking sense, what Gödel argued is the clue to how he demonstrated his conclusion (and this is the basic reason why those who do not possess highly developed mathematical skills can actually grasp what he accomplished). As noted above, Gödel argued that "if arithmetic is consistent, then it is incomplete" (Nagel and Newman 1956, 1694). Hofstadter's paraphrase of the central proposition in Gödel's paper strikes the same notes: "All consistent axiomatic formulations of number theory include undecidable propositions" (Hofstadter 1980, 17).

The decisive idea intrinsic to the incompleteness theorem is the notion of *undecidability*. Mathematicians, and in the sense in which we are now speaking that includes just about everyone, do not like undecidability, especially when they work so hard to close all the loopholes in reasoning and thus tie up all the loose ends as neatly as possible. Hofstadter has a remarkable paragraph that sums up the manner in which Gödel argued, showing how the complex procedures of symbolic logic that Bertrand Russell and Alfred North Whitehead developed in the *Principia Mathematica* could be made to say things that cannot be settled within the structure they developed:

> Gödel had the insight that a statement of number theory could be *about* a statement of number theory (possibly even itself), if only numbers could somehow stand for statements. The idea of a *code*, in other words, is at the heart of his construction. In the Gödel Code, usually called "Gödel-numbering," numbers are made to stand for symbols and sequences of symbols. That way, each statement of number theory, being a sequence of specialized symbols, acquires a Gödel number, something like a telephone number or license plate, by which it can be referred to. And this coding trick enables statements of number theory to be understood on two different levels: as statements of number theory, and also as *statements about statements* of number theory.
>
> (Hofstadter 1980, 18)

As Hofstadter puts it, Gödel succeeded in developing "a way of transporting the Epimenides paradox into a number-theoretical formalism" (Hofstadter 1980, 18). That is to say, he developed a way of utilizing the logical complexity of a system no less than that developed in the *Principia Mathematica* to show that the system is capable of making statements whose truth it cannot settle. Thus this system, and any system like it, is "incomplete"—"there are true statements of number theory which its methods of proof are too weak to demonstrate" (Hofstadter 1980, 18). Or, as Hofstadter puts it (in a formulation that is the clue to the entirety of his discussion of not only Gödel but also of Escher and Bach), what is at stake is the fact that "provability is a weaker notion than truth, no matter what axiomatic system is involved" (Hofstadter 1980, 19).

The yield of Gödel's work for understanding any human inquiry into any subject of reflection, including all attempts to make the human yearning for ultimacy intelligible, is of immense significance. What is at hand is the conclusive demonstration of the fact that consistency and incompleteness go hand in hand. This is the exact opposite of much that we have been led to believe. Both mathematics and philosophy, to say nothing of theology, have always struggled to complete the systems with which they were, and are, preoccupied. And whereas the history of ideas is replete with unfinished efforts, it is hardly devoid of the dream that given time and strength the systems at hand could be put into final form. On this side of Gödel, that dream is unmasked as an illusion.

Any line of theological reflection that takes this seriously must be intrinsically open-ended in brand new ways. The very conclusions we were forced to consider with Heisenberg before us are driven even deeper with Gödel unavoidably in our midst. No theology can be convincing if it ignores "how human minds work," to appropriate Hofstadter's phrase, but this now means that even this sense of being convinced is itself never capable of a final formulation. The fact is that theologians have been notoriously worse than mathematicians in disliking incompleteness. Small wonder, then, that now that the word has become intrinsically positive, the theological task is forced into new modes of thought and onto a new ground, one with a new horizon. To ponder the sense in which Heisenberg's uncertainty principle redefines precision for us and Gödel's incompleteness theorem leaves indelible marks on our understanding of how we think is to uncover the absolute necessity for radically new theological reflection in unavoidably cogent terms. Little did Troeltsch know just how new the new thoughts we now must think would become. Little could Bonhoeffer and Lehmann know how far we would have to go in order to take the context of contextual theology as seriously as now we must.

Why is this issue of the manner in which we think so crucial? Why must we take so seriously what is now being disclosed about the way in which we do our thinking? The answer is not a new one. Christian theological reflection has always had the epistemological question breathing down its neck. This was and remains the basic point to the

Protestant Reformation: The biblical word, not the overwhelming power of the magisterial function of the hierarchical church, was and remains the only clue to stability as the search for ultimacy attempts to order its reflections. It is one thing to admit that the line from ethics to theology has disclosed inexhaustible panoramas. It is another to recognize how drastic it is to know that the effort to reflect on these systematically is open-ended.

The contextual intertwining of ethics and nature is at once unexpected and hoary with precedents, but this must be stated with precision. The genuine note of surprise this entails has to do with the fact that ethics and nature are *contextually* intertwined. They have long been held to be closely interrelated, so much so that vast terrains of theological argumentation seeking to ground ethical judgments in the orders of nature quickly come to mind. None of these, though, are contextual in the sense in which we have been using the term. For in its most recent form, the summons to the contextualization of theology has emerged from the struggles for liberation that so deeply mark our time. And in its most robust theological roots, it has been on the grounds of a theological ethic based on Christology that it has found its decisive depths. To say, then, that the *contextual* intertwining of ethics and nature is *surprising* is to underscore the sense in which the all-consuming struggle for the oppressed, and against the oppressor, encounters on its own theoretical bases the possibility, and even the necessity, of dealing with theology and the natural sciences.

A *polemical* note, then, is close at hand. Not all the theologians of liberation will welcome this addition to an already urgent and compelling agenda. The trouble with this view is that it overlooks the fact that revolution, either in the streets or wherever, will be abortive if it presupposes a world that no longer exists. The pervasive mode of confrontation, always present in the fight against the oppressors, will tragically lose its fire if it simplistically assumes that a state of war still exists between either religion and science, or between theology and scientific reflection. At the opposite extreme can be found those who would use the possibility of a fresh intertwining of ethics and nature as an excuse to avoid the predicament of the disenfranchised. Such a view cannot prevail in the face of the recognition that the very same process of contextualization that informs the overlap of theological reflection and the natural sciences is present in the ferment out of which the theologies of liberation emerge. Given this phenomenological similarity between the two, it is impossible not to hear the resonance between them, and the polemical note in the contextual intertwining of ethics and nature confronts and rejects the denial of this resonance, however this denial is stated.

A note of promise emerges directly from what we have just seen. In that the same process of contextualization operates within both the ethical and the natural domains of theological reflection, the findings of each obtain for the other. What is adequate, true, incisive for theological ethics is equally significant for the theology of the natural, and the reverse is also the case. Now this is indeed promising, for what it indicates is the possibility of formulating both the *cosmic* dimension of the theologies of liberation, and the *existential* dimension of this cosmic claim. This evokes memories of the intrinsic connection between *covenant* and *creation* that pervades both the Old Testament and the New, but we are now confronted with the risky necessity of reasserting this in our own terms, even though these will run far beyond the purview of even the biblical witness.

Hence the challenge now before us. We must find new ways of understanding the contextual nature of ultimacy itself. That is to say, we now know, and know that we know, that the God of the gospel is the God of all the contexts.

THE GOD OF THE CONTEXTS

Why does authentic theological reflection always arise contextually? Why is it restive with its conclusions, so that they are always tentative in character, summoning new creativity and stretching it toward unforeseen frontiers? Why is such contextual reflection intrinsically expansive, so that it cannot settle for even its own presuppositions regarding the arenas within which it is to function?

There is only one answer to all these questions. The God of the gospel is the God of the contexts. The God of whom the Bible speaks can be heard only *in context*. This is why this God is always becoming new. This God is alive. No preoccupation with any given context will disclose in itself the voice of this living God. The contextual character of theology is *not* derived from the context. It is rooted in the contextual character of ultimacy itself. The movement in question is God's own. "I am with you always [all of you, in all places, in all times], to the close of the age" (Matt. 28:20). The continuum, which is plural and open-ended, is revelatory, because God is in the continuum. That is why revelation is processive. Revelation is necessarily processive; that is, it is never capable of reaching completion because God is always on the move, always having more to say, always evoking new hearing. The subject matter of theology is God. God is alive. For us God exists *only in context.*

Two decisive insights lie in the background of what I will now attempt, one from the work of Paul Lehmann and one from that of Joseph Sittler. In my reading, the key to Lehmann's understanding of contextual ethics, as this unfolds in his *Ethics in a Christian Context*, lies embedded in the following insistence: "There is no formal principle of Christian behavior because Christian behavior cannot be generalized. And Christian behavior cannot be generalized because the will of God cannot be generalized" (Lehmann 1963, 77). For Lehmann, both the question of the will of God and the attempt to live it are so immersed in the complex realities of life that the connection between them can be discerned only in terms of the contexts within which decision arises. But the matter may not be left here. The fact is that Lehmann's contextual ethics evokes a contextual theology. If the will of God cannot be generalized, neither can the understanding of what the very word "God" means. This is the real complexity Lehmann's work exposes.

What, however, constitutes this complexity? For Lehmann, the perplexity of faithful wrestling with ethical decisions is not just a matter of wrestling with the vicissitudes of the situation. This is what differentiates his version of contextual ethics from so-called situation ethics. Speaking of *koinonia* ethics, as he characteristically has from the beginning of his efforts on these issues, Lehmann worked out a truly crucial formulation in the following comprehensive terms:

> The complexity of the actual human situation, with which a *koinonia* ethic tries seriously to deal, is always compounded of an intricate network of circumstances and human interrelationships, bracketed by the dynamics of God's political activity on the one hand and God's forgiveness on the other.
> (Lehmann 1963, 141)

This formulation is informed by Lehmann's incisive grasp of the political character of the biblical imagery concerning God (see Lehmann 1963, 86ff.). Memorable though this is, it only points toward the depths of his insight. The insight into the political character of biblical imagery concerning God, like the vicissitudes of the situation, is only one discernible cluster within a set of four complex factors, all of which must be considered together. All four of these are indicated in the passage just quoted. For Lehmann, the context of contextual ethics has to do with the full range of God's complex relationship to humanity. In any incisive unfolding of this context the complexities of circumstance, the nexus of human interrelationships, the dynamics of God's political activity (without which those in the *koinonia* do not know God), and the dynamics of God's forgiveness (without which the *koinonia* cannot continue), all combine and must be understood in connection with each other. Each of the four components is fluid because each is alive. Or, to put it another way, both the theology and the ethics of theological ethics must be understood contextually, because only a theology that is itself contextual can support an ethic that is necessarily contextual.

The second set of theological insights informing this present attempt is caught up in a conclusion reached by Joseph Sittler in his *Essays on Nature and Grace*. Here, setting out a striking differentiation between the "cause of grace and the occasions of grace," he develops a remarkable formulation:

> The disclosure of grace in the enormous paradox of the cross is the "focal point" for man's encounter with grace. The grace of God is humanly, historically, and episodically incandescent in Calvary. That occasion, indeed, was and is so crucial an occasion that the mind and devotion of the devout is tempted to forget, in its grateful Christocentrism, that Jesus was not centered in Jesus at all. He is called the Christ precisely because of that. Our theology can be Christocentric as regards the reality and crucial occasion of grace precisely because that Christology lives within the grace of the Holy Trinity.
>
> (Sittler 1972, 87–88)

Thus Sittler epitomizes with rare precision the manner in which Christology refuses to be confined to its immediate meaning, and this is what classically generated the Trinitarian perspective at the base of the Christian tradition.

Sittler is right. Where Christology is treated at depth, it generates the doctrine of the Trinity. We must now face a new understanding of what this entails. We are not where the church was when this doctrine received its classical formulation. And we are not where the church is now if we think that all that it has before it is either the manifold contemporary struggles for liberation, urgent though these are, or the relating of theology and postmodern science, awesome though this is becoming. As we have already noted, Sittler's argument is that the ecological crisis cannot be treated in ethical terms alone. This is what generates his insight into the intrinsically expansive character of Christology itself. In seeing this he moves far beyond the limits of even the high Christologies of the neo-orthodox milieu in which his labors initially took shape. Thus the passage continues:

> The holy occasion of the discovery of the grace of God may indeed be the mountaintop experience, but the place and content of the experience is not identical with the experience in its origin and fullness and destiny. That is why the occasion must be both absolutely valued and absolutely qualified. For the decisive context of life is time as continuity, and not time as moment; continuity, not break; steadiness, not staccato; what goes on and not only what shakes up.
>
> (Sittler 1972, 88)

The genuinely new implications of the contextual intertwining of ethics and nature can hardly find more compelling language than what is at hand when Lehmann and Sittler are read side by side. The theologies of liberation have to do with "what shakes up." So does the contextual theology of Lehmann. The theology of the natural has to do with "what goes on." This is what Sittler came to see. What happens when the two are combined? Can there be an even deeper confrontation than we have known so far? Can there be an ethicizing of the natural? Both questions must be answered with a resounding "Yes!" but the price of this conviction is the labor of understanding what this means. In that what unfolds knows deep precedents beyond which it must move, and in that ultimacy itself is present in the same contexts within which we must seek our new becoming, we can only risk implementing the full realization of what we first learned from Ernst Troeltsch. The understanding of the essence of Christianity is changing once again. Faith can only await the next turning of a revelatory process that has always been on the move.

Processive revelation is limited—but only by God. What is disclosed presupposes prior revelation while transcending it. The structure of processive revelation is that of God's own revelatory activity. The revelatory vectors have been and will always be operative in intertwined becoming. So interwoven are these three vectors that we discern them in distinction from each other only as they are all present in interrelationship. In any given historical context, all that has gone before is both tied to precedents and yet freed from them. The reality of this complex dynamism is grounded in liturgy in such a way that reflection can only point to that which moves beyond its reach. The plausibility of reflecting on a moving reality is grounded in the faithfulness with which it celebrates the past while transcending it.

Three biblical names identify each of these three revelatory vectors—Father, Son, Spirit. Just as the biblical witness speaks only as it is being transcended, so the tradition has always faced the necessity of extrapolating the meaning of each of these names. The time is at hand to wrestle with this problematic in process modes of thought, for only such thinking can embrace the intertwining of ethics and nature, and the vision of God it necessitates. To attempt this now is to know that the order in which the names are considered must be reversed, and the delineations of the vectors must be in fluid, verbal terms. The following discussion seeks to clarify this claim, and it unfolds in terms of the following schema, deliberately cast in confessional terms:

I believe in the relating God
    (who, in the tradition, is named God the Spirit);
I believe in the liberating God
    (whom the tradition knows as God the Son);
I believe in the creating God
    (whom the tradition calls God the Father).

2

THE RELATING GOD

The biblical name for the relating God is "Spirit." This is why we are beginning with the third article of the creed. All that we say about God depends on our being in relationship with God. The issue has been with us at least since the breakthrough of the Protestant Reformation. In faithful reflection, we must take our lead from the Bible, but apart from the presence of the Spirit the Bible is mute.

This was central to Calvin's epistemology. Faithful reflection is the locus of true creativity and devotion, and such reflection is informed by scripture. But the authority of scripture upon which humanity is dependent for its knowledge of God itself depends upon the "secret testimony of the Spirit" (*Institutes* I, vii, 4 [78]).[1] Viewed from the standpoint of the present, the manner in which Calvin argued his point has striking significance, for his formulation indicates that we ourselves are directly involved in the authentication of the bases of our conviction. Led by the Spirit, we establish the connection between the witness of the past and our own context of faithful reflection:

> They who strive to build up firm faith in Scripture through disputation are doing things backwards. . . . [E]ven if anyone clears God's Sacred Word from men's evil speaking, he will not at once imprint upon their hearts that certainty which piety requires. . . . [T]he testimony of the Spirit is more excellent than all reason. . . . The same Spirit, therefore, who has spoken through the mouths of the prophets must penetrate into our hearts to persuade us that they faithfully proclaimed what had been divinely commanded. Isaiah very aptly expresses this connection in these words: "My Spirit which is in

you, and the words that I have put in your mouth, and the
mouths of your offspring, shall never fail" [Isa. 59:21].
(I,vii,4 [79])

The Spirit is thus the link between the witness of the past and our
present search for ultimate meaning, and relationship to God the Spirit is
the precondition for hearing the voice of God in the word of scripture.
This is the relational vector that pervades Calvin's masterwork, the *Institutes of the Christian Religion*, and is the heart of his creativity. The point of
departure of this work, from its first edition in 1536 through its final, and
therefore definitive, edition in 1559, sees Calvin assert that the knowledge
of God and the knowledge of humanity are inseparably intertwined:

> Nearly all the wisdom we possess, that is to say, true and
> sound wisdom, consists of two parts: the knowledge of God
> and of ourselves. But, while joined by many bounds, which
> one precedes and brings forth the other is not easy to discern.
> (I,i,1 [35])

That God and humanity must be understood together is Calvin's primary assertion. It can be argued that the entirety of his thought seeks to
explicate this. It is certainly the case that this is true of the *Institutes*.
This is why any comprehensive analysis of this work must make constant reference to Calvin's well-known delineation of true piety:

> Now, the knowledge of God, as I understand it, is that by
> which we not only conceive that there is a God but also grasp
> what befits us and is proper to his glory, in fine, what is to our
> advantage to know of him. Indeed, we shall not say that,
> properly speaking, God is known where there is no religion
> or piety. . . . I call "piety" that reverence joined with love of
> God which the knowledge of his benefits induces.
> (I,ii,1 [39, 41])

Given this, the point to Calvin's reflection is clear—he seeks to explore
the *relationship* between God and humanity. "Piety" characterizes the
life of all who live in this relationship.

CALVIN'S SHIFT

No facet of the complex line of discussion in the *Institutes* can be treated
at depth apart from this pervasive relational vector. To interpret Cal-

vin's thought with this in mind is to encounter the restive creativity informing the successive editions of the *Institutes*.[2] From the vantage point of the present, the most significant instance of the operation of this creativity is his treatment of the doctrine of election. Reflection on this vexatious, and profoundly misunderstood, doctrine forces our faith into its most far-reaching understanding. As we shall see, Calvin himself is much closer to our modern struggles than the received interpretation of his work implies. Our task is to get in touch with the dynamism of his theological creativity on the assumption that this is more significant than the conclusions he himself reached, because these always point beyond themselves toward further reflection. It is his creativity that we must extrapolate now.

The Doctrine of Election

The issue at hand turns on the question of the place of the discussion of the doctrine of election in the argument of the *Institutes* as a whole. From the initial edition in 1536 until the next to last edition in 1550, Calvin discussed election (that is to say, predestination, because the terms are interchangeable in his thought) immediately following the treatment of the doctrine of providence. This had the effect of treating election as a function of the power of God. This is the locus of the regnant view that the austere, predestining, sternly sovereign God is the distinctive idea from this figure. But this view, dominant though it has become, fails to take into account the fact that at the apex of his productivity Calvin was beginning to change his mind.

At least two factors inform what was happening in his thought. The first is that with the 1559 edition for the first time Calvin ordered the progression of the discussion in terms of the sequence of the Apostles' Creed, unfolding the *Institutes* in four books. In a loose, rather than rigid, sense, Book I has to do with God the Father; Book II, with God the Son; Book III, with God the Spirit; and Book IV, with the church and civil government. The second factor has to do with the insertion of a new chapter epitomizing his Christology in Chapter vi of Book II. This chapter is of decisive significance for interpreting the *Institutes* as a whole, and thus for understanding why he did what he did with the doctrine of election in the last edition of this, his central work.

The opening lines of the chapter find Calvin making exactly this claim:

> The whole human race perished in the person of Adam. Con-
> sequently that original excellence and nobility which we
> have recounted would be of no profit to us but would rather
> redound to our greater shame, until God, who does not rec-
> ognize as his handiwork men defiled and corrupted by sin,
> appeared as Redeemer in the person of his only-begotten
> Son. Therefore, since we have fallen from life unto death, the
> whole knowledge of God the Creator that we have discussed
> would be useless unless faith also followed, setting forth for
> us God our Father in Christ.
>
> (II,vi,1 [340–341])

Thus everything that precedes this chapter depends upon it, otherwise
the preceding discussion as a whole will be misunderstood. And lest
there be any confusion on what this means for seeing one's way
through the doctrine of election, Calvin moved the discussion of the
doctrine to a different point in the unfolding of the *Institutes* as a whole.

Why did he do this? I am convinced that we can answer this question in terms of two decisive specifications concerning Christology that
Calvin sets out in this new chapter. The first of these has to do with the
impasse of attempting to discern the depths of our knowledge of God
apart from the fact of Christ:

> Even if God wills to manifest his fatherly favor to us in many
> ways, yet we cannot by contemplating the universe infer that
> he is Father. Rather, conscience presses us within and shows
> in our sin just cause for his disowning us and not regarding or
> recognizing us as his sons.
>
> (II,vi,1 [341])

Thus contemplation of the powerful God who creates the universe
cannot deliver us from the voice of doom pervading our consciences.
Awe alone is not the antidote for our sinfulness. Hence the second
specification:

> Christ himself bade his disciples believe in him, that they
> might clearly and perfectly believe in God: "You believe in
> God; believe also in me" [John 14:1]. For even if, properly
> speaking, faith mounts up from Christ to the Father, yet he
> means this: although faith rests in God, it will gradually dis-
> appear unless he who retains it in perfect firmness intercedes
> as Mediator.
>
> (II,vi,4 [346])

The slight, but explicit, shift of focus here must not be overlooked. Calvin is not preoccupied with the sinfulness of humanity in speaking of Christ the Mediator. He is concerned, rather, with the limit of the human capacity. Thus his crucial point is as follows:

> Even if many men once boasted that they worshiped the Supreme Majesty, the Maker of heaven and earth, yet because they had no Mediator it was not possible for them truly to taste God's mercy, and thus be persuaded that he was their Father.
>
> (II,vi,4 [347])

We now have the decisive point concerning Calvin's theological creativity before us. If he means what he says, and most assuredly he does, then the doctrine of election can no longer be left in close juxtaposition to the doctrine of providence. If it is, Calvin's very point regarding our need of Christ the Mediator will be denied by the sequence of the argument. For God's choice of us as hearers of the gospel, and that is what the doctrine of election is all about, is a function of the relationship between God and us, and not a function of God's omnipotence.

Thus the doctrine of election must unfold on this side of the christological section, rather than before it. Moreover, Calvin does not place the discussion of this doctrine in immediate juxtaposition even with the heart of his Christology, namely, the assertion that the Christ is the Mediator between God and humanity. Rather, it is taken up in the culminating chapters of Book III. Election is a matter of understanding the experience of the faithful in the presence of the Spirit. To read Calvin this way is to make him our companion in our own attempt to understand ultimacy in our midst.

I concede immediately that what must now be asserted is controversial and problematical—controversial because it challenges some of the most widely argued and firmly held convictions regarding Calvin's theological legacy, and problematical because it suggests insights that were only beginning to take shape in Calvin's own reflection and were probably incapable of surfacing in his time and place. But if we are to bring forward his creativity as we attempt to discipline our own, we have no choice but to forge ahead. For in our own efforts, some of his conclusions are more important than others, and the exercise of judgment and selectivity cannot be tamed. Life and thought in terms of belief in the relating God confronts the faithful imagination with precisely this demand. Had this not been the case in Calvin's day, neither the Reformation nor his own work would have taken shape.

Note, then, at least two things about the discussion that sets in with Chapter xxi of Book III of the *Institutes*. First, the infamous language of so-called double predestination remains in place. Hence the chapter title: "Eternal Election, by Which God Has Predestined Some to Salvation, Others to Destruction" [920]. But notice along with this the surprising overtone of the opening move of the discussion, namely, Calvin's appeal to the perplexity attending the preaching of the gospel—that not all hear it:

> In actual fact, the covenant of life is not preached equally among all men, and among those to whom it is preached, it does not gain the same acceptance either constantly or in equal degree. In this diversity the wonderful depth of God's judgment is made known.
>
> (III,xxi,1 [920–921])

All those who attempt to live in the presence of the relating God, and especially those charged with the proclamation upon which conviction concerning this presence is based, know full well what Calvin is talking about. This is why it makes sense. It is an appeal to Christian experience. Hence the ironic contradiction in Calvin's case. For part and parcel of his faithful experience, as well as for many now, is the conviction that the clue to the reality of God is the omnipotence of God. Hence, if some do not believe, the only reason can be that God does not want them to, for if God wanted them to they would believe. Now the problem is simply this: Is this contention in touch with Christian experience?

Calvin tries mightily to claim that it is. The overwhelming, though terrifying, line of reflection just noted, solidly in place at least since the relentless logic of St. Augustine, remains cogent for Calvin:

> We shall never be clearly persuaded, as we ought to be, that our salvation flows from this wellspring of God's free mercy until we come to know his eternal election, which illumines God's grace by this contrast: that he does not indiscriminately adopt all into the hope of salvation but gives to some what he denies to others.
>
> (III,xxi,1 [921])

Calvin rings the changes on this theme with a tenacity that matches the unflinching stating of the case that took shape at St. Augustine's hand.

Nothing may undermine the contention that our salvation is strictly and solely the function of the mercy of the powerful God.

That this conviction is part of the experienced conclusion reached by Calvin can hardly be denied. But what forces a probing consideration of the issues at hand is the fact that it made more sense when it was stated in close juxtaposition with the doctrine of providence, as it did in the editions of the *Institutes* prior to 1559, than it does in the context of life before God the Spirit, which is where he placed it in the panorama of the final edition. This brings us to the second point to be emphasized concerning Calvin's discussion of the doctrine of election. Whereas the insistence on double predestination remains in place, it is confronted with the fact that our conviction is based, not on an argument from the raw power of God, but on the fact of our calling.

Now to be sure, Calvin had said this, too, from the early editions of the *Institutes* forward, but this appeal finds its true home only when it is placed at the culmination of Book III. Note carefully the key problem being addressed—doubt versus faith:

> Satan has no more grievous or dangerous temptation to dishearten believers than when he unsettles them with a wicked desire to seek it outside the way.
>
> (III,xxiv,4 [968])

What precisely is this false lead? It is nothing short of the attempt to fathom the depths of ultimacy itself:

> I call it "seeking outside the way" when mere man attempts to break into the inner recesses of divine wisdom, and tries to penetrate even to highest eternity, in order to find out what decision has been made concerning himself at God's judgment seat.
>
> (III,xxiv,4 [968])

Focus on the Calling

Anxiety concerning the question "Am I truly saved?" can be overcome only by concentrating on our relationship with God, that is to say, on our calling:

> Just as those engulf themselves in a deadly abyss who, to make their election more certain, investigate God's eternal plan apart from his Word, so those who rightly and duly ex-

amine it as it is contained in his Word reap the inestimable
fruit of comfort. Let this, therefore, be the way of our inquiry:
to begin with God's call, and to end with it.

(III,xxiv,4 [969])

Did Calvin himself succeed in the effort to end the consideration
of election with the understanding of the calling? At best we can say
only that he made a beginning on this. For the full implication of such
thinking would entail removing completely the language of double predestination, and obviously this has not yet occurred. But if the calling is
the overriding concern, then responsibility, not dividing the world into
common and preferred, is the point to the doctrine, and this does indeed set in in Calvin's thought. One of the fascinating clues to this is his
reiteration of the problematic of preaching:

> If the same sermon is preached, say, to a hundred people,
> twenty receive it with the ready obedience of faith, while the
> rest hold it valueless, or laugh, or hiss, or loathe it. If anyone
> should reply that this diversity arises out of their malice and
> perverseness, I still will not be satisfied, because the nature of
> the former would be occupied with the same malice if God
> did not correct it by his goodness. Therefore, we shall always
> be confused unless Paul's question comes to mind: Who dis-
> tinguishes you? [I Cor. 4:7]. By this he means that some excel
> others not by their own virtue but by God's grace alone.
>
> (III,xxiv,12 [979])

Can this concern be taken any further? Indeed it can, as is evident
in the sequence of concerns that dominate Calvin's creativity from this
point on to the end of the *Institutes*. Systematic thinkers know that the
order in which topics are taken up is the decisive clue to their significance for the one conducting the argument. This is why the argument
from the structure of the final edition of the *Institutes* is so important.
Why did Calvin move the doctrine to the culmination of his discussion
of life in the presence of God the Spirit? And how must the subsequent
discussion be read once this has happened?

Once the doctrine of election is treated, Calvin turns to a culminating chapter for Book III, "The Final Resurrection." This will always be at
the heart of the preaching of the gospel, and for Calvin this entails a
decisive claim. He had paved the way for this in the discussion of election itself by saying that it is in Christ alone that our certainty both of
the presence of the Spirit and of our own salvation resides:

If we seek God's fatherly mercy and kindly heart, we should turn our eyes to Christ, on whom alone God's Spirit rests. . . . Now what is the purpose of election but that we, adopted as sons by our Heavenly Father, may obtain salvation and immortality by his favor? No matter how much you toss it about and mull it over, you will discover that its final bounds extend no farther. . . . But if we have been chosen in him, we shall not find assurance of our election in ourselves; and not even in God the Father, if we conceive him as severed from his Son. Christ, then, is the mirror wherein we must, and without self-deception may, contemplate our own election.

(III,xxiv,5 [970])

Later, this metaphor of the mirror comes into play again, for in Christ's resurrection we behold the "pledge" of our own:

Now whenever we consider the resurrection, let Christ's image come before us. In the nature which he took from us he so completed the course of mortal life that now, having obtained immortality, he is the pledge of our coming resurrection. . . . As we have said that in this mirror the living image of the resurrection is visible to us, so is it a firm foundation to support our minds, provided we are not wearied or irked with a longer delay; for our task is not to measure minutes of time as we please but patiently to wait until God in his own good time restores his kingdom.

(III,xxv,3 [990–991])

This is the gospel we have to proclaim. Those who hear it are the elect. Note well that preoccupation with the nonelect is transmuted into passion for the hearing of the gospel. Note well, also, that this is the bridge from the discussion of the doctrine of election to the discussion of the church.

In saying this we lay hold of the decisive vector along which the creativity of the *Institutes* unfolds. For the church, along with the parallel structure of civil government, is in fact the context within which the experience of election takes shape:

The basis on which we believe the church is that we are fully convinced that we are members of it. In this way our salvation rests upon sure and firm supports.

(IV,i,3 [1015])

But there is more to see, for in focusing the implications of this conviction sharply, Calvin is actually moving beyond the doctrine of double predestination, which he was not yet ready to do in Book III.

How so? We can see this in three steps. First, the ground of this conviction is in election itself: "First [our salvation] stands by God's election, and cannot waver or fall any more than his eternal providence can" (IV,i,3 [1015]).

But second, note the remarkable disclaimer that follows close on the heels of this affirmation:

> Here we are not bidden to distinguish between reprobate and elect—that is for God alone, not for us, to do—but to establish with certainty in our hearts that all those who, by the kindness of God the Father, through the working of the Holy Spirit, have entered into fellowship with Christ, are set apart as God's property and personal possession; and that when we are of their number we share that great grace.
>
> (IV,i,3 [1015–1016])

How is the church, where alone this "certainty in our hearts" is nourished, to be discerned? This is the third step, Calvin's delineation of the marks of the church:

> Wherever we see the Word of God purely preached and heard, and the sacraments administered according to Christ's institution, there, it is not to be doubted, a church of God exists.
>
> (IV,i,9 [1023])

Note well the positive ring of this progression. Risk more than that. Note that Calvin does *not* define the church simply in terms of the certainty of election. He defines it rather in terms of the responsibility of the elect, for the decisive issue concerns what they must *do*. And this passion will not be settled until he has developed an understanding of civil government that is similarly informed. Note further, then, that certainty concerning the nonelect plays no role in this progression. Calvin does not need it. He has moved beyond it. In short, he has begun his own extrapolation of the received tradition.

Calvin could take it no further than this. The inscrutable will of God alone distinguishes between elect and nonelect. The context of the Renaissance/Reformation was not enough to force into the open the full implication of treating the doctrine of election as a function of the experience of believers.[3] Only life on this side of the Enlightenment could do that.

We are on this side of the Enlightenment. In fact, we are on this side of the radical revision of many enlightenment insights, all of which are pointed toward with the current term "postmodern." Is Calvin of any help to us, seeing that we are where we are? The answer is a re-sounding Yes! For when one takes seriously the place of the doctrine of election in the culminating argument of his prolific theological productivity, it emerges that the real focus of the significance of the doctrine does not have to do with the so-called nonelect, but with the self-understanding of the elect themselves. This is why we must take Calvin's own creativity further than he did. In this light, then, we redefine the doctrine. The doctrine of election concerns those who hear the gospel. Having heard it, what are they to do? They are to proclaim it. What about those, then, who, for any reason, do not hear this same gospel? Our task is to bend the full momentum of our imaginative creativity in the direction of seeing to it that they do. That many will not remains the fact of the case. But let us be clear. If that be so, let it not be because of timid weakness on our part. The point to God's choice of us—for that remains the only reason why we do indeed hear God's voice—is not a category whereby we consign to the inexhaustible pit of eternal damnation those who do not respond. Not only is this category not needed, given the claim of all and everything for the love of the relating God; it is an undermining of the very ground of the concern. We believe in the power of the loving God, whose passion for relating to us is alone the reason we hear the voice of the Spirit. We know, and know that we know, that the God of love possesses a power that cannot deteriorate to an ultimacy of caprice. We can have no use for an idea of divine damnation. We have too much work to do to worry about this. In saying this, we put on the mantle of Calvin himself. This is where his faithful reflection was going, too.

BARTH'S BREAKTHROUGH

It is probably too debatable to claim that Karl Barth's discussion of the doctrine of election is the most significant treatment to occur since Calvin's effort. Such a claim would leave out of consideration the vast development of orthodox Calvinism and all that that has generated. What must be seen, however, is this: It is with Barth's discussion that the doctrine finds its home in our postmodern world.

In his excellent work, *The Knowledge of God in Calvin's Theology*, Edward Dowey makes the incisive remark that Calvin was an epistemologist, not a metaphysician.[4] This is a decisive clue not only to Calvin's thought, but also to Barth's; and in fact it may well attend any Protestant effort to clarify what, on this side of Barth, will always be known as *kerygmatic theology*. As we have already seen, for Barth the sole task of theology is the clarification of the proclamation of the gospel. On this basis he will find it necessary to make an epistemological move beyond Calvin, insisting that the doctrine must be understood christologically. This move is at the very heart of his revision of the doctrine of election, which he takes up in *Church Dogmatics*, II/2. I, for one, am convinced that this discussion is not only the fulcrum of the massive argument of the *Church Dogmatics* as a whole; it is the clue to the entirety of his work.

One can hardly be accused of overstating the case, given the thesis with which paragraph 32, the initial section of II/2, begins:

> The doctrine of election is the sum of the Gospel because of all words that can be said or heard it is the best: that God elects man; that God is for man too the One who loves in freedom. It is grounded in the knowledge of Jesus Christ because He is both the electing God and elected man in One. It is part of the doctrine of God because originally God's election of man is a predestination not merely of man but of Himself. Its function is to bear testimony to eternal, free and unchanging grace as the beginning of all the ways and works of God.
>
> (CD, 3)[5]

The Electing God

Immediately we encounter the complex problematic of dealing with the received translation of Barth's work. The thesis itself must be rigorously probed. In the first place, in dealing with Barth, as well as all on this side of the rise of sensitivity to women's liberation, the obvious point must be asserted that *humanity* is elected in Jesus Christ. Neither Barth, nor his translator, reckoned with the fact that the time was at hand in which we must be explicitly concerned with the issue of the inclusiveness of our language about God. All of humanity is involved in the election of God. Given the unlimited reach of this claim in the light of Barth's recasting of the doctrine of election, this must be asserted at the outset. There is no invisibility in the humanity that is the object of the grace of God.

Along with this, indeed accompanying it, is a serious question that must be put, not to Barth, but to the translator, G. W. Bromiley (granted that huge debts of gratitude are owed to him and the considerable array of collaborators who shared with him the massive task of putting the entire *Church Dogmatics* into English). The subject matter of Chapter VII of the *Church Dogmatics* is the doctrine of election, not the doctrine of predestination. As has already been said, the terms "election" (*Erwählung*) and "predestination" (*Praedestination*) stand in apposition, but that means that the intentionality of a given theologian must be given strict respect. When Barth wants to use the term "predestination," he does so. Given where the tradition has been, it is utterly misleading to use it when he does not. Barth claims that the doctrine of *election* is the sum of the gospel: "Die Erwählungslehre ist die Summe des Evangeliums . . . " (*KD*, 1).

This is faithfully rendered by Bromiley. Why, then, does the term "predestination" appear later in the translation of the thesis? The heart of Barth's entire revision of the doctrine of election is contained in an astonishing claim: "It [the doctrine of election] is part of the doctrine of God because originally God's election of man is a predestination not merely of man but of Himself" (*CD*, 3). This is not what Barth said. His words are as follows:

> Sie [die Erwählungslehre] gehört darum sur Lehre von Gott, weil Gott, indem er den Menschen wählt, nicht nur über diesen, sondern in ursprünglicher Weise über sich selbst bestimmt.
>
> (*KD*, 1)

In the translation of this passage, the term "predestination" relates to the German verb *"bestimmt."* The fundamental meaning of this verb is "to decide" or "to determine." Now to be sure, Barth's sentence is difficult to put precisely into English—so difficult, in fact, that one's own theological propensities will operate in the very process of translating.

This will be no less the case for me than it is for Bromiley. But he seeks to assert the traditional doctrine of "predestination" wherever he can. I seek to understand the primordial decision of God, a decision to love all humanity, whatever the cost. The interpretation of the lasting significance of Barth's revision of the doctrine of election turns on how this crucial formulation is understood. I translate it as follows: "It [the doctrine of election] is part of the doctrine of God because God's election of humanity is, in a primordial manner, a decision not only regarding humanity but also regarding God's own self-understanding."

My use of Whitehead's term "primordial" here is deliberate. Calvinist orthodoxy did not follow Calvin's removal of the doctrine of election to Book III of the *Institutes*. This then left the proximity between the doctrines of creation and providence, on the one hand, and the doctrine of election/predestination, on the other, in control of the meaning of the claim at hand. The term "predestination" thus came to have the decisive overtones of *spatial remoteness* and *predeterminism*. As we shall see, Barth's entire effort turns on the rejection of this distortion. Accordingly, a different term must be used to indicate the antecedent character of the sum of the gospel.

To assign this duty to the term "primordial" brings into the open one further problem in the translation of the thesis of paragraph 36. In the final sentence, Barth speaks of the function of the doctrine as being that of bearing witness to the eternal, free, and *continual [beständigen]* grace that is the beginning of all the ways and works of God. The translation speaks of God's "unchanging" grace. This is far too static for me and, I think, for Barth. The grace of God is continual, in the midst of all the fluctuation we know as reality. To say that it is "unchanging" is indeed how we have said this, in English, until now. We can no longer leave the case there. The stability of God's grace has to do with the trustworthy duration of God's primordial decision. The dependable continuity of the grace of God informs our faith. This is why Barth spoke of God's *beständigen Gnade* (KD, 1). The primary meaning of the term is "steady, constant, continual," not "unchanging."

The epitomizing formulation of Barth's revision of the doctrine of election occurs virtually at the outset of II/2. The term "predestination" is in order:

> The truth which must now occupy us, the truth of the doctrine of predestination, is first and last and in all circum-

stances the sum of the Gospel, no matter how it may be understood in detail, no matter what apparently contradictory aspects or moments it may present to us. It is itself evangel: glad tidings; news which uplifts and comforts and sustains.

(*CD*, 12)

Barth moves immediately to indicate what this affirmation excludes. The truth at hand is neither "neutral" nor "a mere theorem." Moreover, "it is not a mixed message of joy and terror, salvation and damnation." How so? Here we encounter one of Barth's most significant and reiterated assertions: The Yes and the No of the gospel are *asymmetrically* related. One can never grasp, or be grasped by, the grace of God apart from this:

> Originally and finally it is not dialectical but non-dialectical. It does not proclaim in the same breath both good and evil, both help and destruction, both life and death. It does, of course, throw a shadow. We cannot overlook or ignore this aspect of the matter. In itself, however, it is light and not darkness. We cannot, therefore, speak of the latter aspect in the same breath. In any case, even under this aspect, the final word is never that of warning, of judgment, of punishment, of a barrier erected, of a grave opened. We cannot speak of it without mentioning all these things. The Yes cannot be heard unless the No is also heard. But the No is said for the sake of the Yes and not for its own sake. In substance, therefore, the first and last word is Yes and not No.

(*CD*, 13)

Thus the No of the gospel has no independent existence. It cannot be understood apart from what it negates. In this sense it is dependent on the gospel that it denies. Gone, then, is the effort to understand the negation as the opposite equal of the claim of the gospel. Gone too, then, and for that reason, is the terror that our passion for symmetry necessarily generates. If the Yes and the No of the gospel are equally weighted, only the No will be heard.

Calvin, too, was sensitive to this problem, as we have already seen, but he did not go far enough for Barth. Indeed, the baseline of Barth's critique of Calvin turns on this very point:

> What is revealed to us in Scripture is as such necessary and useful and worthy to be known by all. On no account, then,

must the doctrine of predestination be withheld from believers. . . . Calvin was right. But although his point was right, he could have made it more emphatically and impressively if his understanding of predestination had been less speculative and more in accordance with the biblical testimony; if it had been a strictly evangelical understanding. And with its *parallelismus membrorum*, with that balanced assertion of the two-fold dealings of God, as a doctrine of double predestination, this is precisely what it is not.

(*CD*, 18)

Hence the impasse, and for Barth this is precisely why we must move beyond Calvin: "In such a form it is inevitable that the No should become much the stronger and ultimately the exclusive note" (*CD*, 18). The problem with the received tradition focuses here, and it is precisely this distortion that Barth sought to confront and remove:

The task which confronts us is rather a critical one, even in face of the very best tradition. . . . If the doctrine is to shed forth its light, then the shadow must be dispersed. The dispersing of this shadow will be our definite objective in the polemical discussions throughout this whole chapter. We cannot be too soon, or too radical, in the opposition we must offer to the classical tradition, or rather in the attempt to do justice to the particular and justifiable and necessary intention which underlies that tradition. And we introduce the first and most radical point with our thesis that the doctrine of election must be understood quite definitely and unequivocally as Gospel; that it is not something neutral on the yonder side of Yes and No; that is not No but Yes; that it is not Yes and No, but in its substance, in the origin and scope of its utterance, it is altogether Yes.

(*CD*, 13)

Barth spent his life spelling out what this entails. He would go to whatever lengths proved necessary in this inexhaustible interpretative effort. So must we. As we shall see, our effort must move beyond even Barth's precisely because of the claim he made.

Why can we not be too radical in challenging the classical tradition in this light? Why is it the case that the point at hand cannot be overstated? These two questions are necessarily joined together. To ask one is to ask the other. The tradition itself has been the greatest enemy of the very truth it has sought to protect and proclaim. We are at the very baseline of Barth's revision of the doctrine of election when we listen to the manner in which he clarifies this assertion:

> Starting from Jn. 1:1f., we have laid down and developed two statements concerning the election [*Erwählung*] of Jesus Christ. The first is that Jesus Christ is the electing God. This statement answers the question of the Subject of the eternal election of grace. And the second is that Jesus Christ is elected man. This statement answers the question of the object of the eternal election of grace. Strictly speaking, the whole dogma of predestination [*Praedestinationsdogma*] is contained in these two statements.
>
> (*CD*, 145; see also *KD*, 157)

This leads him to a very concise and incisive statement:

> Im Angang bei Gott war dieser Eine, Jesus Christus. Und eben das ist die Praedestination.
>
> (*KD*, 157)

> [In the beginning with God was this One, Jesus Christ. And that is predestination.]
>
> (*CD*, 145)

There are countless formulations such as this in the vast writings of Karl Barth. For it is simply the case that he was a man with a single idea, one that receives an infinite set of expressions. Even so, the statement before us is as close as any to his epitomizing confessional affirmation. Accordingly, he literally means it to be that in speaking of Jesus Christ as electing God and elected man a relationship is established "which cannot be broken and the perfection of which can never be exhausted" (*CD*, 145).

Claims such as this are truly radical, for that which is inexhaustible cannot be overstated. Intelligibility alone rules what one says. Accordingly, it can come as no surprise that Barth commences his elaboration of this claim by addressing the epistemological issue, and what marks the drastic character of his insight is the fact that he must challenge the whole tradition in this light:

> We may begin with an epistemological observation. Our thesis is that God's eternal will is the election of Jesus Christ. At this point we part company with all previous interpretations of the doctrine of predestination.
>
> (*CD*, 146)

That Barth was never timid in pressing his arguments contributes to all the legends concerning his aggressive, even abrasive, vigor. But although this would seem to be irrepressibly present in treating his discussion at this point, it is the least significant aspect of the matter at hand. Why was he so exercised on all this? The answer has to do with the fact of the gospel as the basis of all Christian conviction. The trouble with the tradition, according to Barth, is that at the heart of faith it finds a great mystery, one that is twofold, we might say, given the gospel itself. For the impasse of the tradition is that in all its forms "the Subject and object of predestination (the electing God and elected man) are determined ultimately by the fact that both quantities are treated as unknown" (*CD*, 146). Thus:

> We may say that the electing God is a supreme being who disposes freely according to his own omnipotence, righteousness and mercy. We may say that to Him may be ascribed the lordship over all things, and above all the absolute right and absolute power to determine the destiny of man. But when we say that, then ultimately and fundamentally the electing God is an unknown quantity.
>
> (*CD*, 146)

Hence the other side of the impasse: To argue simplistically from the a priori of God's omnipotence is to wind up with the unknown God, simply because that is where one begins. The issue is genuinely epistemological in character, for how does one know that this God is omnipotent?

> We may say that elected man is the man who has come under the eternal good-pleasure of God, the man whom from all eternity God has foreordained to fellowship with himself. But when we say that, then ultimately and fundamentally elected man is also an unknown quantity.
>
> (*CD*, 146)

The claims of the tradition are grand indeed, but how do we know, and know that we know, that they are sound? Here the tradition falls silent, and that silence undermines the very ground of the conviction itself. Indeed, all too often the apparent blessedness of the comfortable masquerades as the real reason why the convicted can speak with such conviction. The Deuteronomic redactors tried this argument; the brilliant author of Job refuted it once and for all. The fact is that at the heart of the faith is the reality of the relating God. To say that this is just the presence of the Great Mystery is to have no gospel at all. But to argue thus is to stand before the armored columns of established conviction with nothing in one's hand but a piece of paper with the gospel written on it. For the tradition ignores the hollow claims in the name of the Great Mystery by simply rushing by them. This may be the reason behind the fact that so many of today's theological students, old and young, shy away from discussion of election and predestination as if these were the marks of the plague. Obscurity, mystery—these are not the code words for the gospel. We do not believe in the great Question Mark. Thus, the tradition to the contrary notwithstanding, "Our thesis that the eternal will of God is the election of Jesus Christ means that we deny the existence of any such twofold mystery" (CD, 146).

This emphatic denial is rooted in the twofold affirmation at the base of Barth's doctrine of election. Each of these affirmations relates to one or the other aspects of the twofold claim that Jesus Christ is both electing God and elected humanity in one. The first of these excludes once and for all the idea of the absolute decree, issued from the remoteness of eternity and evoking the logical symmetry of the doctrine of double predestination. The close proximity of the acting out of God's love for us, not the remote vagueness of God's decision so to act, is the heart of the gospel. Given this, Barth can make his unequivocal claim: "There is no such thing as a *decretum absolutum*. There is no such thing as a will of God apart from the will of Jesus Christ" (CD, 115). Thus the doctrine of election is part of the doctrine of *God*. For: "There is no such thing as Godhead [*Gottheit*] in itself. Godhead is always the Godhead of the Father, the Son and the Holy Spirit" (CD, 115).

The troublesome word "Godhead" is deeply rooted in the tradition, from the time of the ancient church forward. But its use in this translation must be questioned, because the term is hopelessly opaque for many in the present. The point to the doctrine of election is that, in the light of the gospel, what the faithful mean by the term "God" is focused, once and for all, in the fact of Jesus Christ. Accordingly, there may be no shared time between doubt and faith, insofar as the question doubted is whether God does indeed love us. This is clear: "As we believe in Him and hear His Word and hold fast by His decision, we can know with a certainty which nothing can ever shake that we are the elect of God" (CD, 116).

This affirmation itself is a clear example of what I mean in speaking of the *extrapolation* of past insights as a necessarily central component of the theological task. Barth's move beyond the tradition is explicitly informed by the appeal to the basis of our conviction itself. If the gospel holds, the entire idea of the absolute decree must be rejected, in spite of the hoary and convoluted history of its use (see *CD*, 106ff.). Note carefully the fact that this idea falls because of epistemological considerations. Given the gospel, it can and must be said that "God's eternal will is the election of Jesus Christ" (*CD*, 146). The challenge to the tradition, then, is at the very heart of the issues at hand. What do we mean by the term "God"? Do we mean the God of love we know, because we are known, in Jesus Christ? Or do we mean the God who may or may not love us? The second question can arise only if the gospel is not understood or is understood and not believed. This extrapolation is one Barth would not merely countenance; he would demand it.

Elected Humanity

We will not sense the truly radical way in which Barth follows out the logic of his insight, however, unless we lay hold of the second affirmation at hand. Jesus Christ is not only electing God; Jesus Christ is also, at one and the same time, elected humanity. Barth is right in insisting that this second affirmation must be stated with precision, for here he moves to one of, if not *the*, most profound insights to come from the full range of his work as a whole. The claim that Jesus Christ is elected humanity means two things: First:

> It tells us that before all created reality, before all being and becoming in time, before time itself, in the pre-temporal eternity of God, the eternal divine decision as such has as its object and content the existence of this one created being, the man Jesus of Nazareth, and the work of this man in His life and death, His humiliation and exaltation, His obedience and merit.
>
> (*CD*, 116)

But second, along with this:

> It tells us further that in and with the existence of this man the eternal divine decision has as its object and content the execution of the divine covenant with man, the salvation of all men.
>
> (*CD*, 116)

73

Here is the decisive basis of Barth's so-called universalism. Note, however, that what is at stake is the universal significance of the election of Jesus Christ. This, and this alone, is central. The universalism of the gospel is not an implication of the goodness of humanity. It is the direct significance of the action of God. This is why it is so crucial to understand that the doctrine of election is part of the doctrine of God.

How far may we take this claim? There is no limit, provided that we remain explicitly in touch with its epistemological base. The gospel itself, not some hypothesis regarding the God not known in Jesus Christ, and not some hope regarding human nature, demands this. So Barth insists. As has already been noted, Barth was a man with a single idea. Once his basic point is clear, the remainder of what he writes corroborates the insight at hand by deepening the clarification of its implications. There are three crucial instances of this process with reference to his affirmation of the universal significance of the gospel: (1) his understanding of the relationship between Israel and the church, as this is stated in Romans 9–11, (2) his discussion of Judas Iscariot, and (3) the basis of his understanding of the relationship between the Election of God and the Command of God, the two chapters comprising *Church Dogmatics*, II/2.

Israel and the Church

A compact line of reflection sets out the basis of Barth's understanding of Israel and the church. Jesus Christ is both "the crucified Messiah of Israel" and "the risen Lord of the Church" (*CD*, 198). But because we are saying two things about Jesus Christ, the relationship between Israel and the church, however one understands the contrast between them, is one of basic unity:

> Israel is the people of the Jews which resists its election; the Church is the gathering of Jews and Gentiles called on the ground of its election. This is the formulation which we have adopted and this or a similar formulation is necessary if the unity of the election of the community (grounded in the one election of Jesus Christ) is to remain visible. We cannot, therefore, call the Jews the "rejected" and the Church the "elected" community. The object of election is neither Israel for itself nor the Church for itself, but both together in their unity.
>
> (*CD*, 199)

The difference between them, then, must be understood christologically, for "it is in the twofold determination of Christ himself that this

74

difference has its basis": Israel being seen from the side of Jesus Christ "as elected man as such"; and the church, from the side of Jesus Christ "as electing God as such" (CD, 199). This leads Barth to the fundamental contention that he will maintain with relentless consistency:

> The antithesis between the two cannot be formulated in exclusive terms. . . . The ineffaceable differentiation of the two forms of the community has certainly to be noted. But it has also to be noted that thereby its indissoluble unity is also brought to light.
>
> (CD, 200)

This contention turns on the detailed discussion of Romans 9–11, which accompanies, and virtually transcends, the text of Barth's own argument. In fact, this is one of those points in the *Church Dogmatics* as a whole where the notes are more important than the text, because it is in them that the decisive formulations occur. In commencing this discussion, Barth rightly notes that "the doctrine of predestination has only too often been presented without a coherent consideration of this *locus classicus*" (CD, 202). At the outset, Barth insists that "the Church lives by the covenants made between God and Israel" (CD, 203). How else can we put it, given the context of the coming of Jesus Christ?

> It is from Israel that this man has come and been snatched. Not from Greece, not from Rome, not from Germany, but from Israel! It is independent either of Israel's unbelief or the faith of the Church. It cannot be destroyed by Israel's unbelief and therefore it is not to be denied in the faith of the Church but openly confessed: "Salvation is of the Jews" (Jn. 4:22). . . . the Church does not dispute, but asserts and teaches in defiance of all Gentile arrogance, the eternal election of Israel.
>
> (CD, 204)

Here we encounter one of the priceless insights of Barth's contention that the doctrine of election must be understood as part of the doctrine of God. The issue of the difference between Israel and the church cannot be worked out simply on the basis of human considerations alone. Israel and the church are tied together not only by their common origin in the electing action of God, but by the fact that Israel necessarily *precedes* the church. Accordingly, neither Israel's rejection of the Messiah nor the church's confession of faith in the Lord may be understood apart from each other.

A key formulation regarding this central matter occurs in Barth's interpretation of the parable of the potter (Rom. 9:19ff.), which is the context in which Paul distinguishes between vessels of wrath and vessels of mercy. The point is that *both* Israel and the church are necessary, given the purpose of God as we know this in the gospel. If, now, this purpose is the pivot on which the distinction turns, we are *not* dealing with the ruthless exercise of absolute power:

> He uses them both [Israel and the Church] as witnesses to Jesus Christ, each in its own way. This is how the potter, the God of Israel, deals in and with his people—not according to the caprices of His omnipotence [*den Launen seiner Allmacht*] but in the determinate purpose, corresponding to His name and nature, of His own justification in the death and man's justification in the resurrection of Christ, in the revelation of the way taken by Him in His advance towards the day of His future. Two things are necessarily revealed on this way, that Israel is the place of His glory, and this glory is His own and not Israel's.
>
> (*CD*, 223; see also *KD*, 246)

Here, once again, we encounter the asymmetrical relationship between the Yes and the No of the gospel:

> If to the right He says Yes, He does this for His own sake. . . .
> If to the left He says No, he does this for the sake of the Yes.
> . . . [T]he relationship between the two sides of the one divine action is one of supreme incongruity, supreme a-symmetry, supreme disequilibrium.
>
> (*CD*, 224)

If this is indeed the case, then the church itself most radically misunderstands the fact of its own election if it presumes a superior and autonomous role in this relationship. This is the heart of Romans 9–11, and it is the central reason behind the long discussion Barth devotes to his line-by-line analysis of Paul's argument. Given the fact that Paul was Saul, there can be little doubt that we are at the core of the understanding of the gospel reached by one of the most important of all the progenitors of the Christian tradition as a whole. How tragic, then, that this is misunderstood in that prevailing distortion of the doctrine of election, the *sum* of the gospel, as Barth insists, which sees God's decisive choices as functions of omnipotence rather than universal love.

Even the language of scripture itself must be held to this interpretation. Speaking of Romans 9:22, where Israel is spoken of under the metaphor "vessels of wrath," Barth relentlessly insists on his basic point: Because Jesus Christ is "the secret of Israel's history," it follows that

> the meaning of its history cannot, then, be perceived in a juxtaposition of two different purposes of God. The existence of the "vessels of wrath," the existence of Israel standing at last before us as a single "vessel of wrath" embodied in the "traitor" Judas Iscariot, has no end in itself.
>
> (CD, 227)

That we must deal with Judas Iscariot before we have finished with the issue at hand is clearly indicated here. For the moment, though, note the insistence that Israel's history, and therefore its rejection of the Messiah, has *no end in itself.* One can only evade this conclusion by ignoring Romans 9–11. This is surely ironic, because the Letter to the Romans is decisively central for at least a Protestant understanding of the gospel as a whole. In Barth's remarks we encounter the most trenchantly argued theological insistence that anti-Semitism is categorically contrary to Christian conviction. In dealing with Israel and the church, we are not dealing with two histories, but one. For the church to deny Israel is for the church to deny its own origin.

It is precisely this issue that Saul-become-Paul wrestled with at the apex of the Letter to the Romans. We cannot have the great blessings of the doctrine of justification by faith alone through grace, with which the letter begins, without pursuing the original argument to its basic conclusion. Does the coming of Jesus confessed to be the Christ deny God's electing word to Israel? Paul says No; so, therefore, does Barth. At stake here is the careful reading of Romans 11. Saul-become-Paul asks and answers his own agonizing question, Has God rejected his people? Paul cannot undo his own origin. Neither can the church. This is the inexorable conclusion toward which he moves. The chapter begins with a reference to Elijah and the remnant of seven thousand who with him did not bow down to Baal. Barth is mindful of this when he ponders verse 13, Paul's statement "I am speaking to you Gentiles." Concerning this he observes:

> In the first instance, of course, the reference is to the Christians among Paul's Gentile hearers. Yet Paul certainly regards these Gentiles as representative of the whole Gentile world. . . . Regarded christologically and eschatologically the Church is always both *all* Israel—not only the seven thousand but also the hardened rest—and *all* the Gentile world, those who have already become believers and those who are yet to become so.
>
> (*CD*, 280)

This crucial passage, buried so deeply in an extended note that it is likely to be overlooked, contains Barth's radical explosion of the doctrine of election. In Barth's own indication of the implications of this remark, we encounter a frontier that extends beyond even his own penetrating exploration, as we shall see. What we learn from him is the direct consequence of his claim, following Paul, that Israel and the church do not comprise two histories. They must be understood together. More than that, without Israel the church cannot understand itself!

> The Church can understand its own origin and its own goal only as it understands its unity with Israel. Precisely in its Gentile Christian members it must perceive that it would itself be forsaken by God if God had really forsaken Israel.
>
> (*CD*, 284)

Nor may we consign the significance of this contention to a simplistically chronological progression, which is all too often the manner in which Christians today speak of "the Judeo-Christian" tradition. The significance of the point at hand, both in Paul's day and in Barth's and ours, is the *present*, not the past:

> Israel is still the possession and work of God, and as such the presupposition without which there would be no Church, and no Gentile Christians. . . . The conclusion following from this insight will again be that precisely in its Gentile Christian members the Church would have to regard itself as forsaken if it tried to think and say this of Israel or even of the hardened in Israel.
>
> (*CD*, 285)

The point defies overstatement. The word of God to the church cannot be true if the word of God to Israel is—not *was*, but *is*—a lie. Not only do we not believe in a capricious God; we do not believe in a schizo-phrenic one either. We do not believe in the Ultimate Liar.

Nor do we believe in the ultimate victory of unbelief. How can we, given the gospel? This is the conclusion that Barth did not refuse to press and that lays him open to the charge of universalism. For him, the issue turns on how we are to understand the hardening of Israel's heart. Recall the text in Romans 11:

> Lest you be wise in your own conceits, I want you to under-stand this mystery, brethren: a hardening has come upon part of Israel, until the full number of the Gentiles come in, and so all Israel will be saved; . . . As regards the gospel they are enemies of God, for your sake; but as regards election they are beloved for the sake of their forefathers. For the gifts and the call of God are irrevocable.
>
> (Rom. 11:25–26a, 28–29)

To read these lines in the light of Romans 11 as a whole is to know that the contrast between elect and hardened *within the chosen* qualifies once and for all how the latter are to be understood. They can only be known in the light of the grace that generates the differentiation:

> If with the making of this contrast between the elect and the hardened in the chosen people there vanishes even the last semblance of the idea that God's elect owe it to themselves that they are such; if this contrast brings all the more clearly into the view the nature of the free goodness of the electing God, this obviously means that some light necessarily falls even upon the darkness of the hardened.
>
> (CD, 276)

That indeed some light does fall upon the darkness of the hard-ened is a function of the fact that God needed their transgression. If this is so, the transgression is itself qualified, for it is taken up into the un-folding purpose of the expansion of the grace of God:

> God needed the Jews for the sake of the Gentiles. He needed their transgression. In order to bring about this transgression he hardened them. Thus their hardening has become an inte-gral part of salvation-history in a way that is decisive even for the Gentiles. . . . This must be noted by Gentile Christians . . . who would like to regard the hardened as forsaken. God has so little forsaken them that it is for their sake that He has

stretched out His hand to the Gentiles. The existence of the Gentiles as recipients of salvation has the meaning and purpose of a summons to these hardened Jews and therefore of a confirmation of their eternal election.

(CD, 279)

The insight at hand is incontrovertible. If the election of God is to transcend the ethnic limitations of the election of Israel, it must do so in a way that leaves intact the original call. Otherwise, the integrity of God's purpose, which is the origin of the integrity of Israel's identity, would be denied. Accordingly, the expansion of the covenant to include those beyond the limitations of Israel's identity necessitates understanding the contrast between Jew and Gentile in positive terms. The integrity of the initial election is durable. Hence the emergence of a broadening, more inclusive election will be born only in struggle. The birth of new creativity will be marked by pain. How, though, does the new reality transcend the pain of the birth of this emergence?

The gospel itself, the proclamation of the crucifixion and resurrection of Jesus Christ, informs the contrast at hand and thus conditions the transcendence of Israel by insisting on its positive meaning. Cross and resurrection involve both Israel and the church, not just the latter. Paul spoke of the wild olive shoot now grafted onto the tree as being there only by God's act (Rom. 11:17–24), an act manifesting the power of God to restore the discarded branch: "God has the power to graft them in again" (Rom. 11:23b). Despite the confusing character of the metaphors, Barth's comment is decisive:

> This reference to the omnipotence of God in Paul, as in the other witnesses of the Old and New Testaments, is not to be understood as an appeal to or a reliance on the infinite potentiality of the divine being in general. He does not build vaguely and arbitrarily on the postulate that with God everything and all things must finally be possible. It is from an optimistic estimate of man in conjunction with this postulate of an infinite potentiality in the divine being that the assertion of a final redemption of each and all, known as the doctrine of the *apokatastasis* ["restoration"], usually draws its inspiration and power. Paul does not start from this point and therefore he does not get the length of this assertion.
>
> (CD, 295)

Thus the crucial point does not turn on generalizations but on the astonishing particularity of the gospel itself. This alone is the ground of a universalism that both can and must be stated. But it is a universalism of the loving God whose power carries forward each and every relationship the relating God has, does, and will risk. Barth's expression of this contains one of the most memorable insights in the *Church Dogmatics* as a whole:

> Both at this point and in what follows the thought of the future of this man and of the omnipotence of this God is, therefore, a thought of faith, a concrete thought of hope which neither overestimates man nor infringes the freedom of God. But in this very concreteness it has force and precision; it can and must be thought and expressed. In view of the relation of this God to man it is impossible to expect too much from God.
>
> (*CD*, 295)

Here, then, is the gospel according to Barth: "We can never believe in unbelief; we can believe only in the future belief of those who at present do not believe" (*CD*, 296).

Everything in Barth's thought at large pivots on this insight. The gospel has to do with all humanity. Those who hear the gospel, then, have only one certainty, and it is this faith they have to proclaim. This is Barth's extrapolation of the doctrine of election. That it bears the marks of a concern profoundly central in Calvin's thought is clear. But that it moves not only toward the conclusion Calvin's thought itself generates, but beyond it is also clear. If Israel's rejection is caught up in a future that transcends it, we have a principle that can be infinitely extended into realms and times beyond even the farthest horizons of either Paul, Calvin, or Barth. This is how far the asymmetrical relationship between the Yes and the No of the gospel can and must be carried. We need, however, the two further steps already mentioned if we are to grasp and be grasped by the power of the gospel of the love of God. For Barth confronts the depths of this gospel in wrestling with the fact of Judas Iscariot, and he states what must be regarded as the principle of the infinite expansion of this gospel in formulating the relationship between the Election of God and the Command of God. We need these, too, if the task before us is to be handled with the courage the creativity of the relating God demands.

That the doctrine of election must be understood as part of the doctrine of God informs the moves we have just examined in Barth's discussion. So to think places the distinction between elected and rejected in relationship to the relating God. In this sense the contrast is decisively relativized. Does this apply to individuals as well as to the communities, Israel and the church? If it does not, the insight disappears into the realm of the remote, and the doctrine at hand can hardly be maintained as "the sum of the gospel." Accordingly, Barth presses the case at hand to its full conclusion.

Again we encounter the Yes/No theme so central in his line of reflection. The issue can be grasped only christologically: "It is strictly and narrowly only in the portrait of the one Jesus Christ that we may perceive who and what a rejected man is" (CD, 352). What does it mean to say this? For Barth there is only one answer, and it is drastic indeed:

> He is *the* Rejected, as and because He is *the* Elect. In view of His election, there is no other rejected but Himself. It is for the sake of the election of all the rejected that he stands in solitude over against them all. It is just for them that He is *the* rejected One. . . . Thus Jesus Christ is the Lord and Head and Subject of the witness both of "the elect" and also of "the rejected." For all the great difference between them, both have their true existence in Him.
>
> (CD, 353)

Both the elect *and* the rejected are involved with God in Jesus Christ. The whole claim of the gospel is here stated. In Jesus Christ God relates to *all humanity*, not the good, not the elect, but humanity as whole, good and bad, elected and rejected. This is the primordial reality—that fallen humanity is confronted from the beginning in Jesus Christ as electing God and elected humanity. Whatever is meant by the negative terms must be derived, then, from the positive ones. The No has no independent meaning because it has no independent reality.

Those who hear the gospel must know this. Their entire outlook upon those who do not depends on how well they understand this ultimate claim. The very purpose of their hearing—that is, of the relating God's relating to them—is that the circle of those who do hear be expanded. Just as God says Yes to them, so they must affirm the world:

> One thing is sure. The elect man is chosen in order that the circle of election—that is, the circle of those who recognize and confess Jesus Christ in the world—should not remain stationary or fixed, but open up and enlarge itself, and therefore grow and expand and extend. What is given him in his election and calling is undoubtedly the task not to shut but to

> open, not to exclude but to include, not to say No but Yes to
> the surrounding world; just as he himself is undoubtedly one
> to whom it was opened, who was included, to whom Yes was
> said—the Yes of the unmerited, free and eternal grace and
> love of God.
>
> (CD, 419)

Explicitly before us, then, is the fact that the gospel itself entails an inexhaustibly inclusive and expansive capacity at its very center. The ultimate is open to us; ultimate openness is the mode of our relationship to the world. So, therefore, the passage continues:

> It is by and in this Yes that he must live with others. He repre-
> sents and reflects the gracious God, and Jesus Christ and His
> people, as he causes them to hear this Yes. If he says No he
> also says Yes; even when he closes he opens; even when he
> excludes he includes. He will face others wrathfully but
> never contemptuously, with indignation but never with mal-
> ice, angered but never embittered, a guest and a stranger but
> never an enemy.
>
> (CD, 419)

We are not dealing with the ideal state, here, but the concrete reality of the daily life of the one who hears the gospel. Thus one cannot deny those who resist the word simply because of the nature of the word itself. Such a person can never renounce the fact that she or he is "a lost soul to whom the grace of God has been revealed and come" (CD, 419). So understood, then, the doctrine of election is the most practical of all Christian doctrines. That this is a far cry from the prevailing estimate of this doctrine's significance is no doubt true, but this neither can nor should be reason for ignoring it. The claim, note well, is not simply that we should relate to others positively because God so relates to us. Rather, it is that our own rejection of relationship has been taken into account by God from the beginning of all things and thus decisively contained in advance. So to understand the No that hearers of the gospel will find themselves driven to utter unleashes an inexhaustible power, for it places such negation at the disposal of the affirmation of ultimacy itself. Such negation is never the final word. Neither, then, is a sentimental reading of the affirmation at stake:

> Nowhere does the New Testament say that the world is
> saved, nor can we say that it is without doing violence to the

New Testament. We can say only that the election of Jesus Christ has taken place on behalf of the world, i.e., in order that there may be this event in and to the world through Him.

(*CD*, 423)

Behold the true power of love. Those who know this love are restrained in their reading of the rejected. "We can take his existence seriously only as it is taken seriously by God Himself" (*CD*, 453). The ultimate limit on the individual's use of the No is the fact that the rejected themselves exist in Jesus Christ:

> The shadow is itself sinister and threatening and dangerous and deadly enough. Yet it is this within the limit set for it by God. It is more important, urgent and serious to see its divinely imposed limit than the horror which is peculiar to it within this limit.
>
> (*CD*, 453)

Obviously, light and shadow are irrevocably related. The Yes and the No of the gospel are related in this way. So, then, must be the relationship between those who hear the gospel and those who do not. For this is how the relationship between God and the rejected unfolds:

> The rejected man exists in the person of Jesus Christ only in such a way that he is assumed into His being as the elect and beloved of God; only in refutation, conquest and removal by Him; only in such sort that as he is accepted and received by Him he is transformed, being put to death as the rejected and raised to his proper life as the elect, holy, justified and blessed. . . . With Jesus Christ the rejected can only *have been* rejected. He cannot *be* rejected any more.
>
> (*CD*, 453)

The light limits the shadow, then, for shadows by definition have a derivative reality. The gospel has to do with just this limit. This is the power of the inexhaustible relationship of the love of God:

> The faith of the elect . . . denies the actuality and asserts the passing of the existence of the rejected. It is faith therefore— together with Jesus Christ—which marks the limit of the shadow.
>
> (*CD*, 454)

The elect know only one finality—the finality of the gospel itself. This yields the final limit of the rejected:

> He can lie, but he can lie only against the Gospel. He has no truth of his own to assert against it. . . . He can reproduce, but he cannot again perpetrate, the sins for which Jesus Christ died. . . . He may deny and blaspheme the transformation, the renewal of life, which has come to him also in the resurrection of Jesus Christ, but he cannot now evade the sign under which his own life is placed by it.
>
> (*CD*, 453–454)

Judas Iscariot: One of the Elect

To understand the rejected's rejection of the gospel in this light—to view this rejection as shadow, not light—to confront every No, even one's own, in terms of the Yes in which it is rooted—this marks the elect. But can this truly be maintained in the presence of humanity's capacity for the ultimate rejection of ultimacy itself? Only if we face this will we have plumbed the depths of the claims now before us in Barth's reading of the doctrine of election as the sum of the gospel. And this, in turn, can only happen if we hear him wrestle with a subject comfortably ignored by most. This subject is Judas Iscariot and the stubborn fact that he was one of the Twelve.

The ingenious nature of the long note Barth devotes to this tragic figure is indicated in its opening lines:

> The character in which the problem of the rejected is concentrated and developed in the New Testament is that of Judas Iscariot, the disciple and apostle who "betrayed" Jesus. We observe at once that . . . the New Testament does not seek or find the rejected at a distance, but in the closest conceivable proximity to Jesus Christ himself. . . . The counterpart of the elect is not really an opponent who confronts and opposes the kingdom of God from outside.
>
> (*CD*, 458–459)

And even this is not emphatic enough. More than proximity is at hand. Judas Iscariot was not an imposter who worked his way into the inner circle. He was one of the elect. We are not dealing with a "mole"; we are dealing with one of the chosen:

> The New Testament account of Judas does not say that
> among the genuine apostles there was one who was an apos-
> tle only in appearance, or that among the presumed and sup-
> posed elect there was one who was actually rejected. What it
> does say is that it was one of the genuine apostles, one of the
> genuinely elect, who was at the same time rejected as the
> betrayer of Jesus.
>
> (*CD*, 459)

The significance of this parallels what we have already seen Barth
make of Romans 9–11 regarding the contrast between Israel and the
church. But here there is an added dimension that stands out with stark
and unavoidable lines. Judas is indeed *"the* great sinner of the New Testament" (*CD*, 461) precisely because he is one of the Twelve. He can only
misunderstand Jesus by virtue of his close proximity to him. His reserva-
tions concerning Jesus are rooted in his own passion to follow him: "He is
not opposed to Jesus. He even wishes to be for Him. But he is for Him in
such a way . . . that actually he is against him" (*CD*, 463). But because he
is one of the Twelve, his act is one of which they all are capable:

> None of the other apostles handed Jesus over. But for all that
> Judas and the other apostles belong together as closely as
> possible. . . . What Judas did affects them also. To be sure,
> they have not actually done it or co-operated with him. But
> the point is that they obviously could have done it. The possi-
> bility of doing it was their possibility too.
>
> (*CD*, 471)

Barth holds that this is the only way to treat the confusion of the Twelve
when Jesus confronts them with his impending betrayal. The cry "Lord,
is it I?" is on the lips of all because all were capable of doing what would
be done. Even more intractable is the import of the inclusion in the
record of the account of Peter's denial, an account that will always undermine any effort to treat Judas in isolation:

> Peter no less than Judas was inclined to be independent in
> face of Jesus, as is shown in the story of his denial. . . . The
> basic flaw was revealed in Judas, but it was that of the apos-
> tolate as a whole.
>
> (*CD*, 475)

But whereas we may not treat Judas in isolation, the fact remains
that his transgression knows no parallel. Though he embodies a flaw in

the apostolate as a whole, he alone perpetrates his rejection of ultimacy by handing over Jesus to his death on the cross. There is not a trace of a suggestion that Judas may be regarded "as an example of *apokatastasis* ['restoration']" (*CD*, 476). In saying this, Barth reaches a major clarification of what he calls "the situation of proclamation":

> The Church will not then preach an *apokatastasis*, nor will it preach a powerless grace of Jesus Christ or a wickedness of men which is too powerful for it. But without any weakening of the contrast, and also without any arbitrary dualism, it will preach the overwhelming power of grace and the weakness of human wickedness in face of it.
>
> (*CD*, 477)

The situation of proclamation is that all that the church can be certain of is the Yes of the gospel itself. Whether this entails the ultimate restoration of those who reject it is left to God alone:

> We may not know whether it [the power of grace] led to the conversion of Judas or not, but this is how it always is in the situation of proclamation. The rejected cannot escape this situation and its relation of opposites. He cannot extricate himself from this order. He will necessarily confirm it and even in his own way be active in it. And in the New Testament this divine determination of the rejected is unambiguously clear even, and especially in, the person and act of Judas.
>
> (*CD*, 477)

How so? Well may we ask, and in fear and trembling, for the absence of all too many of the genuinely faithful from the struggle to understand the significance of Judas Iscariot may well be the root of the misunderstanding of the doctrine of election itself. We leave a great mystery in place of the overwhelming power of grace at the core of the proclamation. The mystery as to whether Judas himself is restored is not to be confused with an uncertainty regarding the power of grace. And this power receives marvelous exemplification in the role played by Judas's betrayal in the unfolding of the gospel of love. To leave open the question of Judas's restoration is *not* the last word to be said concerning Judas, nor is it the final issue regarding the significance of his heinous sin for our own self-understanding.

This is the point at which Barth's close scrutiny of the biblical text pays one of its richest dividends. Judas *delivers* Jesus into the hands of his executioners. The word for this deliverance, *paradosis* ("handing over"), is the word from which we get our word "tradition." What is at stake here is no mere play on words. Rather, it is the clue to a profound appraisal of the fact that Judas, one of the Twelve, marks each of us with an indelible hue. In his act of deliverance he plays an *active* role in the coming to pass of the central acts of the gospel, the crucifixion and resurrection of Jesus Christ:

> It is no mere semantic accident what the word "delivery" (παράδοσις), which has this purely negative meaning when applied to the act of Judas, is elsewhere used positively to define and describe the apostolic ministry, as this consists in the faithful and complete transmission into a second set of hands—the hands of others in space or time who had not originally received it—of the unchanged and undiminished message of Jesus, the record of His words and deeds and death and resurrection, the knowledge of the will of God manifest in Him for the being and ordering of the Church.
>
> (CD, 482)

If this is so, there is an inescapable question on the table, and Barth is never reluctant to pick up such questions when the biblical record includes them and forces them into the open when the text is meticulously scrutinized. The question is this:

> Are we not forced to ascribe a positive meaning to the act of Judas, to the extent that in all its faithlessness it foreshadows the act of faithful apostolic tradition? Was it *only* an attempt on the royal freedom of Jesus? Was it only a service of the devil, the transference of the Son of God to powerlessness, to the power of sinful men?
>
> (CD, 483)

This is the point at which the case of Paul, in its own way as significant as that of Peter, comes into the discussion. For Saul-become-Paul is one who had also stood in radical opposition to the coming of the gospel:

> The activity of Paul—himself a converted Saul, himself once a deliverer like Judas—shows that an active participation in the positive task of the apostolate cannot be denied even to the apostle Judas and his handing-over.
>
> (CD, 488)

As Barth himself indicates, this is a dangerous deduction, and it is dependent on the real heart of the matter, the claim that there is a relationship between the acts of Judas, and Paul and Peter, and thus by implication the apostolate as a whole, on the one hand, and God's own act, on the other. For God, too, hands over Jesus. To hear the gospel is to know, inescapably, irrevocably, inexorably, that God's act in Jesus Christ has to do with the ultimate redemption from the possibility of the ultimate rejection of grace. Here, most basically, the Yes precedes the No; light informs the understanding of the shadow. And it is in the hands of this God that decision concerning the rejected remains:

> Whatever God may inflict on them, He certainly does not inflict what He inflicted on Himself by delivering up Jesus Christ. For He has done it for them, in order that they should not suffer the judgment which accompanies the cleansing of the world's sin, and therefore should not be lost. It cannot be our concern to know and decide what has or will perhaps become of them, for they also stand in the light of what God has done for the world.
>
> (CD, 496–497)

In the light of the divine handing-over, all human involvement in the hearing and the proclamation of the gospel of Jesus Christ, including the rejection of this same gospel, is clarified once and for all:

> If all the darkness of the divine judgment and rejection of sinful men is only the inevitable shadow of the judgment and rejection which God decreed from all eternity and executed in time when He did not spare His only Son, it is also clear that all the gracious light of the commission and ministry in which sinful man may proclaim the Gospel to other sinful men is only the reflection of the radiance of the eternal mercy in which God willed to take sinful man to Himself, and actually did take him to Himself by the handing-over of His Son.
>
> (CD, 497)

And so the dangerous deduction is not only in order; it is necessary. Judas, one of the Twelve, plays out a necessary, active role:

> The act of Judas cannot . . . be considered as an unfortunate episode, much less as the manifestation of a dark realm beyond the will and work of God, but in every respect . . . as one element of the divine will and work. In what he himself

> wills and carries out, Judas does what God wills to be done.
> He and not Pilate is the *executor Novi Testamenti.*
>
> (*CD,* 502)

The issue now before us has overwhelming implications for understanding the risks of the calling to proclaim the gospel. This is why Barth's radical revision of the doctrine of election will never be understood unless one follows through his grasp of the contrast between Israel and the church to his relentlessly penetrating analysis of the record regarding Judas Iscariot, one of the Twelve. We are not potential Jesus Christs. Only insanity can pretend this. But we are all potential Judas Iscariots. Only evasive dishonesty can avoid this. And if we know a prevailing redemption, as did Peter and Paul, the grace of God alone will be the source of our new becoming. From this, though, come conclusions that sound extravagant indeed:

> In one sense Judas is the most important figure in the New
> Testament apart from Jesus. For he, and he alone of the apos-
> tles, was actively at work in this decisive situation, in the ac-
> complishment of what was God's will and what became the
> content of the Gospel. Yet he is the very one who is most
> explicitly condemned by the Law of God. He is the very one
> who might cause us to stray completely from the insight that
> in the New Testament no one is merely rejected—because he
> seems so unequivocably to act as one who is rejected and
> only as such among the elect apostles.
>
> (*CD,* 502)

In the New Testament "no one is merely rejected." *This* is what we must make of Judas. To be sure, regarding him "veneration is as misplaced as contempt" (*CD,* 502). But a deep understanding of what it means to stand before God as the recipient of God's grace is the direct result of working through Barth's unparalleled discussion of this figure. Only those who know that they are potential Judas Iscariots, precisely because they do hear the gospel and are compelled to proclaim it, will indeed run the risk of exposing their version of that same gospel before the scrutiny of the relating God, for the sake of a savable, redeemable world. It is for *all* humanity that God comes to us in Jesus Christ our Lord. What does it mean, then, to say that God redeems fallen humanity, primordially, before all things?

> The rejected as such has no independent existence in the
> presence of God. He is not determined by God merely to be

rejected. He is determined to hear and say that he is a rejected man elected. This is what the elect of the New Testament are—rejected men elected in and from their rejection,
men in whom Judas lived, but was also slain, as in the case of
Paul. They are rejected who as such are summoned to faith.
They are rejected who on the basis of the election of Jesus
Christ, and looking to the fact that he delivered Himself up
for them, believe in their election.

(CD, 506)

These are the closing lines, not only of the note on Judas, but of the
chapter on election that lies at the base of Barth's thought as a whole.
This is how far we must go if, with Barth, we claim, that "we can never
believe in unbelief; we can believe only in the future belief of those who
at present do not believe" (CD, 296).

Election and the Command of God

We now have before us the basic components of Barth's doctrine of
election. But to leave the discussion of his thought at this point would
leave in place the possibility of a deep misunderstanding. This doctrine
does not stand in isolation in his thought. Precisely because it is the sum
of the gospel, it must pervade the discussion of all other themes in the
Church Dogmatics. This can be shown almost at random. Cut into the
Church Dogmatics at any point and the asymmetrical relation between
the Yes and No of the grace of God in Jesus Christ will be noticeably in
operation. But even to leave the matter with this is out of order. For in
the transition from the first to the second of the two chapters comprising Church Dogmatics, II/2, Barth sets out the decisive implication of all
that we have heard him say.

Chapter VIII of Church Dogmatics, II/2, begins with these words:

In the true Christian concept of God with man the doctrine
of the divine election of grace is the first element, and the
doctrine of the divine command is the second. . . . For God
is not known and is not knowable except in Jesus Christ. . . .
He does not exist, therefore, without the covenant with man
which was made and executed in this name. God is not
known completely—and therefore not at all—if He is not
known as the Maker and Lord of this covenant between
Himself and man.

(CD, 509)

To say this is to insist, explicitly, that God's self-understanding intrinsically involves humanity. No trace of a dependence of God on humanity may be countenanced. But at the same time, it is impossible to overstate the issue at hand. For God's self-confinement to this relationship is a function of the freedom of God. Willingly, God is understandable only in terms of this relationship:

> We dare not encroach on the freedom of God by asserting that this relationship [*Beziehung*] of His with man is essential, indispensable, and inalienable. But we cannot avoid the free decision of His love in which God has actually put Himself into this relationship, turning towards man in all the compassion of His being, actually associating Himself with man in all the faithfulness of His being.
>
> (*CD*, 509; see also *KD*, 564)

Faithfulness, not necessity, defines this ultimate relationship. The constancy and fidelity of God's relating to humanity, not the shackling to rigid inflexibility, is the point to Barth's caveat. But given the warning, note well the radical claim. That God does indeed stand in relationship to humanity is the priceless gift the doctrine of election clarifies. Precisely because this is the sum of the gospel, the doctrine itself cannot stand in isolation. The very expansive inclusiveness of the Yes of the gospel, which we have watched Barth unfold, transcends even the attempt to state the sum of the gospel:

> To say divine election, to say predestination, is to name in one word the whole content of the Gospel, its sum. For that reason the doctrine of election belongs to the doctrine of God. For how can we really speak about God without speaking directly, if only summarily, about the Gospel?
>
> But the concept of the covenant is not exhausted by the doctrine of election. The partner in this covenant is man.
>
> (*CD*, 510)

In a word, then, because the doctrine of election has to do with the relating God, it can only point beyond itself to the manifold dynamics of this relationship.

Given this, Barth's own critical distance from Calvin's efforts to revise the doctrine is transcended, but transcended in such a way that the move beyond Barth's own frontiers of reflection is inexorable. When Calvin and Barth are read in close juxtaposition with reference to the doctrine of election, the resonance between their creativities cannot be denied. It is this resonance that we must extend by way of extrapolating the line of development itself. When Calvin moved the doctrine to the conclusion of his analysis of life in the Spirit, he anticipated Barth's even more radical intensification of the significance of the doctrine. Relationship pervades Calvin's reading of the doctrine, too. And he, too, places the doctrine at the service of clarifying the responsibility of the elect—the ordering, that is, of the lives of those who hear the gospel.

Here we must move explicitly and with the utmost care and precision. What precisely was Barth's critical distance from Calvin? Barth applauds Calvin's moving of the doctrine to the end of Book III in the final edition of the *Institutes,* but here a basic problem emerges, for he does not see Calvin as subordinating providence to predestination, rather than the reverse of this (see Barth 1957, 46). This ambiguity is hard to avoid, for as Barth himself indicates, the tradition that thought itself to be following Calvin most rigorously has always done precisely that. It has read predestination in terms of providence, with the drastic misunderstanding, that of reading predestination as predeterminism, solidly entrenched in a virtually unassailable position. That Calvin had a lot to do with this can hardly be denied. But neither dare we overlook what we have already demonstrated, namely, Calvin's own disquiet with this understanding.

Now Barth knows this, too, but he is troubled:

> Calvin never connected the doctrine of predestination with that of God. . . . What Calvin did appear to find in the doctrine of election was this—a final (and therefore a first) word on the whole reality of the Christian life, the word which tells us that the existence and the continuance and the future of that life are wholly and utterly of the free grace of God.
>
> (*CD,* 86)

This is the problem with Calvin, for Barth. As far as he is concerned, Calvin's failure to connect the doctrine of election with the doctrine of God yields an impasse:

> The electing God of Calvin is a *Deus nudus absconditus* [a "hidden God only"]. It is not the *Deus revelatus* [the "revealed God"] who is as such the *Deus absconditus* [the "hidden God"], the eternal God. All the dubious features of Calvin's doctrine result from the basic failing that in the last analysis he separates God and Jesus Christ, thinking that

what was in the beginning with God must be sought elsewhere than in Jesus Christ.

(*CD*, 111)

Now is this in fact the case? Is this the "last analysis" regarding
Calvin's efforts? I think not. And what is more, I wonder whether Barth
would really leave the case there; for he himself links his own efforts to
Calvin's, and he does this at the very point where he focuses his most
trenchant argument regarding rejected humanity as well as elected humanity as being within the reach of the electing God:

> We can and should recognize the fact that however we regard
> man, as creature, sinner or Christian, we must always regard
> him and understand him as one who is sustained by the hand
> of God. Neither in the height of creation nor in the depth of
> sin is he outside the sphere of the divine decision. And if we
> see in this decision the divine election, this means that he is
> not outside the sphere of the election of grace.
>
> (*CD*, 90)

In insisting on this, Barth appeals to the "intention" of Calvin. I think
he is right in so doing. I think this because he and Calvin are moving in
the same direction:

> We believe that in so doing we shall not be disloyal to the
> intention which activated Calvin especially as he drew up
> those different outlines. We shall rather be taking up and re-
> alizing the very same intention.
>
> (*CD*, 90)

I am convinced that Barth's reading of Calvin does not give suffi-
cient attention to the fact that Calvin's developing understanding of
Christology informs his final moves regarding the doctrine of election.
The God of whom Calvin speaks in *Institutes* II,vi is not the hidden God
but the revealed God. This is the God whom the elect experience in the
relationships described at the culmination of Book III. The God concerning whom the doctrine of election is necessary is the relating God
we know in Jesus Christ. This is as true for Calvin as it is for Barth.

With Barth, this relationship is an expanding one, for he cannot
rest his case until he has settled accounts with both the contrast between Israel and the church, and the fact of Judas Iscariot. This, then,
puts the No of the gospel at the service of the proclamation of this

expansion. Watch this move carefully, for this is the point at which the doctrine of double predestination in its classical form completely disappears. Given the line of development from Calvin to Barth, the question of the rejected is settled, once and for all, in the doctrine of election considered as intrinsic to the doctrine of God. From this point forward, the decisive contrast, from the standpoint of the elect, is no longer that between elect and rejected. It is rather the contrast between those who have heard the gospel and those who have not. That *some* of the latter have indeed rejected the gospel is clear enough. But this may no longer be said of all those who do not respond to the proclamation of the good news concerning the inexhaustible grace of God.

Thus we arrive at the discussion of those who do not hear the gospel. It does not begin here. The gospel has to do with all humanity, not because the relationship between Israel and the church entails a comprehensive theory of the history of religions, nor because even the tragic case of the heinous sinfulness of Judas Iscariot is beyond the reach of the Yes of the gospel, but because the relating of the relating God is the primary subject the gospel addresses. It is intrinsic to the relating of the relating God that *all* humanity is to be part of the relationship.

THE SPIRIT AND THE CONTEXTS

Calvin was right. It is the case that the doctrine of election makes sense only in the context of the doctrine of the Spirit, the third article of the creed, for life in the presence of ultimacy has to do with the experience of the responsibility of the chosen. Barth was wrong in failing to see that Calvin's move, as well as his own, forces the doctrine of election into the closest relationship possible to the doctrine of God. The very connection between election and command that informs the progression of *Church Dogmatics*, II/2, can unfold only in terms of the *experience* of faith. We will never know how Barth would have handled this in the unwritten Volume V of the *Church Dogmatics*, but one thing is clear: He would have to concede that he was closer to Calvin than he realized in his treatment of election.[6] For the God of whom the gospel speaks is the *relating* God, and it is only in terms of relationship that this God can be confessed. Response and relationship go hand in hand, for both God and humanity. As human contexts change, so does the understanding of God—and in that sense so does God. Revelation proceeds. This is why each succeeding time and place must confess anew what it means to serve the living God.

In our time, on the basis of the gospel itself—in terms, that is, of *kerygmatic*, not *apologetic* theological reflection—we arrive at the conclusion that in speaking of the relating God we know in Jesus Christ, we are speaking of the God of the religions. At a remarkable, and I am convinced inadvertent, moment, this claim received *confessional* status. This occurs in paragraphs 9.41 and 9.42 of the Confession of 1967 of the Presbyterian Church (U.S.A.):

> The church in its mission encounters the religions of men and in that encounter becomes conscious of its own human character as a religion. God's revelation to Israel, expressed within Semitic culture, gave rise to the religion of the Hebrew people. God's revelation in Jesus Christ called forth the response of Jews and Greeks and came to expression within Judaism and Hellenism as the Christian religion. The Christian religion, as distinct from God's revelation of himself, has been shaped throughout its history by the cultural forms of its environment.
>
> The Christian finds parallels between other religions and his own and must approach all religions with openness and respect. Repeatedly God has used the insight of non-Christians to challenge the church to renewal. But the reconciling word of the gospel is God's judgment upon all forms of religion, including the Christian. The gift of God in Christ is for all men. The church, therefore, is commissioned to carry the gospel to all men whatever their religion may be and even when they profess none.
>
> (*The Book of Confessions*, 9.41–9.42)[7]

These are radical words indeed, especially given their context in a formally adopted confessional document. Perhaps we had to wait until this century and these decades before the import of giving confessional status to such a claim can be given its due. For the church to relativize itself by placing itself on a par with "the religions of men" is truly astonishing. Even more so is the possibility of faithful, confessional recognition of the principle of expansive inclusion that the gospel of reconciliation entails.

The relating of the relating God—the reach of God the Spirit—cannot be restricted, even by those so touched that their lives are committed to the proclamation of the gospel of Jesus Christ. This portends creative liberation from the myopia of cultural imperialism that has so shackled the universal mission of the church. Our certainty resides only in the conviction that the gospel must be heard by all. The form of the response of others to God resides within the relating to them of the relating God, even as it has with us. The God we know, and are known by, in Jesus Christ is the God of the religions. The end of the curse of triumphalism has long been the yearning hope of those who recognize integrity in any attempt to serve ultimacy in the midst of humanity. What we are coming to see is that the end of triumphalism is intrinsic to the gospel itself.

To be grasped by the presence of the relating God is to know both liberation from past limits and the challenge of new creativity. For the relating God is the liberating God, and the creating God, and the relating of the relating God cannot be known apart from this liberation and without this creativity. This has always been the case. To be confronted by God is to be opened to God's own future becoming. We know the precedents of those who have been so confronted before. We must know, therefore, that the future will contain those who must move beyond our efforts. There are implications to what we now see that can only be proleptic in our imaginative efforts to live out our faith. For we are confronted by the freedom of God, even as those of old were and those of tomorrow will be. The revelation of the relating God is processive in character. We have always been summoned beyond the frontiers of yesterday's certainties, for the God who inspired those risks has new risks to run, evoking the response of the faithful to a presence always new. We are known by, and therefore know, this ultimacy. We therefore know, and know that we know, that we must always be willing to think thoughts that have never been thought before in order that the gospel may be heard by all.

3

THE LIBERATING GOD

We reach the center of our discussion. Christology always informs the center of Christian theological reflection. This seems a truism, but those who know their way around the history of Christian thought know full well that this is not the case. Moreover, it is noteworthy that the point is hoary with age and knows myriad expressions. Myopia always plagues the vision of those who think that it is unique to any given period or any given theological persuasion.

Granted that, we have now examined at length two instances of the claim at hand. Both for Calvin and for Barth, christological reflections are at the center of the discussion. In the former case, this receives its sharpest focus with the new christological chapter at the heart of the argument of the last edition of the *Institutes* (in Book II, Chapter vi). In the latter case, it informs the transition from the writing of *Die christliche Dogmatik* (in 1927) to the massive unfolding of *Die kirchliche Dogmatik,* beginning in 1932 and receiving its decisive expression in II/2 (1942).

Now regarding each of these instances, an important observation must be noted with great care: The statement of the christological fulcrum of the argument is not the delineation of the content of Christology; it is an indication of the necessity of developing this discussion in such a way that it informs everything else that must be said. In the case of Calvin, this unfolds in his delineation of the threefold office of Christ in the culminating chapters of Book II of the *Institutes.* In the case of Barth, it provides the extensive subject matter of *Church Dogmatics,* IV/1, IV/2, IV/3/First Half, and IV/3/Second Half, and in fact even this prolonged discussion was not completed.

In similar fashion, we now arrive at the point at which Christology proper is before us in the present discussion. Our task is to ponder the *liberation vector* intrinsic to understanding the God of the contexts. The liberating God is known in the New Testament as God the Son.

Such language is recent, given the rise of the theologies of liberation. But recent though it is, it is irrevocably a part of the language of theological reflection today, resisted only by those who serve one or another of the establishments that seek to reduce the theologies of liberation to the minor realm of recent fads. As has already been indicated, these maneuvers are doomed to failure, for the struggles against racism, sexism, and classism/colonialism/imperialism are not figments of the imagination. They are permanent developments, and they will be quieted only with the complete overcoming of the captivities these painful terms indicate. Indeed, they will not disappear until oppression in all its forms disappears.

RELATIONSHIP AND LIBERATION

On the cutting edge of contextual theological reflection today, it is quite common for the claim to be made that Jesus of Nazareth, confessed to be the Christ, is the Liberator. Why is this claim so often made in this context? In dealing with this question, we must be mindful of our reflections, at the outset of this discussion, concerning the simultaneity of the emergence of theological reflection presupposing the permanence of each of the indicated three struggles. No successful claim as to which causes the other two can be maintained because they have unfolded synergistically. Given that, there are two proleptic developments that took shape in the initial phases of the appearance of the theologies of liberation. The clarification of each of them will aid in understanding both the now permanent character of the confession that Jesus the Christ is our Liberator, and the decisive implications this has for the doing of theology.

The first of these is Frederick Herzog's argument that our theological reflection must now unfold under the regimen of what he calls the *analogia liberationis*. This gains cogency if we have in mind its precursor, Dietrich Bonhoeffer's remarks concerning what he called the *analogia relationis*. (I must indicate immediately that this juxtaposition is my own, not Herzog's.) The second is the *praxis methodology* that is in operation across the full spectrum of the theologies of liberation.

Bonhoeffer's notion of the *analogia relationis* was worked out in his lectures on Creation and Fall, which he gave at the University of Berlin during the winter of 1931–32. These lectures entailed a theological analysis of the opening three chapters of Genesis. The proposal itself informs his interpretation of Genesis 1:27:

> The "image . . . after our likeness" is . . . not an *analogia entis* in which man, in his being *per se* and *a se* [An-und-für-sich-sein], is in the likeness of the being of God. There is no such analogy between God and man. . . . The likeness, the analogy of man to God, is not *analogia entis* but *analogia relationis*.
>
> (Bonhoeffer 1965, 38; see also Bonhoeffer 1955, 7)

In this light, Bonhoeffer insisted that humanity's reflection of ultimacy cannot be understood in individualistic terms. That humanity is created "male and female" is the concrete embodiment of this fact (see Bonhoeffer 1965, 38). It is in relational terms, according to Bonhoeffer, that the uniqueness of humanity is to be understood. And these relational terms can be authentic only if in freedom they reflect the freedom of God.

Even in this very early work, one of the most central affirmations of Bonhoeffer's theological reflections as a whole received memorable formulation:

> From the beginning the world is placed in the sign of the resurrection of Christ from the dead. Indeed it is because we know of the resurrection that we know of God's creation in the beginning, of God's creation out of nothing. The dead Jesus Christ of Good Friday—and the resurrected *kurios* (Lord) of Easter Sunday: that is creation out of nothing, creation from the beginning. . . . There is absolutely no transition or continuity between the dead and the resurrected Christ except the freedom of God which, in the beginning, created his work out of nothing.
>
> (Bonhoeffer 1965, 19)

Thus the *analogy of relationship* arises as the way to deal with the relational character of the freedom of God. This is Bonhoeffer's priceless insight. As is the case with all analogies (and one can never touch this issue without being aware of the convoluted character of the history of analogy in Christian thought), what is going on here is a specification of the language appropriate to the subject matter of Christian theological reflection. In simple terms, Bonhoeffer insists that relational language alone is appropriate for this kind of thinking. His thought as a whole demonstrates this, for the concern pervades everything that he wrote. It is interesting to note that this suggestion had striking influence on Barth. From *Church Dogmatics*, III/1, forward he explicitly adopted Bonhoeffer's suggestion (see Barth 1960, 194–195).

Frederick Herzog does not indicate any connection between his proposal of the *analogia liberationis* and Bonhoeffer's insistence on the *analogia relationis*, but for obvious reasons the connection is irresistible. In effect, Herzog intensifies Bonhoeffer's specification concerning the language appropriate to reflection on the relationship between God and humanity. The proposal lies at the heart of Herzog's remarkable commentary, *Liberation Theology: Liberation in the Light of the Fourth Gospel* (1972), and it focuses his claim that this gospel delivers humanity out of individualism into the struggle for freedom. Commenting on the passage "So if the Son makes you free, you will be free indeed" (John 8:36) he writes:

> Once man grasps corporate freedom he is on the way to becoming man. On his own, man remains in the state of concealment. It takes an act of liberation—responded to by faith—to unshackle us from our self-contradiction. Only through liberation from the concealment of privatism can we be set on the road to becoming human. This occurs in the unconcealed one who uncovers the new direction of our destiny toward a new future: "So if the Son liberates you, you will be free indeed" [John 8:36]. As for the *Reformation* justification by faith was the interpretative key to the Christian life; for the *Liberation* today, liberation by the Son is the key. This is the core thought of the Fourth Gospel for our age. Man can only be grasped through the analogy of liberation (*analogia liberationis*), in accord with his liberation in Christ. Man is not something static, finished, but a process of ever-increasing freedom, a growth into greater freedom.
>
> (Herzog 1972, 126)

Herzog's claim is drastic indeed, as is the case with all proponents of theologies of liberation. The breakthrough that has occurred has irreversible hermeneutical significance for the understanding both of the biblical texts and of the history of Christian thought at large. Herzog's intensification of Bonhoeffer's specification irrevocably crosses a frontier and envisions new horizons. In his judgment, the struggles for liberation parallel the Reformation itself, and he is not reluctant to press his case relentlessly. An epistemological current runs through Bonhoeffer's suggestion: If relational words are not used to express the human involvement with ultimacy, whatever is said is untrue. This current sears the wires in Herzog's case. The only truly relational words for him are liberating words. His commentary on the Fourth Gospel manifests this. The concern pervades all that he has written since then.

ORTHOPRAXIS:
THE EMERGENCE OF A NEW REGIMEN

But now, given all this, what is the content of Christology under the regimen of the *analogia liberationis*? Are we not still where we were in speaking of the christological fulcrum of theological reflection? That is to say, have we done anything more than specify the formal centrality of Christology in insisting that only liberating words are appropriate in such an undertaking? Were we to leave the discussion where it now is, these questions could only point to the fact that much remains to be done if they are to be taken seriously. But the new efforts now in order defy hasty analyses, for liberation is a contextual affair, and its exact meaning will vary with the contexts within which it can emerge only by way of struggle. Liberation—that is, vis-à-vis racism—is not precisely the same as liberation from the curse of sexism; and the struggle against each of these, to say nothing of the combination of them, is intensified when the problematic of classism/colonialism/imperialism is taken into account. Christology itself has always defied simplistic discussions; and in the time of the rise of the theologies of liberation, this is even more intractable and unavoidable than it has ever been before. How then do we proceed?

Action/Reflection

This is the point at which we must now reckon with the fact that the theologies of liberation operate with *praxis methodologies*. In one way or another, all theologies of liberation presuppose the central insights of Paulo Freire's seminal work, *Pedagogy of the Oppressed* (1972). Freire's discussion is addressed to the problematic of teaching adult, illiterate serfs in Brazil how to read. It is painful indeed to know that this truly

102

ground-breaking discussion takes as its point of departure the simple assumption that illiteracy is not rooted in a lack of intelligence. Freire develops a pedagogy of dialogue on this basis and in the process unmasks the demonic character of indoctrination (by whomever mounted) with devastating precision. In commenting on this pedagogy, Freire wrote one of those incisive paragraphs that will leave indelible marks on the thinking of any who grasp what he is saying:

> As we attempt to analyze dialogue as a human phenomenon, we discover something which is the essence of dialogue itself: *the word.* But the word is more than just an instrument which makes dialogue possible; accordingly, we must seek its constitutive elements. Within the word we find two dimensions, reflection and action, in such radical interaction that if one is sacrificed—even in part—the other immediately suffers. There is no true word that is not at the same time a praxis. Thus, to speak a true word is to transform the world.
>
> (Freire 1972, 75)

At this point Freire attached a footnote so crucial that it is in fact intrinsic to the formulation before us:

$$\left.\begin{array}{l} \text{Action} \\ \\ \text{Reflection} \end{array}\right\} \quad \text{word} = \text{work} = \text{praxis}$$

Sacrifice of action = verbalism
Sacrifice of reflection = activism

(Freire 1972, 75)

The equations in the footnote are intrinsic to the insight in the formulation. Given the formulation, we cannot escape the radical epistemological claim being made. Only transforming words are true. This resonates with both Bonhoeffer's *analogia relationis* and Herzog's *analogia liberationis*. The combination of these two insights with the addition of Freire's formulation is irresistible. Relational words are true only if they are liberating, for then they will be involved in the transformation of the world. Hence we perceive the significance of the equations, for they unmask the false leads. Action and reflection must inform each other, lest we wind up in the blind alley of verbalism, on the one hand, or activism, on the other. The theologies of liberation do not have to do with either verbalism or activism. The point to rigorous attention to language is the transformation of a world that hides behind self-understandings that are untrue. The point to the demand for action against the forces of oppression is the insistence that there will be no cessation of the effort until the systems of oppression are recognized, defeated, and replaced. Thus the demand is for thought rooted in and informing concrete activity, and for action that necessitates new reflection and as yet untested ideas. In short, what is envisioned is action/ reflection, in synergistic interrelationship, committed to the coming of a new day.

Two works exemplify the issue at hand, and each of them plays a continuing, significant role in the development of the theologies of liberation. The first of these is Letty Russell's *Human Liberation in a Feminist Perspective: A Theology* (1974); the second, Juan Luis Segundo's *The Liberation of Theology* (1976).

At the conclusion of her work, Russell sets out a comprehensive formulation of the praxis methodology explicitly implemented throughout her discussion:

> This book itself is an experiment in liberation theology. . . . It is an experiment, not just because that is where we are in the search for human liberation, but because this is always the nature of liberation theology. The method of this type of theology is that of asking questions and exploring possible alternatives through action-reflection. In this sense, every exercise in theological praxis is a new beginning in a continuing process and never a conclusion.
>
> (Russell 1974, 184)

Experiments are always open-ended. The force of Russell's argument is that this is the permanent reality of any theology of liberation. This will account for its openness to a variety of possible formulations of the central concerns of the faith, simply because these are always understood in connection with the contexts that evoke them. Her insight is the direct correlate of the point of departure for her discussion. Liberation, as she insists, defies a simplistic definition:

> [The] *situation variability* of liberation means that in every situation, every culture, every subculture, the things *from* which people would be free and things *for* which they long are different. For every woman who longs to be free from the drudgery and boredom of her home, there is another woman who longs to be free from the drudgery and boredom of a job that keeps her out of the home, and another who wishes she has a home or a job!
>
> (Russell 1974, 26–27)

To work in terms of a praxis methodology is to encounter the intrinsic necessity of a plurality of interrelating conclusions, all of which resonate with each other. Indeed, they are so interrelated that it is the continuum of the interrelationship that provides the matrix whence the action-reflection nexus derives its vibrant productivity. More than that, theological reflection operating in terms of a praxis methodology will not be hostile to this plurality of emerging insights. Quite the reverse, it will be restive if they are not continually arising, for then it will know that it has deserted its authenticating integrity, namely, commitment to the arrival of a new day. We are back where we were with Freire. The only true word is a *transforming* word.

Juan Luis Segundo, S.J., uses the term *orthopraxis* to emphasize the normative significance of praxis methodology for liberation theology. In so doing he focuses his discussion of *The Liberation of Theology,* one of the most important works to emerge from the South American struggle against classism/colonialism/imperialism. The crucial instance of his use of this term occurs in his appraisal of the significance of the work of the North American black theologian James Cone:

> Unless I am mistaken, [Cone] is asserting that orthodoxy possesses no ultimate criterion in itself because being orthodox does not mean possessing the final truth. We only arrive at the latter by orthopraxis. It is the latter that is the ultimate criterion of the former, both in theology and in biblical interpretation. The truth is truth only when it serves as the basis for truly human attitudes. "Doers of the truth" is the formula used by divine revelation to stress the priority of orthopraxis over orthodoxy when it comes to truth and salvation.
>
> (Segundo 1976, 32)

Thus the right formulation, the right opinion, is replaced by the right action/reflection process as the norm of true theological reflection. This is not to say that this dispenses with the importance of correct formulations. The disciplining of our language about God is of absolutely prime significance for the struggle against oppression. But it is to say that the search for this rigorous, exacting precision in our reflection is itself a function of the struggle. It is in the midst of this involvement, and all that it demands, that we discover the theological insights informing the involvement itself.

Now this is not a new idea, of course, but what *is* new is the term *orthopraxis* as the focusing term for the regimen at hand. Here the liberation theologians have made one of their most significant finds. Indeed, this yield may prove to be the decisive component in the argument for the irrevocable, inexhaustible, and indispensable development of the theologies of liberation in the history of Christian thought at large. Why so? Orthopraxis typifies a theological reflection that not only welcomes pluralism; it presupposes it. Given the fact that liberation is situation variable, as we have heard Russell insist, a theology concerned with orthopraxis is the only theology worth attempting.

Segundo's close attention to the work of James Cone exemplifies this concern and demonstrates its creativity. His high estimate of Cone's work turns on his own understanding of the "hermeneutic circle" in operation in the theologies of liberation. This circle is informed by "two preconditions": "They are: (1) profound and enriching questions and suspicions about our real situation; (2) a new interpretation of the Bible that is equally profound and enriching" (Segundo 1976, 9). These preconditions in turn generate the "four decisive factors" in the hermeneutical circle as Segundo understands it:

> *Firstly* there is our way of experiencing reality, which leads us to ideological suspicion. *Secondly* there is the application of our ideological suspicion to the whole ideological superstructure in general and to theology in particular. *Thirdly* there comes a new way of experiencing theological reality that leads us to exegetical suspicion, that is, to the suspicion that the prevailing interpretation of the Bible has not taken important pieces of data into account. *Fourthly* we have our new hermeneutic, that is, our new way of interpreting the fountainhead of our faith (i.e., Scripture) with the new elements at our disposal.
>
> (Segundo 1976, 9)

In Cone's work, Segundo finds the demands of such a hermeneutic met in every detail. In that sense, his work shows what it means to close the hermeneutical circle (see Segundo 1976, 25ff.). The true importance of this appraisal will be apparent only to those who see the point to orthopraxis as the concern of true theology. Segundo does not agree with Cone on all points; he resonates with Cone's intentions. Orthopraxis in one context will recognize a kinship with orthopraxis in another. Thus Segundo observes:

> I have no intention . . . of disputing Cone's interpretations of the Scriptures. Sometimes I am in agreement with him, some-

times I am not. Be that as it may, I think that his theological
efforts afford us a fine example of the hermeneutical circle.
(Segundo 1976, 33)

Agreement is not the issue. Convergence of efforts is. The integrity of
involvements in a spectrum of contexts pervades the spectrum itself.
The continuing becoming of this plurality is the precondition for the
kind of theological reflection that seeks orthopraxis as its authenticating
characteristic.

To see this much is to be in touch with why Segundo calls his book
The Liberation of Theology. A style of theological reflection that is as
open as this to the efforts of others in different contexts is free indeed.
But we have only seen part of the picture so far. Segundo is incisive in
reckoning with what all theologians of liberation encounter. This is the
fact that the struggle against oppression necessarily is one that cannot
be controlled by any one point of view, including those of Christians
involved in the struggle:

> The real problem of Christian unity, in my opinion, comes
> down to this: When will we manage to break that conserva-
> tive, oppressive, undifferentiated unity of Christians in order
> to establish an open dialogue with all those, be they Chris-
> tians or not, who are committed to the historical liberation
> that should serve as the basis for the "service of reconcilia-
> tion" in and through real justice?
> (Segundo 1976, 44)

The depths of Segundo's contribution are reached in his answering of this question. The "break" he contemplates is not simply with
conservatism, or even oppression, surprisingly enough, though each of
these will be combatted ruthlessly. The decisive creativity is to move
beyond "undifferentiated unity." Precisely this concern informs
Segundo's appraisal of Cone. But to move beyond the assumption of
such unity is to know the absence of certainty, and this is the doorway
to the liberation of theology.

Theology as the Corrective of Sociology

Segundo's insights turn on his critique of the sociologists. This is a function of his insistence that Christians do not monopolize the struggle
against oppression. To be involved in such struggles is to encounter

agreements, and disagreements, with both Christians and all others who find themselves sharing the involvement. Segundo is not being facetious when he entitles a crucial chapter "In Search of Sociology." Sociological insights are absolutely pivotal for the liberation of theology, so much so that only the intersecting convergence of sociological and theological reflections can serve the emergence of theology committed to the struggle for liberation. However, these insights are not to be found in the United States, where specialization has informed the desertion of ideology in sociological reflection (see Segundo 1976, 48ff.); nor from the Marxists, where Marx's oversimplified critique of religion offers no help in the positive efforts now at hand. In the former instance, "overly specialized sociology leaves theology in the lurch, forced to formulate its own hypotheses in a field not its own" (Segundo 1976, 49). In the latter, "those [Marxist] analyses have little to tell us about the greater or lesser potential of the superstructures to abet the process of liberation" (Segundo 1976, 61). In this light, the real risk of the political character of the theologies of liberation comes into sharp focus:

> Changing the world presupposes an assurance that our projected new image of it is better than the one operating at present, and that it is also feasible. . . . But consider where these presuppositions lead us, given the existing situation of sociological science. . . . Two choices seem open to us: either we must deny theology any possibility of directing us towards liberative hypotheses and options, thereby restricting it to its hoary certitudes; or else we must move forward without sufficiently scientific certitudes of a sociological nature, with the result that theology plunges headlong into politics.
>
> (Segundo 1976, 69)

In a word, the liberation of theology rescues us from the false security of "hoary certitudes" and delivers us into the risks of relevance—risks precisely because certainty is not their verifying characteristic.

The risks of relevance are the direct result of the ideological character of political involvement. This is the "headlong plunge" to which Segundo is referring. How can such a risk be a liberation? Here he encounters the problem that all do when the term "ideology" moves to center stage. It has its pejorative meaning, of course, and Segundo uses it this way more than once. But it must have a positive use as well, if his argument holds, and his version of this point has a disarming clarity:

> No one can enter into the revolutionary process without forming some idea for himself of the goal of the process and the proper means to be used to achieve it. To keep our explanation clear and simple here, I shall label the latter process as *ideology*. Note that here the term does not have . . . pejorative connotations. . . . By "ideology" here I am simply referring to the system of goals and means that serves as the necessary backdrop for any human option or line of action.
>
> (Segundo 1976, 101–102)

We must not move too quickly in construing this simply as a plea for concreteness, for left in these terms, the risk of relevance is tamed. What is at stake is a fundamental judgment concerning the nature of authentic theological reflection. This is reflected in Segundo's citation of two key passages from one of the pivotal documents of Vatican II, *Gaudium et spes*:

> The first passage deals with the orientation of faith, not towards other-worldly certitudes, but towards historical problems and their solutions: "Faith throws a new light on everything, manifests God's design for man's total vocation, and thus *directs the mind to solutions which are fully human*" (*Gaudium et spes*, no. 11). Are we to assume from this that the faith *possesses* such solutions? Vatican II unexpectedly rejects such an assumption, the standard assumption of classical theology: "In fidelity to conscience, Christians are joined with the rest of men *in the search for truth, and for the genuine solution* to the numerous problems which arise in the life of individuals and from social relationships (*ibid.*, no. 16)."
>
> (Segundo 1976, 110)

Such a search can never know finality. This is the real risk of relevance, and deliverance into this insight liberates theology from its obsessive preoccupation with having the last word. For Segundo, what this involves is the radical revision of our understanding of revelation itself. His commentary on these two citations discloses this as the heart of his book:

> The latter passage by itself, and even more so when combined with the first passages cited, forces us to a different conception of revealed truth. It is not a *final* truth, however absolute it may be. Instead it is a fundamental element in the search for *the truth*.
>
> (Segundo 1976, 110)

So understood, faithful reflection is a "process of learning to learn," and as such,

> it is always in the service of historical solutions to human problems—even though the latter solutions will always be provisional and incomplete. Faith, then, is a liberative process. It is converted into freedom for history, which means freedom *for ideologies.*
>
> (Segundo 1976, 110)

A more emphatic move in the direction of insisting on the processive character of revelation can hardly be found than this assertion. Even so, further specifications are in order. Segundo's illuminating discussion presupposes Freire's radical epistemological claim: The only true word is a transforming word. Others can quote *Gaudium et spes,* with anything but liberation in mind. But if true transformation is not the point of their citation, the fact is that they fail the test of orthopraxis. Accordingly, a *substantive* claim concerning the nature of authentic theological reflection is at hand. A theology that is not liberating is not good theology. Such a theology does not speak of the liberating God.

One must wonder, then, concerning a contention made early in Segundo's discussion, that seemingly conditions his argument as a whole. This is the claim that "it is a fact that the one and only thing that can maintain the liberative character of any theology is not its content but its methodology" (Segundo 1976, 39–40). Is this really the case? Have we been listening to an argument that has only a formal point to make? I think not. Segundo is convinced that with the advent of the theologies of liberation an irreversible process has set in (see Segundo 1976, 3). This is very much at stake in his interpretation of the two key passages from *Gaudium et spes* we have just noted. If theology is a process of learning to learn, then it is intrinsically open-ended and incapable of closure. Moreover, it is necessarily tentative in its conclusions, not because these are merely formal in character, but because they are always interrelated with the issues and contexts evoking them. The risky character of the political options we must now run inhere in the shaky sociological bases upon which they must be mounted. We must do what the times demand—knowing full well that we are vulnerable to those who can mount their case for doing little, or nothing at all—by pleading known certainties in the face of the provisional character of contextual insights. To be delivered into history is to know that this uneasiness is permanent:

> The fact is that the major problems of man are definitely not tackled on a plane of certain knowledge, after which we must decide whether they are also to be framed in terms of some specific historical context. The real situation is just the opposite. We live and struggle in the midst of decisive contextual conflicts without science being able to provide any ready-made option in advance.
>
> (Segundo 1976, 76)

This is not simply a case for a methodological procedure. It is much more radical than that, for it makes a substantive claim.

To assert a contextual methodology for theology is to demand a theology that is itself contextual in its very nature. We are at the same point with Segundo that we have already been with Bonhoeffer and Lehmann. Segundo follows this to its logical conclusion with a remark that touches the very heart of Christian faith:

> Jesus is not an historical monument. If he were alive and active today, he would say many things that would differ greatly from what he said twenty centuries ago. Without him, but not without his Spirit, we must find out what he would say to free us if he were alive today.
>
> (Segundo 1976, 86–87)

The relating God and the liberating God are one and the same. But to know this is to know, and know that we know, that tomorrow must say the same thing, including us as part of the past that must be transcended if the transforming word that is then in order is to be spoken and heard. The method and the content coincide.

This leads to the final question to be put to Segundo, though we stand on the shoulders of his argument to see it. Brilliant though his interpretation of *Gaudium et spes* is, dare we leave his decisive suggestion as it stands? Recall his contention that we are forced "to a different conception of revealed truth." He also recognizes: "It is not a *final* truth, however absolute it may be. Instead it is a fundamental element in the search for *the truth*" (Segundo 1976, 110). Revealed truth is not just an element, even a fundamental one, in the search for truth. Revealed truth is so tied to the search that apart from it there is no revelation. Revelation itself is processive in character. Our debts to Segundo can never be repaid. To discern the fact that orthopraxis entails the liberation of theology is priceless, because it enables us to know what it truly means to be disciplined in our work. Only a liberated theology can be liberating. But the depths of this insight cannot be reached if revelation itself is only one of a set of elements comprising the search for truth. We have yet to be grasped by, for we have not yet grasped, the revelatory nature of the search itself. And this we will never know until we understand the living character of revelation.

TOWARD THE LIBERATING CHRIST

We must move from liberation Christology to liberating Christology. Even the understanding of the uniqueness of Jesus of Nazareth confessed to be the Christ that emerges from the liberation struggles can deteriorate into sectarian rigidities. Witness the running problem of taking seriously what we first learned from Russell. Liberation is indeed situation-variable, that is, contextual, and therefore it may never be frozen to any set of resonating instances. Until this dynamism is given its due, there will be no quantum move beyond simply changing the places of the oppressed and the oppressors in the attempt to move into a new day. For if this is all that happens, when the struggle quiets, the hegemony of injustice will remain intact.

Now it cannot be claimed that this problematic has not been recognized before. Segundo's discussion itself is a prime case in point. To argue for the process of "learning to learn" as intrinsic to theological reflection is to insist on the never-ending character of such efforts. Segundo eloquently states this on the closing page of the book in a set of three brief paragraphs under the heading "General Conclusions?":

> The question mark is very much in order. As the reader probably realizes, my aim in this volume has not been to dissect a dead corpse but to examine the living organism known as theology.
>
> (Segundo 1976, 241)

So this brief conclusion begins. Watch carefully its closing lines:

> Whether they are followed or not, the pathways opened up here lead into a long and unforeseeable future. The only thing that can be said for sure is that they take their cue from flesh-and-blood human beings who are struggling with mind and heart and hand to fashion the kingdom of God out of the human materials of our great but oppressed continent.
>
> (Segundo 1976, 241)

What happens when we follow this long road? Can we reach its end with only the hermeneutics of suspicion as our guide? No, for then we would be dependent on that of which we are suspicious, with the result that our reflections would always be derivative in character.

The Man for Others

Here a new question surfaces. How do we differentiate between being dependent on that of which we are suspicious, and being intrinsically linked to the contexts within which we work? Or, to put the question more specifically, at what point does theology engage its own contextual character, and what does it discern in this engagement? It engages its own contextual character when it takes up the question of the content of its Christology, and in this engagement it discerns a living, liberating reality.

Once again we must listen to Bonhoeffer, for he is one of the first to see what is involved. In his letter of August 3, 1944, one of the truly arresting insights he left us reached formulation. He was in the midst of sketching an "Outline for a Book," which he never got to write, even in the fragmentary form it would have taken in his prison cell, had he been granted a few more months of work. This letter contains his final word on Christology:

> Who is God? Not in the first place an abstract belief in God, in his omnipotence, etc. That is not a genuine experience of God, but a partial extension of the world. Encounter with Jesus Christ. The experience that a transformation of all human life is given in the fact the "Jesus is there only for others." His "being there for others," maintained till death, that is the ground of his omnipotence, omniscience, and omnipresence. Faith is the participation in this being of Jesus (incarnation, cross, and resurrection). Our relation to God is not a "religious" relationship to the highest, most powerful, and best Being imaginable—that is not authentic transcendence—but our relationship to God is a new life in "existence for others," through participation in the being of Jesus. The transcendental is not infinite and unattainable tasks, but the neighbour who is within reach in any given situation. God in human form—not, as in oriental religions, in animal form, monstrous, chaotic, remote, and terrifying, nor in the conceptual forms of the absolute, metaphysical, infinite, etc., nor yet in the Greek divine-human form of "man in himself," but

"the man for others," and therefore the Crucified, the man
who lives out of the transcendent.

(Bonhoeffer 1967, 121)

In these lines, written for himself as he contemplated the next
writing he would attempt, Bonhoeffer leaves us both a tentative outline
and a question. The outline is a function of the question itself. If Jesus
the Christ is the Man for Others, who are these others? One cannot fill
in the content of the new christological title, the Man for Others, without specifying the others themselves.[1] Thus Bonhoeffer's adherence to
his own principle of the *analogia relationis* yields this specific sense in
which Christology cannot be developed without contextual analysis.
Indeed, one could go so far as to say that the whole idea of the incarna-
tion has to do with the contextualization of God.

How do we proceed further down this line of thought? Or, to put
it another way, how do we implement Herzog's *analogia liberationis*?
Segundo's answer is clear. We do so by way of the regimen of orthopraxis. But how do we discipline this, for surely orthopraxis does not
unfold any more automatically than the orthodoxy it seeks to transcend.

This is the point at which the theologians of liberation need to
think carefully about the concepts with which they work.[2] Reflection
plays an equal role with action in the orthopraxis loop. For those
caught up in the struggle against oppression there is an understandable reluctance to do anything more than work with the ideas at
hand. But this overlooks the possibility that there are better, and
surely more incisive, ways of thinking than the tradition automatically assumes. What at first may look like a sleight-of-hand maneuver must be taken with deadly seriousness. What precisely does it
mean to concur with Segundo regarding the fact that theology really
has to do with a process of learning to learn? This question brings
into the arena of consideration a work that may well prove to be the
most significant contribution to date from the process camp to the
theologies of liberation—Delwin Brown's *To Set at Liberty: Christian
Faith and Human Freedom* (1981).

Brown's introductory considerations pivot on an illuminating discussion of the existentialism and Marxism of Jean-Paul Sartre. His basic
point is that it was the latter that made Sartre's existentialism operational. In a word, he was driven "to the construction of a philosophy of
human freedom that recognizes both external conditioning and the individual's creative self-making" (Brown 1981, 26). This is the sense in

which "Sartre's combination of existentialism and Marxism enables each to enrich the other" (Brown 1981, 26). Why is this so important?

> The task is to understand freedom as being essentially affected by external circumstance—diversity or conformity, poverty or plenty, liberty or slavery. Otherwise, one would have one's freedom regardless of external conditions; the connection between freedom and, say, economic security would merely be a "habit of mind." Sartre's move to Marxism is a rejection of so ephemeral a freedom. Social and economic conditions create needs, not merely because we happen to think that they do, but because such conditions somehow exercise real agency even over freedom. Our question is, how?
>
> (Brown 1981, 27)

How does the context exercise agency over freedom? This question surfaces with great intensity when one ponders the fact that for Sartre, and despite the fact that Marx himself was better on the issue than many of his followers, the context itself remains static and inert. The long-standing view remains intact:

> The Aristotelian tradition had viewed matter as potentiality, thus ensuring a place for activity in its conception of nature; a natural thing, in part material, is by its very nature in process, possessing within itself a principle of agency. In the sixteenth and seventeenth centuries, however, there emerged a new view which identified the physical world with matter, and more significantly deemed matter to be wholly actual and thus in itself changeless.
>
> (Brown 1981, 27–28)

Can an inert context evoke new thought? Yes. But it cannot offer any criterion whereby the validity of such new thought can be appraised. This was the problem with Descartes:

> For the new view, matter is movable, but contains within itself no principle of motion. Consciousness, as self-creative and dynamic subjectivity, must be wholly removed from the inert physical world. Thus there arose the Cartesian dualism of mind and matter with its concomitant problems.
>
> (Brown 1981, 28)

Now the decisive point emerges. For all his brilliance, even Sartre does not transcend this impasse. And by implication neither will we, however intense our efforts at what for us is central to theological reflection. Bonhoeffer's Man for Others will be crucified again and again if the context is so inert that there are only superficial means for differentiating between saint and villain:

> These problems recur in Sartre's Cartesianism. How can a passive physical environment impose needs upon the free, self-creative self, as Sartre now wishes to say? They cannot. Judgments of value, including those pertaining to need, are impositions of an active subjectivity upon a passive material world. . . . [O]n this view the judgments of the oppressed are no less arbitrary than those of the oppressor.
>
> (Brown 1981, 28)

The Dynamic Concept of Nature

This is the point at which process modes of thought demand technical attention, for this kind of reflection presupposes a context that is, in some sense, alive. The key figure in the emergence of process thought is Alfred North Whitehead (1861–1947). At the culmination of his career, this celebrated mathematician turned his attention to setting out the philosophy long implicit in his work. In so doing he presupposed the emergence of what we have elsewhere called postmodern science, and its dynamic concept of nature. Contextual thinking is impoverished to the point of impotence if it assumes that social conditions alone supply the content of the word "context." We do well to recall Segundo's heroic facing of scientific uncertainty in advocating a theologically informed involvement in the political option. The promise of the suggestion now before us is a far more knowledgeable deliverance into the contextual ferment in which we are involved. The fact is that the uncertainty plaguing Segundo is not really uncertainty at all. It is rather that tentativeness which is the real mark of reflection that sets in under the regimen of orthopraxis. In this sense, it is the mark of his integrity. Segundo is a process thinker, whether he admits it or not. All liberation theologians should be. Close attention to the understanding of reality as being dynamic in character can only strengthen those who seek to implement orthopraxis. The reflection orthopraxis evokes is dynamic, too; that is, it is open-ended, fully expecting to be transcended as orthopraxis itself continues on its manifold ways.

Insight into this claim depends upon a basic grasp of Whitehead's central affirmations, and Brown's succinct summation is one of the most helpful to be found. This turns on two key points, which, as we shall see, lead to further implications that are crucial for our present line of thought. The first of these points focuses Whitehead's relational understanding of reality:

> Whitehead shows, first, that the actual entities constituting reality at every level are relational or social. This means, for one thing, that the ingredients—the "what"—of each presently becoming actual entity is dependent upon the actualities and latent possibilities given in the past, immediate and remote. The relational character of actual entities also means that the way these ingredients are synthesized in the present—the "how"—is contributed to by the past.
>
> (Brown 1981, 30)

The second point in Brown's twofold summation of Whitehead's thought has to do with the notion of novelty that is intrinsic to Whitehead's reflection, and it must be admitted that this is open to profound misunderstanding. First, the point itself:

> There is novelty as well as repetition in the temporal process. Whitehead believes that novelty, on the physical level as well as in "mental" processes, is best accounted for by attributing to all actual entities at least some minuscule measure of self-directedness.
>
> (Brown 1981, 30)

Brown's words are chosen carefully. To account for novelty in the temporal process one faces a choice hoary with prior, intense reflections. One can either regard novelty as an intrusion into the order of reality, and thus as an accidental interference into the stable realm we regard as the truly real, or one can regard novelty as the clue to the unfolding dynamism that is reality itself. Whitehead argued for the latter choice. In so doing, he risked the idea that some sense of what Brown calls "self-directedness" must be ascribed to all the components interacting in reality as it unfolds. This can lead to the charge of panpsychism as intrinsic to Whitehead's thought. Such a charge is the hallmark of those who opt for the stability of the known, rather than risky involvement in the as yet unknown, as the mark of certainty in the midst of change.[3]

In this light Brown moves to a key summation:

> In addition to being relational, therefore, Whitehead also argues that actual entities are autonomous. They are not socially

> related and autonomous in precisely the same respects, of
> course, and the balance of sociality and autonomy varies enor-
> mously among actual entities. Repetition, and thus social de-
> pendence, dominates overwhelmingly in the actual entities
> making up physical processes or what we ordinarily call "na-
> ture." Here the capacity for novelty, and thus the exercise of
> autonomy, remains for the most part unactualized potentiality.
> In "higher" or more complex processes, and especially in the
> self, the measure of autonomy becomes an increasingly signifi-
> cant factor, interfaced with the inheritance of the past upon the
> present becoming. Here, particularly, the power of the past
> upon the present is that of influence—the "power of persua-
> sion," Whitehead sometimes calls it—and not determination.
>
> (Brown 1981, 30)

One of the chief characteristics of process modes of thought is the fact
that the new is regarded, not as an enemy, but as a friend. We are not
being asked to bow down before the god of innovation, but we are
being confronted with a challenge originating in the very nature of reality itself. The genuinely new is intrinsic to the intersection of the past
and the present, on the way to an as yet unrealized potentiality inherent
in all that is at hand. The process is indeed the reality.

Two important implications of this twofold summation of Whitehead's thought spring immediately into Brown's discussion. The first is
that we are part of the nature that is unfolding, and our thought is itself
a clue to this unfolding reality:

> In the physical sciences (physics especially) the deterministic
> model has now given way to a looser, more dynamic concep-
> tion of physical relationships. This development strengthens
> the notion that freedom and creativity—in some very embry-
> onic form, no doubt—characterize the entire physical pro-
> cess, physical as well as mental. This notion is further
> strengthened if we assume, as apparently we must, that the
> mind is part of nature. For if this is true, the autonomy so
> central to our intuitive understanding of mentality tells us
> something about the nature of things no less than does the
> repetition that dominates the physical processes.
>
> (Brown 1981, 30)

The second implication Brown indicates is perhaps even more significant than the first. Process modes of thought can deliver Sartre from
the impasse of his adoption of Marxist insights, for these at best only
partially make his existentialism operational. The context is *not passive*

in nature. It is alive with movement, even intentionality in some sense. Hence Brown's claim unfolds: "Our purpose here has been to show that Whitehead's philosophy can give to Sartre's understanding of freedom the cosmological setting that it requires in order to gain coherence" (Brown 1981, 31).

What does this processive cosmology have to do with freedom? It gives it both the context and the creativity it must have if it is to become what it promises. This will prove to be as true for the theologians of liberation as it is for Sartre. This is the real point to Brown's discussion as a whole. On the basis of what we have seen, he develops his case for the contention that context and creativity are related as the two polar elements of freedom. Freedom must be understood as creativity, for more than simply the release from bondage is at hand. This creativity is neither "the possession of an elite few," nor is it "the masses' frenzied pursuit of novel content for its own sake"; rather, it is "an essential element of *every* human event, however much (and for whatever reason) it might have been repressed and obscured" (Brown 1981, 32).

One could well recall Freire's insight here. The reason that the only true word is a transforming word is that truth and creativity go hand in hand. Each proceeds toward ever-new horizons, into ever-renewing depths of reflection. Brown does not cite Freire here, but the two sets of insights strengthen each other. The creativity that freedom must have cannot unfold apart from a living context. "Ideologies of the privileged carefully ignore this fact, pretending instead that the quality of freedom is a constant, unaffected by external circumstance" (Brown 1981, 33). This pretense must be exposed. Creativity and context stand in perfect balance as polar elements of freedom, for "the context is a 'framework' that 'conditions' but does not determine creativity" (Brown 1981, 33). Thus Freire's combination of word and work is strengthened. But so is the link between process modes of thought and the action/reflection nexus orthopraxis presupposes, and it is in this light that Brown's basic conclusion gains its real usefulness:

> Creativity and context are the polar elements of freedom. Conceptually, they presuppose each other. They are thus abstractions. In process philosophy there is no context that is not creatively appropriated, however small the margin of creativity. Likewise, there is no creativity that escapes the profound weight of the past, its context, as the source and lure for its present becoming.
>
> (Brown 1981, 34)

The formulation now before us informs the theological dimension of Brown's discussion, both its inner core and its inexhaustible reach. "The poles of freedom . . . are creativity and contextuality. Each alone is an abstraction. Together they constitute freedom" (Brown 1981, 51). God, he argues, is "the supreme instance of freedom" (Brown 1981, 57), and this is entirely in accord with the spectrum described by the two terms "creativity" and "context." The God of the biblically informed tradition is the God whose *aseity* (God's being understood solely in terms of itself) and *agape* (God's being regarded as unintelligible apart from relationships to all creatures and all creation) must be inseparably interrelated. This contention informs the theological heart of Brown's discussion:

> God is free because God is contextual creativity. If creativity is an intentional spontaneity grounded finally in itself, God's *aseity* is the supreme instance of creativity, for God's reality and character are rooted in the infinite potentiality of the divine reality. If contextuality is openness to surrounding circumstance, God's relatedness is the supreme instance of contextuality, for God opens the divine life to the full concreteness of the entire temporal order. No being is more independent and more dependent, more absolute and more relative, more creative and more contextual. No being is more free. And no being *can* be more free. In no other experience can the world be more fully and vividly ingredient, for no experience can be more inclusive than pure *agape*. In no other experience can the contextual data be more creatively taken into itself, for no experience can be more autonomous than pure *aseity*. God is unsurpassable freedom. Such is the logic of the Christian witness.
>
> (Brown 1981, 51–52)

Myriad insights stem from this formulation, each of them indicating the fact that process modes of thought can, and must, do for the theologians of liberation the same thing that Whitehead's thought could do for Sartre's. Brown explicitly demonstrates this in terms of Latin American theologies of liberation, but he indicates that the point also carries with reference to the work of both black theologians and the feminists who work on the theological front (see Brown 1981, 132 n. 64). Clearly enough, to argue that God is contextual creativity will be nonsense for those who persistently construe "context" in static terms and "creativity" as being above the impact of circumstance. But even more deeply, to argue that God must be understood in terms of the creativity/context spectrum brings a new depth to the struggles against oppression, whatever their forms.

Thus, to think of God in process modes of thought is to discover, or perhaps rediscover, the sense of urgency that attends the proclamation of the gospel of the liberating God. As Brown observes, the minimizing of the understanding of lostness, the trivialization of the doctrines of sin and salvation, inevitably leads to a superficial optimism that the reality of oppression denies. The fact is, however, that "life has its tragedy that no future can undo. All is not saved; some things are lost" (Brown 1981, 57). Neither an understanding of God cast in terms of static remoteness nor a reading of the context reduced to passive situational terms can do justice to awesome depths of this remark:

> It is important to see . . . that the reality of lostness is not grounded in the arbitrary whim of a deity who could have had it otherwise. The losses of freedom are rooted in the requisites of freedom and the unrepeatability of time, both matters of metaphysical necessity. Freedom neglected or prevented is freedom lost forever. It is irretrievable, not because some regnant deity, miffed at human insolence, wills or even permits its loss, but because a freedom missed for whatever reason is an unactualized freedom, and a freedom that is never actual, is not. No reality, not even God, can save that which is not.
>
> (Brown 1981, 57–58)

Attending this sense of urgency is its direct counterpart, an equally moving sense of commitment. Informed as it is by the conceptual clarification for which Brown contends, this dimension, embodied in the closing lines of the book, discloses the deepest strength of theology in process modes of thought. God is on the same side of an unfolding future that we are. Hence our involvement in the present must respond to and, within the limits of our own capacities, match ultimacy's commitment on the long road toward a new day:

> Freedom has no timetable. Its history is not guaranteed. Thus a Christian language faithful to freedom eschews speculative chronologies of the future. It does not seek to discern the signs of the end time. "Of that day and hour," it says, "no one knows" (Mark 13:32). Its certitude is the God whose purpose and faithfulness are revealed in Jesus, the messiah of freedom. A Christian theology for freedom does not know of

freedom's future. Believing in the God of freedom, it knows
of freedom's worth. Thus, unequivocally, it calls us to the
service of every freedom everywhere.

(Brown 1981, 129)

Brown's contribution as a whole enables us to see that we are
given the exciting possibility of understanding context as being something that is itself alive, and that in manifold ways. Russell's insistence
on the situation-variability of liberation is now far more radical than it
may have sounded at first. To say that the Christ is the liberating God is
to say that the identity of the Christ is intrinsically tied to the reality of
the liberation of a given set of "others." That is how far-reaching
Bonhoeffer's suggestion actually is. If we read Freire's insistence that
the only true word is a transforming word in this light we can, and
must, then claim that the basic reason why this is so is that the transforming Word is the liberating Jesus Christ. In so doing we will have
crossed a frontier toward which Segundo's labors drive us: Theology is
an inexhaustible process of learning to learn because we are summoned
to reckon with the liberating God, whose liberating work continues to
unfold. Such reflection will always face the necessity of moving beyond
fixed certainties into fluid, tentative conclusions along the way.

Theology under the regimen of orthopraxis and theology in process modes of thought thus intersect in irrevocable ways. The latter
gives to the former the knowledge that the living context demands
open-ended and, therefore, tentative reflection. The former demands
from the latter that relational thinking and liberating thinking are one
and the same thing. For the understanding of Christology, the result is
clear. The relating God is the liberating God. Our task now is to see that
this insight is not restricted to these times, these generations, these
places. In fact, it can lay claim to the support of the tradition that has
delivered us into the present, within which our witness must become
what it must become.

THE HISTORICAL/THEOLOGICAL CONTEXT
OF CHRISTOLOGICAL REFLECTION

Our faith stems from the historical character of Christianity. This can
hardly be denied. But how is it to be harnessed? We are not the first to
ask this question; but manifold though the precedents are for the reflec-

tion now demanded, there is something genuinely new about the manner in which we must deal with it. In Brown's incisive discussion, the notion of context carries a pronounced historical component. The context is not simply the present; it is the present in the light of the past that has engendered it. This can be, and often is, heavily deterministic for the simple reason that the polar elements of freedom, creativity, and context relate erratically:

> The relative efficacy of creativity and context varies markedly in human experience as it does in the full span of the natural order. The balance between our sense of autonomy, deriving from the exercise of creativity, and our sense of being determined, deriving from the power of our material context over us, is by no means a constant one, either. Sometimes the creative pole, and thus the awareness of autonomy, dominates. Sometimes context overwhelms us, and thus the feeling of being formed by our past. Often the blend of the two baffles self-analysis. "I choose," we may wish to say of such times, "yet not I but the past that lives within me."
>
> (Brown 1981, 36)

For faithful reflection, the historical/theological component of the context is as important as the immediately circumstantial complex. All too often only the latter is thought of as being the source of the demand for new creativity. This fails to reckon with the fact that yesterday's insights were also evoked by the interplay between creativity and context, for they were the result of yesterday's freedom. Orthopraxis is actually a new and precise way of discerning what has always been in operation in one fashion or another. Failure to grasp this will generate a hopelessly ahistorical way of appraising the problematic now before us. The fact is that the key doctrines now demanding reconsideration and reformulation have always sprung from the concrete involvement of the faithful in a given time and place. To speak of the liberating God is not new; it is only a new way of speaking of the decisive reality in the continuum of the tradition. This must be grasped lest the proposals now at hand be written off as the momentary flashes of restive, irritable innovationism.

There is yet an even deeper problem. To suggest that orthopraxis is just a new name for an old reality is only half true, for the notion does indeed contribute not only a new methodology but also a new content to the ongoing theological reflection that attends the life of the church. If this is not reckoned with carefully, the charge of co-option is unavoidable. Even worse, new theological efforts will simply yield a new, sectarian rigidity while arguing for an open-ended process of learning to learn. The result will be a new stifling of the freedom that both authentic theological reflection and informed action presuppose.

Historical Conditioning

The only way to deal with the complex issue at hand is to address the historical/theological dimension of the context that evokes new creativity. In so doing, our initial task is to wrestle with the meaning of the phrase "historical theology." Characteristically, this phrase is read as if the words comprising it were reversed, for usually we mean "theological history" when we use it. That is, we mean a theologically informed wrestling with the emergence of the continuum of Christian thought at large. This, of course, will always be needed. But what does it mean to take the phrase in a quite literal sense? What is *historical* theology—theology, that is, that takes its historical conditioning so seriously that it can claim that the action/reflection nexus has always been the root of theological creativity?

The prototypical effort to do precisely this, which has yet to be superseded, was that of Ernst Troeltsch. His massive work *The Social Teaching of the Christian Churches* has been before us earlier in this discussion. It demands attention again, for Troeltsch was the first historical theologian, in the sense in which we must now use the phrase. This is focused sharply in one of the key insights informing not only this immense work, but also Troeltsch's own efforts to deal significantly with the question of an adequate Christology for modern Christian conviction. It is an insight capable of succinct formulation: *Cult and community precede dogma and idea.*

The idea pervades *The Social Teaching*. Its key formulation, as one might expect, emerges when Troeltsch focuses the difference between himself and Harnack on how the emergence of Christian doctrine is to be understood. At a key turning point in his discussion, Troeltsch noted that medieval Catholicism added three decisive dogmas to the received tradition. These were "(1) the dogma of the universal episcopate of the Pope, (2) the dogma of the supremacy of the spiritual power over the temporal, and (3) the dogma of the impartation of grace through the seven sacraments" (Troeltsch 1931, 226). In a crucial footnote, Troeltsch noted that Protestant historians of doctrine characteristically leave the first two of these to the realm of church history, treating only the latter as a matter properly considered as a doctrinal issue. Harnack, he argued, had improved on this by insisting that "psychological explanation" rather than "dialectic development" should inform the history of doctrine (see Troeltsch 1931, 387 n. 98). He then set out his incisive observation:

> We need to go farther along this line, and realize that it is precisely the modern sociological research and discoveries which here considerably enlarge the range of psychological conditions for the formation of thought. Church law and ritual need to be included in the history of dogma—at least as far as the Catholic Church is concerned—for in both these spheres there lie the chief roots of dogma. The worship of Christ and the Christian Sacrament of Holy Communion preceded the doctrine of Christ in the Early Church, and to a great extent conditioned it. The same holds good of the law of the Church. A purely intellectual conception of the Faith is much less important than people think. When the churches are studied sociologically, however, it is then precisely that it becomes plain that the cultus provides the real means of unity, and the system of law the form of unity; it is only natural that these fundamental sociological elements should be reflected above all in dogma, and that the purely logical theoretical speculative elements rather accompany the whole system as the special concern and interest of the theological experts.
>
> (Troeltsch 1931, 387 n. 98)

Troeltsch's point is crucial, not only for the understanding of the history of doctrine, but for the construction of new theological thought as well. This is the sense in which it is not only helpful, it is necessary, to argue that orthopraxis and the principle that cult and community precede dogma and idea are two ways of saying the same thing. All that is missing in Troeltsch's formulation is the term "orthopraxis" itself.

Troeltsch knew that the difference between himself and Harnack was indeed of decisive significance. Late in his career, while commenting on the relationship between his work and that of Max Weber, he observed:

> I may on this occasion refer also to my book, The Social Teachings of the Christian Churches and Groups, 1912, which places alongside the great, essentially ideological-dogmatic presentation of Christianity which Harnack has given, an essentially sociological-realistic-ethical [presentation].
>
> (Troeltsch 1922, 369 n. 190. My translation; see Reist, 1966, 39 and 227 n. 33)

With this formulation, the real point at hand emerges with all its intrinsic forcefulness. An ideological-dogmatic understanding of the history of doctrine will inexorably yield an ideological-dogmatic theological creativity. A sociological-realistic-ethical theology will invariably emerge from an understanding of the theological tradition that is sensitive to the fact that cult and community precede dogma and idea. Note well, however, that for the latter, the action/reflection nexus, not just action, is the domicile of normative considerations. The very term "cult" assures this. Worship is not just a matter of reflection, of course, but it is impossible without it. On this anvil the Reformation was hammered into shape. The fact that preaching, not just the Eucharist, is at the center of liturgy embodies this concern.

In 1911, as *The Social Teaching* was being completed (it was published as a completed work in 1912), Troeltsch wrote out his central understanding of Christology in a monograph entitled "The Significance of the Historical Existence of Jesus for Faith."[4] No Jesus, no Christianity—this is Troeltsch's argument. His case pivots on a central claim: "Now one perfectly clear result of the history and psychology of religion is that in all religion what really counts is not dogma and idea but cult and community" (Morgan and Pye 1977, 194). When the pristine Christian community transcended its relationship with Judaism and then broke with it completely, it inexorably became a "Christ cult." Troeltsch's formulation of what it means to say this must be noted in detail:

> It is not the worship of a new God but the worship of the old God of Israel and of all reason, in his living and concrete highest revelation. . . . No matter what emerged later from this earliest form of the Christian community as a Christ cult, the original motive is clear. The need for community and the need for cult had no other means than the gathering to worship Christ as the revelation of God. The dogma concerning Christ which emerged from this Christ cult was only meant to show and give access to the one eternal God in Christ in order to create a new community.
>
> (Morgan and Pye 1977, 195)

These are the passages that inform the focusing of Troeltsch's basic insight as we have: Cult and community precede dogma and idea. What is now at hand is the deepening of the insight itself. For Troeltsch, Christianity would never have become the force that it has without community and cult. This is why Jesus has always been, and will always be, central for the Christian faith:

> A cult illuminated by the Christian idea must . . . always centre upon gathering the congregation around its head, nourishing and strengthening it by immersion in the revelation of God contained in the image of Christ, spreading it not by dogmas, doctrines and philosophies but by handing on and keeping alive the image of Christ, the adoration of God in Christ. So long as Christianity survives in any form it will always be connected with the central position of Christ in the cult. It will either exist in this form or not at all.
> (Morgan and Pye 1977, 196)

For Troeltsch, this contention turns on "social-psychological laws" observable wherever religion is in operation. There can be no religious community without a cultic center. Christ is the center of Christianity. This is the significance of the historicity of Jesus for faith.

Christ, the Center of Christianity

To understand, with Troeltsch, the derivative character of dogma and doctrine is to take the decisive initial step in the direction of discerning that orthopraxis is normative for Christian reflection. Here, though, is where we must move beyond him, along the very path he discovered. In so doing we must challenge a basic conclusion he reached, but we can do so only in terms of the steps leading to it and in the name of the horizon it envisions. One of his most memorable formulations focuses the conclusion of the monograph:

> For us "God in Christ" can only mean that in Jesus we reverence the highest revelation of God accessible to us and that we make the picture of Jesus the rallying-point of all God's testimonies to himself found in our sphere of life.
> (Morgan and Pye 1977, 206)

All reflections on the uniqueness and the significance of Jesus of Nazareth confessed to be the Christ must live under this overarching statement, for all of them, without remainder, are derived from the reality Troeltsch describes.

If this is so, we must question his conclusion, for he was convinced that the doctrinal tradition at large was antithetical to his insight. It was not antithetical to this concern; it was exemplary of it. How so? Immediately following the lines just cited, Troeltsch leveled his critique of the tradition:

> And we had best abandon altogether reading this meaning into the christological dogmas of Nicaea and Chalcedon (however elastic they may be). There is no need to bring that page of thought into the foreground. There is nothing in it for preaching, devotion and catechism; academic training in theology can also place it in the background.
>
> (Morgan and Pye 1977, 206)

Troeltsch is right only if the Chalcedonian tradition is understood as an exception to the operation of his fundamental insight—that cult and community precede dogma and idea. But he is wrong *if this tradition is itself a function of this living community,* as most assuredly it was in its origins and development, and continues to be so as a source of creativity today.

What then is the decisive problem, for us, in bringing into play the principle that cult and community precede dogma and idea? It is the problem of making absolute the living formulations of the past and thus forgetting their own derivative nature. It was precisely this absolutism that Troeltsch contended against throughout his life. It was even there in the depths of his differentiation of his understanding of the history of doctrine as over against Harnack's. What he did not see was that the tradition of Nicaea and Chalcedon, too, both can and must be treated as a function of a sociological/ethical/realistic theology. That is to say, it too is capable of being understood and utilized under the regimen of orthopraxis.

Now, can this reading really be maintained in the face of Troeltsch's rejection of it? Yes, indeed. He maintained something that we can and must affirm precisely because of the living tradition of the cultic community that is Christianity:

> It would be good in practical work not to emphasize too much the eternal dependence of millions yet unborn upon the person of Jesus, and instead to bring alive in a practical way how one is oneself bound to him in the present. People who can be happy in their own faith only when they tie all the future millions of years to it know nothing of the real freedom and grandeur of faith.
>
> (Morgan and Pye 1977, 206)

We have already seen something of the explosion of the doctrine of election at the hand of Karl Barth. One could hardly deny his adherence to the very tradition Troeltsch rejects. One cannot dismiss lightly the fact that he would have been at least astonished, if not outraged, to be thought of as exemplary of Troeltsch's insight! What else is *Church Dogmatics* than the implementation of the fact that cult and community precede dogma and idea? What else is the christologizing of the entire range of doctrine than the explication of how we are indeed bound to the Christ in our own present time? What is really at stake here is the fact that no revelation is revealing if it is absolutized. The Chalcedonian tradition has meaning only if it is interpreted in such a way that the Christ to whom it points is the one to whom we are bound in our own present time.[5]

Moreover, we have pondered at length an idea that receives its decisive clarification at the hands of a Jesuit theologian, nurtured in the eucharistic tradition of Catholic liturgy. The Catholic mass is simply unintelligible apart from the Chalcedonian tradition. But grace is grace only as it is lived out, and in this instance it has yielded the incisive notion of orthopraxis. This counters decisively Troeltsch's contention that this tradition has nothing to offer preaching, devotion, and catechism.

The fact is that Troeltsch's alternatives are false, though given the state of the adherents of the Chalcedonian tradition in his day, both Protestant and Catholic, we must not be too quick to fault him for not seeing this. The phrase "God in Christ" means for us exactly what it meant for him. Precisely because cult and community precede dogma and idea, Jesus the Christ is the central focus of God's self-revelation in our spheres of life. To think through Christology under the regimen of orthopraxis demands the liberation of Christology itself. No final statement of the uniqueness and significance of Jesus of Nazareth confessed to be the Christ will ever be found. For the liberating God is the relating God, to the untold aeons of the future as well as to the present contexts, carrying with them as they do both the stimulation and the burdens of yesterday's confessional insights.

THE CHRIST OF THE CONTEXTS

New horizons now beckon christological reflection. They have always been there, and many have suspected their existence long before our time. We can no longer dismiss them as tantalizing suggestions regarding territory as yet unexplored. We now face the necessity of moving toward and even beyond them. If we stay where we are, we are doomed, not to annihilation, but to the relic room of exalted, but rarely visited, museums. Contextual thinking has its own storied past, and by now it takes a robust apparatus to mount its investigation. Too often it still languishes under a supposed singularity of the effort. We are not delivered into the context. We are liberated into the *contexts*. The only possible Christology, therefore, is one concerning the Christ of the contexts. Otherwise we are left in the cul-de-sac of convincing the convinced, the all-embracing effort of the sectarian mind. We should have known this and moved on this front long ago. The New Testament does not contain a single Christology. One can speak only of the Christolog*ies* of the New Testament. Even for a rock-ribbed fundamentalist there are at least seven Christologies in the New Testament: one for each of the Synoptic Gospels, one for Paul, one for John, one for Hebrews, and one for Revelation. And that is the most controversial sentence in this paragraph, for several more clamor for attention, and one's numbering will depend upon the current state of one's reflection on the New Testament documents. What is not controversial is this: We need each and every one of these perspectives, and none is valid unless all are present.

The New Testament name for the liberating God is God the Son. Hence Christology is central in any theological system that appeals to the New Testament as the basis of its efforts. There are three specifications we can now formulate explicitly, and they lead to a fourth implication that cannot be settled within the realm of christological reflection alone. But take care. In moving to these specifications, we are speaking of vectors within a vector, so to say. The relating God is the liberating God. We cannot settle accounts finally in the present line of reflection, because the God whose relating is liberating in character is the creating God whose creativity we must seek to approximate in our own lives. In strict observance of strictures long in place in the tradition, we are not speaking of three Gods in our efforts at large. In fact, given the process modes in which we are moving, we are not thinking of substances in any sense. We are thinking, rather, of the lines of activity along which ultimacy makes itself intelligible to us. Thus the relating God is the liberating God is the creating God, because the becoming of ultimacy has to do with relating/liberating/creating.

In the light of these overarching perspectives, the discussion within the realm of Christology proper likewise has to do with specifications concerning the processive character of the revelation of the liberating

God. These, as I say, are three in number, pointing toward a fourth that cannot be settled within the realm of christological reflection alone.

The Liturgical Life of the Community

The Christ of the contexts is primarily known in the liturgical life of the believing community. This is not to be taken along narrow lines. No priority can be assigned to any of the liturgical constellations that have taken shape within the expanding universe of Christian life, work, faith, and order. For all of them can, and do, appeal to the New Testament for their origins and verifications, and they do so with cogencies that appeal forcefully to their adherents. The forcefulness is most apparent in those whose lives unfold without deviation from their own individual origins, but it is by no means confined to them. What is fascinating is the fact that we are here dealing with the birthright factor in the identities of individual Christians. This simply could not have been recognized apart from the experiences of our own century, with the rise of ecumenicity and the experience of theologically ordered struggles for liberation from oppression.

Each Christian will be dependent on her or his own experience to discern what is at stake here, and thus each will know the limitations of his or her own perspective in the attempt to clarify what is being said. After the unfolding of the ecumenicity that emerged within Protestantism—as my own coming of age theologically unfolded—and then cascaded toward unexpected, long-regarded impossible horizons with the advent of Vatican II and all that it has entailed, it is clear to me that I am as much a child of the Reformed tradition within the heritage of the Reformation as were my mothers and fathers in this lineage. Unlike them I have experienced, and been nourished by, the Catholic mass, to the extent that whereas I am not yet at home there, I am no longer an alien, an unwelcome stranger.

What unifies this spectrum of liturgical life and identity is the centrality, in cult *and* community, of belief in the Lord, Jesus the Christ. However construed, the faith in Jesus the Christ is central for the Christian community. We are hardly the first to recognize this. But we are the first to have been blessed with the opportunity to practice it in ways utterly unknown to our forebears and unwelcome even now to some of our sisters and brothers. Diversity is intrinsic to the intensity attending the liturgical identities of the multifaceted historical reality that is Christianity. What is new is that this diversity is our friend, not our enemy.[6] It is liberating to know this reality and to be known within the contexts comprising it.

Immediately we encounter the obvious, countering reaction to such a line of thought. "Anything goes" will be the charge hurled against this view. "As long as you are sincere, do what you want" will be the invective of the polemicist, always recognizable in the propensity to hold as normative the best possible expression of his or her view, and as final the worst example of all that diverges from it. Genuinely christologically ordered liturgy can have nothing to do with this sectarian reduction. For the liberating God is pleased by all real efforts to respond to the awesome, yet intelligible, presence of ultimacy with adoration, even the adoration of the cross. I know that I am with Christians when I behold their efforts to worship the liberating God. Sometimes that recognition is comparatively easy when I am at home in the liturgical mode; sometimes it is difficult when the liturgical mode is strange, even opaque. But the pivotal recurrence of the name Jesus Christ is enough in itself to restrain hasty retreat, for where liturgy is attempted true witness may be at hand. The liberating God prompts this reluctance to leave too soon. The Christ of the contexts is most persistently evident in the plurality of liturgies the liberating presence of ultimacy engenders. There is a curious proof of this: Christology will never command attention where liturgy is not at least being attempted.

Word and Worship

But how can we be sure that where liturgy is attempted true witness may be at hand? Jesus the Christ, the Lord of the liturgies, cannot be served by liturgy alone. Once again we appeal to Freire. In the liturgical life, it is a recognizable constant that, whatever the form of a given tradition's attempt at worship, word and work go together in such a way that worship cannot complete itself in itself. Of the Word at the center of worship, even the Word of God that is God, it is supremely the case that the only true word is a transforming word. We have already spoken of an awesome adoration that includes even the adoration of the cross. Why is this crucial? The very term "crucial" speaks it! Christology springs from worship; hence Christology will always be *theologia crucis*. As Troeltsch never wearied of saying, there was a community that worshiped the Christ *before* there was a Christology; there was a community that practiced and was sustained by the Eucharist *before* there was a theology of the sacraments.

A theology of the cross can only be lived out, and only in the light of this will it find the momentary significance of a genuine witness that points beyond itself. The decisive issue has to do with that pointing. To what, to whom, and how does it point? Here the confessional life of the church is the inexhaustible source of insight, most recently, and indelibly, in the Theological Declaration of Barmen.[7] The liberating God always delivers us into concreteness. The theologies of the cross do not demand contrived crosses, for only the derangement of messiah complexes would, or could, be guilty of such misunderstanding. But they do indeed evoke the risk of real ones. It was the Theological Declaration of Barmen that ordered the lives of those elements of the church that did oppose the nightmare of the Third Reich to the end. At least one risked cross left its new, indelible mark on the community stemming from *the* cross. It was the gallows of Dietrich Bonhoeffer, whose life and work epitomized what the Theological Declaration of Barmen confessed.

Here we really do encounter the depths of a contention that has already played a role in our reflections. The tradition of Nicaea and Chalcedon does indeed inform the liturgical norms of complex Christianity, simply because the emerging christological consensus embodied in the symbol of Chalcedon makes sense only in the kind of continual reinterpretation its liturgical yield constantly generates. Chalcedon means nothing if it is not continually reinterpreted, for the same reason that liturgy points beyond itself to lives in which what is adored is lived into reality.

The liberating God evokes lives that risk crosses. What was at stake at Barmen was precisely this. We cannot admire Barmen's concreteness without risking our own. Liberation is like that. It permits no counterfeits. Each of the six "evangelical truths" specified in the Theological Declaration of Barmen, with the possibly debatable exception of the fifth one (which simply perpetuated the doctrine of the two kingdoms, so central for traditional Lutheranism), confronted the Third Reich with unyielding clarity. Karl Barth, its principal author, would later claim that this clarity was not clear enough (see Barth 1949, 33–34). But given the realities of 1934, I am not so sure his later case carried. For the witness of Barmen was clear, and the issue was rightly focused. Fascism raises false claims that are primarily *theological* in character. False messiahs, including Hitler and all his imitators since (and without doubt we will face others), can be resisted finally only in the name of the true Messiah, even Jesus the Christ our Lord. But the price is the risk of new crosses. The liberating God offers us precisely this liberation. Christology can speak of meaning only in terms of sacrifice and new reality. The cross is the sign under which we shall always live, move, and know our own becoming.

Movement to New Insights

How can this be true of *us*? How can *we* know this, seeing that we now comprise an ecumenical diversity that is permanent? We can know this is true, and know that we know it, only if the revelation of the liberating God proceeds—moves, that is—beyond our prior insights, along the paths of emergence that engendered them, toward horizons some of which we can only speculate about with fear and trembling. Faith in the liberating God, simply because it is indeed faith, can never know the certainty of false absolutes. We cannot have the Christ if we yearn for absolutes, for living realities defy finality. And the witness of the resurrection is that whereas the risks of real crosses attend the only liberation we may know, these risks are not final, for they speak of ultimacy's ultimate resolution.

The liturgical risk of the Reformation, in all its forms, is focused in the immense significance ascribed to the attempt to proclaim the gospel. For nothing less than the continual effort to reword the Word is entailed in this heavy responsibility. To know that the relating God promises a relationship that is liberating demands a creativity we must now ponder explicitly. Clearly, this is a fourth christological specification, but we cannot deal with it on christological grounds alone. The liberating God is the creating God. The ground of being turns out to be the origin of a becoming that is still under way. Revelation proceeds. The faithful must move, too. We become as we become because God becomes as God becomes.

4

THE CREATING GOD

As we turn to thinking of the creating God, for whom the biblical and traditional name is God the Father, some would assume that we now enter the realm of the doctrine of God in its most primordial sense. Clearly, this is not the case. The doctrine of God has been before us from Chapter 2 forward. The basic contention throughout is that the relating God, the liberating God, and the creating God are one God. We are discussing this confessional affirmation in terms of the three revelatory vectors by which we know the becoming of this God, and we are doing so in terms of the claim that the revelation of this God is processive.

Even so, the problematic now before us is decisive for the discussions of each of the two preceding lines of reflection. Without it they are incomplete, not in the sense that one third of the point at hand has yet to be addressed, but in the sense that without this revelatory vector the other two are irreparably weakened. We must now reckon with the question of relationship between cosmology and theology, or more precisely, the problem of the relationship between theology and the natural sciences. Some of the truly mighty theological voices of our century argue that cosmology and theology are *not* related, at least not at the center of theological concerns. Karl Barth took this view, and it gains cogency for many of the theologians of liberation. Oppression preoccupies the latter. To be concerned about cosmology and theology is, in their view, the private preserve of the comfortable. As we shall see, to maintain this view is to overlook completely the epistemological convergence of concerns rooted in the liberation struggles and those at the center of current reflections about theology in the context of postmodern science. Moreover, to ignore this convergence is to avoid or evade what has already been shown in this present study. The fact is that the contexts within which the contextualization of theology take shape have exploded to include the realm of the natural.

In speaking now of the creating God, we move into the realm of developing a contribution to what must be called a theology of the natural, one that resonates with all that we have seen in pondering the relating and liberating vectors of the God of Christian conviction. A theology of the natural is not to be confused with natural theology, a subject that has an immensely convoluted history all its own, running into our own century in the celebrated argument between Karl Barth and Emil Brunner. At the same time, it must be noted at the outset of our present line of reflection that these two concerns are indeed related. Theological reflection about the natural realm must include pondering the sense in which what we know about the world of which we are a part bears heavily upon how we think about any and all issues, including those having to do with theological reflection, above all in its doctrine of God. The issue is not whether nature is revelatory. It is rather whether there can be understanding of revelation that does not include the natural realm in its purview.

In approaching this question, we must note at the outset, as the "bottom line" of the discussion, that we must move far beyond a long-held conclusion concerning the doctrine of creation. This is the seemingly invulnerable conviction caught up in the phrase *creatio ex nihilo*. The central affirmation focused in this phrase (it has been around since the intertestamental period [see Brunner 1952, 11], and it has informed Christian conviction clear up to our own century) is not simply "creation out of nothing," its literal meaning, but "creation once-and-for-all." Its contrasting opposite has always been *creatio continua*, "continuing creation," and until now this has been rejected. To be sure, the idea that creation initially occurs "out of nothing" may be finding new currency with the advent of the "big bang" theory of the origin of the universe. However, as we shall see, the only case that can be maintained now for belief in God the Creator presupposes a creativity that is still in operation.

The understanding of our world—our own place within it and its place within the universe of which it is a part—is the subject matter of cosmology. This realm of reflection is in great ferment today. Neither the just mentioned big bang theory of the origin of the universe nor popular notions evoked by the term "evolution" are as settled as the lay mind assumes. Hence Barth's warning is germane. Theology is not to be confused with cosmology, for then it will be trapped in the assumptions guiding a current line of cosmological reflection and thus vulnerable to the inevitability of its being superseded by future insights. But what theology cannot ignore is the necessity of understanding the forces that generate the continual development of cosmological inquiry. Humanity will always be insatiably curious about the world of which it is a part. Today that curiosity cannot be engaged by a faith that contends that the natural realm was fixed, once and for all, by ultimacy's creativity in some remote past.

Hence the problem is that of becoming involved in theology's own involvement in the cosmological inquiry and of taking seriously the yield of such an unrestrained engagement in the advancing frontiers of our understanding of the cosmos and our relationship to it. This interrelationship must be seen concretely before its theoretical impact on theological reflection can be appraised. Even this defies a neat progression, for the ontic and the noetic dimensions of becoming involved in this involvement are continually emerging as inextricably intertwined. The initial theological yield of this effort is already susceptible to precise formulation: How do we understand our confessional conviction that the God of Jesus of Nazareth confessed to be the Christ is still creatively involved in the emergence of all that is becoming? How, that is, do we grasp and become grasped by the fact that the relating and liberating God is relating and liberating only in terms of a creativity that is still creating?

THEOLOGY AND BIOLOGY

The intertwining of the ontic and noetic dimensions of the relationship between theology and the natural sciences can be discussed in several different ways.[1] One can discern this nexus in terms of postmodern astronomy, physics, or biology. No doubt it also asserts itself in a host of cognate lines of reflections. The case for focusing the issues at hand in terms of theology and biology turns on a rather obvious point. Here the direct relationship to understanding our humanity itself cannot be avoided. Actually, in the final analysis it also cannot be avoided in terms of astronomy and physics, but it can be deferred there in ways that are untenable when biology is at the center of the discussion.

The fact is that the logic of history supports us in moving as we are, for the emergence of postmodern science—that is, science on this side of Descartes and Newton, transcending while presupposing their decisive accomplishments—began with Darwin, not with Einstein or Heisenberg. The advent of reflection on theories of evolution as irresistible and necessary antedates the breakthroughs concerning relativity and indeterminacy. In saying this, we must be mindful of the quite obvious fact that biology has moved far beyond the ground initially won by Darwin. By now there is a clear consensus on the basic contention, and I am instructed by Arthur Peacocke as to the best epitomization of this. It comes from the hand of the French Nobel prizewinner François Jacob, who sums up the theory of evolution as follows:

> First, that all organisms, past, present or future, descend from one or several rare living systems which arose spontaneously. Second, that species are derived from one another by natural selection of the best procreators.
> (Peacocke 1986, 33 and 167 n. 2)

Peacocke insists that among biologists a formulation such as Jacob's is beyond dispute, and he epitomizes this consensus with his own concise statement: "All forms of life, current and extinct, are interconnected through evolutionary relationships" (Peacocke 1986, 35). Here the truly basic question before us as we think of the creating God emerges. The issue is not whether this is the case, but whether the process to which it points is intentional. To assume that it is indeed intentional is already implied in speaking of "the creating God." But what does it mean to say this?

We have alluded to Darwin, but his work is not the focus of the present discussion. The convoluted conversation generated by his thought is both well known and well charted. We will be preoccupied, rather, with three figures, each of whom are scientifically competent and theologically literate. Their reflections epitomize what happens when science and theology converge. These are Pierre Teilhard de Chardin, Charles Birch, and Arthur Peacocke, who has already helped us on our way. We will deal with each of these in turn.

Pierre Teilhard de Chardin

Teilhard de Chardin was not a biologist, but a paleontologist. The range of his thought, however, was not confined to his specialty. It touched both biology and theology in ways that are decisive for the issues now before us.

138

As Teilhard worked out the extended range of his treatment of the human phenomenon, moving from the realm of beginnings yielding molecular aggregates to the human envisioning of the ultimate omega point, he found that he could not evade or suppress wondering about what he called "the within of things." He was aware that he was shaped, as most of us still are, by the fact that "the apparent restriction of the phenomenon of consciousness to the higher forms of life has long served science as an excuse for eliminating it from its models of the universe" (Teilhard de Chardin 1955, 55). In the face of this, he contended that "things have their *within*; their reserve, one might say; and this appears in definite *qualitative* or *quantitative* connections with the developments that science recognises in the cosmic energy" (Teilhard de Chardin 1955, 54). This contention is one of the central elements in the dynamic of Teilhard's creative attempt to understand the human phenomenon within the context of cosmic reality as a whole.

We cannot reckon with Teilhard's fascination with "the within of things" without coming to terms with his idea of *the suppression of the evolutionary peduncles* (see Teilhard de Chardin 1955, 120). This recurrent phrase is to be found wherever he is attempting to account for the move from one strata of development to the next. It is strikingly similar to the vexatious question of the so-called missing link that plagued evolutionary thought until the marvelous breakthroughs of our own recent decades; but in the case of Teilhard's thought, a daring suggestion could not be suppressed. This has to do with the contention that the emergence of the new is always marked by a fragility that will be eclipsed as the new develops. Here we must listen to him:

> Nothing is so delicate and fugitive by its very nature as a beginning. As long as a zoological group is young, its characters remain indeterminate, its structure precarious and its dimensions scant. It is composed of relatively few individual units, and these change rapidly. In space as in duration, the peduncle (or, which comes to the same thing, the bud) of a living branch corresponds to a minimum of differentiation, expansion and resistance. What, then, will be the effect of time on this area of weakness?
> Inevitably to destroy all vestiges of it. . . .
> It is the same *in every domain:* when anything really new begins to germinate around us, we cannot distinguish it—for the very good reason that it could only be recognised in the light of what it is going to be. . . . In biology, in civilisation, in linguistics, as in all things, time, like a draughtsman

with an eraser, rubs out every weak line in the drawing of life. . . . Except for the fixed maxima, the consolidated achievements, nothing, neither trace nor testimony, subsists of what has gone before.

(Teilhard de Chardin 1955, 120–121)

Because the new can be recognized only in what it is going to be, the suppression of the evolutionary peduncles is automatic in the sense that it is inevitable with the passage of time. Accordingly, we can understand the past only in the light of what has come to pass as the result of the myriad developments that have gone before. Here then we behold the humanistic affirmation so central to Teilhard's reflections. We can no longer think of humanity as the center of all things, but we must think of it as the clue to what has been going on:

Man is not the centre of the universe as once we thought in our simplicity, but something much more wonderful—the arrow pointing the way to the final unifications of the world in terms of life.

(Teilhard de Chardin 1955, 223)

There are two dimensions to this remarkable formulation. First, it points toward the past, insisting that the past makes sense in the light of the present. Quoting a memorable insight from Julian Huxley, Teilhard then adds his own considered insight:

Man discovers that *he is nothing else than evolution become conscious of itself,* to borrow Julian Huxley's concise expression. It seems to me that our modern minds (because and inasmuch as they are modern) will never find rest until they settle down to this view. On this summit and on this summit alone are repose and illumination waiting for us.

(Teilhard de Chardin 1955, 220)

If this is so, humanity is not only caught up in the meaning of the present, it is also the clue to the primordial depths from which it has sprung. The "arrow" was launched in the infinite reaches of that beginning. Is it still going? Yes! So Teilhard would argue. Whatever Huxley may have meant by his words, on Teilhard's lips they become a doxology.

This points inexorably toward the second dimension of the issue at hand. The humanity that is the clue to the past is indeed also the clue to the future. Teilhard cannot conceive of this insight in terms other than those evoked by his faith. This is what he meant by speaking of an omega point yet to appear. The most succinct expression of his real confession of faith is to be found in the brief article written in 1947, "Turmoil or Genesis?" Here he expresses four theorems that later will receive their massive elaboration in *The Phenomenon of Man:*

> *a* Life is not an accident in the Material Universe, but the essence of the phenomenon.
> *b* Reflection (that is to say, Man) is not an incident in the biological world, but a higher form of Life.
> *c* In the human world the social phenomenon is not a superficial arrangement, but denotes an essential advance of Reflection.
>> To which may be added, from the Christian point of view:
> *d* The Christian phylum is not an accessory or divergent shoot in the human social organism, but constitutes the axis itself of socialisation.
>> (Teilhard de Chardin 1959, 214–215)

We must go further than Teilhard de Chardin did, formidable though that assignment is. We know more about what he considered than he did. Some of us will wish to locate the explicitly theological dimension at a different point in the progression than he does, true as he is to his Thomistic training and purview. However that may be, our debt to his efforts defies calculation. If his interpretation of Huxley's insight carries, then is it the case that humanity is the way, or one of the ways, the universe thinks? Is humanity the way, or one of the ways, the cosmos prays? As we will see, we must answer Yes to these questions and then ponder what it means to do so. Theology in the tradition of Anselm and Barth—theology, that is, as faith seeking understanding—is always driven to efforts of this sort. Yet even that tradition, including the recent figure, Karl Barth, must be transcended. For to think through the depths of saying "I believe in the creating God" on this side of the work of Teilhard de Chardin is to ponder dimensions of the ancient faith that could not have become explicit until our own time.

Charles Birch

That we do indeed know more than Teilhard de Chardin did is evident in the work of Charles Birch, work that unfolded during his distin-

guished career as Challis Professor of Biology at the University of Syd-
ney. Here our beginning point is on the biographical front, and happily
we have Birch's own account of the decisive turning point in an article
published in 1975 under the title "What Does God Do in the World?"
This point occurred in the midst of the deepening research demanded
by his study of biology, the discipline to which he committed his life:

> Theology was initially more important to me than science. It
> gave me an interpretation of much that I valued most in my
> experience of growing up. . . . It seemed to me that there was
> an eros, or reaching forth in life, which met a response from
> beyond myself. And when I stumbled upon that question
> asked last century at the height of the Darwinian controversy
> by T. H. Huxley "Is the universe friendly?" I knew that it
> was; God was pressing in on all sides blocked only by us. My
> theology drew solely from the personal.
>
> (Birch 1975, 78)

Crucial in this paragraph, simply because it is likely to be overlooked, is the word "solely." The problem Birch encountered, and he is
surely not alone in this, had to do with the fact that his theology "drew
solely from the personal." This issue would prove to be as much a ques-
tioning of the prevailing use of the term "personal" as it was the discovery of the limits of a received theology. The full force of this would
dawn later, at the culmination of Birch's work. What was happening at
the moment in question was the discovery that his theology no longer
made sense:

> I did not know [my theology] was false until science became
> part of my experience. My undergraduate science did not re-
> ally affect my ideas at all. It was not until I became a research
> student in an active laboratory that I began to try and relate
> science to my concept of God, challenged as I was on every
> count by my laboratory colleagues. Whilst God as personal
> influence was as strong as ever, I had no intellectual defense
> for my beliefs at all, particularly my simplistic and orthodox
> view of God as creator. It threw no light, only confusion, on
> the scientific world-view that I was rapidly assimilating. My
> God had nothing to do in my new world of science. There
> was a breach between my experience of "God as redeemer"
> and my understanding of "God as creator."
>
> (Birch 1975, 79)

Why believe in a God who has nothing to do? That question is heavy enough. Yet it is tame when related to the question it inexorably generates: How can God do the work of redemption if this same God has nothing to do in the world in which redemption must occur?

Providentially, I would say, in the name of the God who does have something to do as both Creator and Redeemer, at just this moment Birch read Whitehead. And as he records it, at this same time, in 1946, he went to the University of Chicago to do research in zoology only to discover there "the richest collection of Whitehead scholars in the land" (Birch 1975, 79). This encounter would lead him to understand that "God participates in the world as it evolves" (Birch 1975, 83), but it would push him even further. It would lead him ultimately to the drastic claim that the human is the clue to nature itself, as well as the context within which alone faith in God as participant could heal the breech between God the Creator and God the Redeemer, which his laboratory integrity relentlessly forced.

"Can Evolution Be Accounted for Solely in Terms of Mechanical Causation?" is the title of an article Birch wrote in 1977, in which we can discern the key move in developing the claim that humanity is the clue to the natural as a whole. His point of departure is Whitehead's observation that "it is orthodox to hold that there is nothing in biology but what is physical mechanism under somewhat complex circumstances" (Whitehead 1925, 102). In Birch's shorthand form, "biology has an orthodoxy; it is mechanism based on physics" (Birch 1977, 13). Biology under the dominance of this idea cannot ponder evolution "in a comprehensive way" because it ignores the contention that "there is a qualitative side to evolution which escapes interpretation that is solely concerned with mechanical causes" (Birch 1977, 13).

It would seem to be the case that this orthodox biology is the predominant view among the practitioners of the discipline and that, given the great advances in this discipline since Whitehead's day, the stranglehold of this orthodoxy is even more unrelenting. Birch was not completely alone in his central concern, and the list of those who were concerned with the qualitative side of evolution included illustrious names indeed: Theodosius Dobzhansky, Sewall Wright, C. H. Waddington, B. Rensch, and W. H. Thorpe (see Birch 1977, 13).

The basic contention Birch advances can be stated simply: If humanity is the result of all that has gone before, humanity is not only dependent upon the prior process; it is also the clue to its dynamism. If humanity is epitomized by consciousness, then this capacity carries with it the irresistible hunch that what has yielded humanity had and has consciousness implicit within it. This is tantamount to insisting that the simplicity that generates complexity must be understood in the light of the resulting complexity itself. Birch's illustration is illuminating:

> Whitehead reversed the situation of the mechanists. . . . We do not start with knowing all about atoms and molecules and then seem to understand the phenomena of biology. It is from observed phenomena in biology that we have to start. . . . It is from these we work back to construct models of similar entities. . . . To use an example of Waddington . . . sodium chloride molecules exhibit properties which we cannot observe by studying sodium and chlorine atoms in isolation. When the compound sodium chloride is formed, it is not that something entirely new is added to sodium and chlorine atoms, but rather we know something more about the nature of sodium and chlorine atoms than we did before.
>
> (Birch 1977, 14)

The central point is clear. Subsequent development always discloses what could never have been known concerning the components involved had the subsequent itself not have emerged. Birch is willing to take this contention to its inexorable conclusion:

> Similarly with the phenomena of life. When certain arrangements of atoms of carbon, nitrogen, hydrogen, oxygen and so on exhibit properties which we recognize by the name of enzymes, or other combinations are able to conduct electrical impulses as in nerve cells, *it is not that something new has been added to these atoms. We have discovered something about the nature of these atoms that we did not know before.*
>
> (Birch 1977, 14; italics mine)

We are now at the very nerve center of Birch's creativity and contribution. The insight before us has a momentum that drives beyond known frontiers with compelling cogency. If it is the case that the process indicated discloses something about the nature of the atoms in question that could not have been known before the process itself unfolds, where then should the study of atoms themselves begin? With the functioning of the atoms directly involved in putting the question!

> We discover that when atoms are organized in particular ways they reveal aspects of their nature not revealed in isolation. Atoms and molecules organized in brains reveal the potentiality of atoms organized in particular ways to give rise to

entities with subjective experience to which we give the
name mind or consciousness. Atoms that can give rise to
brains that think must be different from hypothetical atoms
that could under no circumstances have done this.

(Birch 1977, 14)

The case with Birch is similar to what we saw in Teilhard de Chardin's thought. The implication of Birch's line of reflection is also doubly
valenced, suggesting both an incisive understanding of humanity's
place in the vast sweep of evolution and a yearning question concerning
the ultimate question for theology, the doctrine of God.

The former of these turns on updating evolutionary theory. We do
indeed have before us extremely significant insights that Teilhard did
not have at his disposal. We know something about the DNA molecule.
Birch focuses this in a remarkable volume he wrote in collaboration
with the process theologian John B. Cobb, Jr., entitled *The Liberation of
Life* (1981). (Birch was responsible for the biological side of the discussion, though the text as a whole is the result of scrutiny by both
authors.)

There were three phases in the development of the theory of
evolution by natural selection. The first was the bold outlines
in Darwin's *On the Origin of Species* in 1859. The second had
to wait until 1930 when quite independently three brilliant
geneticists developed the genetical theory of natural selection. These were R. A. Fisher and J. B. S. Haldane in England
and Sewall Wright in the U.S.A. This phase was first highly
theoretical. It came to earth in the studies of Theodosius
Dobzhansky and his students on natural populations, especially of fruit flies. The third phase had its origin in the unrav-
eling of the structure of the DNA molecule by Watson and
Crick in 1953. This opened the door to the interpretation of
mutation and selection in molecular terms.

(Birch and Cobb 1981, 53)

Teilhard himself was quite clear on the initial implication of the
second of these developments. For him, as for Birch, the emergence of
humanity is the emergence of a group, not an individual (see Teilhard
de Chardin 1955, 185). However, Teilhard died in 1955, within two
years of the breakthrough wrought by Watson and Crick, and thus he
could not know that horizons only dimly seen would disclose remarkable corroborations and extensions of reflections such as his. It is the
note of concreteness, as over against intuitive speculation, that marks

the advance of Birch's insights beyond the frontier discerned by Teilhard. Building on the work of Dobzhansky and then Waddington, he argues that we are beyond the impasse of "the hit and miss element of simple models of natural selection" (Birch and Cobb 1981, 55). For him, Waddington's experiments with fruit flies led to an astonishing conclusion:

> If there are genetic mechanisms that tend to fix these changes genetically then we have a much closer relationship between environment and genetic constitution than a simple reading of Darwinism would give. The theory becomes much more credible. Natural selection is not, as is so often stated, the selection of the genotype. It is not even the selection of the phenotype. It is the selection of the *developing phenotype*.
> (Birch and Cobb 1981, 55–56; italics mine)

In this light, Birch makes common cause with Teilhard: "We cannot measure evolution by comparing one individual today with a forebear sometime back." But he is able to go further, in two steps. First:

> The biological understanding of human history is that the decisive qualities that made the difference between the human and the pre-human did not appear first in one individual at a specific moment in history. No such moment and no such individual could have existed. A threshold had to be crossed. But it was no mere hop, step and jump but two or more million years wide.
> (Birch and Cobb 1981, 62–63)

The second step brings into play Birch's own specialty, population ecology:

> A population made the journey. Mutation, recombination of genes and natural selection are phenomena that happen to populations. The human gene pool does not belong to any one individual. It belongs to the total population of human beings alive at any one time. . . . What happens in evolution is not that the type suddenly changes but the mean of the population in many of its characters gradually moves. The species takes a trip. . . . Despite the incompleteness of the fossil record of human origins there is a continuum of transitions between early ape-like creatures, Australopithecines, *Homo erectus* and *Homo sapiens*. The "missing link" is no longer missing.
> (Birch and Cobb 1981, 63)

This bold specification of how our own lives are tied to the emergence of all life adds cogency to Teilhard's intuitive insights. And with that cogency, what we dared to ask in the light of Teilhard's thought becomes even more compelling. Do we quite literally think for the universe, and pray on behalf of the cosmos? These probes come to mind again as we ponder the question Birch himself asks and then answers. What does God do in the world? His answer is that "God participates in the world as it evolves" (Birch 1975, 83). That he is building directly on Whitehead in saying this is obvious. But his own creativity informs his assertion. What is at stake is "a vision of *the world* in relation to God [that] is not provable. It stands or falls by its adequacy to account for and illuminate our experience. But it requires imagination to see it. . . . For the scientist it is not a case of metaphors or no metaphors. It is a case of *which* metaphor" (Birch 1975, 83).

I italicize "the world" in this passage. The ultimate issues with which we are concerned do not simply involve God and humanity. What is before us is the relationship between ultimacy and the cosmos as a whole, together with all that it involves. In the light of Teilhard's thought, and now Birch's, *all* theological questions must be answered in terms of an ultimacy that participates in the life of the cosmos it is creating. The theological creativity in operation in each of these figures forces our conceptual and linguistic capacities into new imaginative realms. The most far-reaching of Birch's own suggestions takes shape in precisely this way:

> Some events have much more significance than others. This is not because God intervened in these events and not in others. To interpret significant events as special acts of God is to turn God into an agent of mechanical causation. It is to replace persuasive love by fiat, acting in accordance with some preordained plan. Significant events are significant because they happen to open up a new realm of possibility heretofore closed. The history of the Jews is rich in such events. The life of Jesus is such an event; it opened up for mankind new possibilities of compassionate understanding, creativity, and human brotherhood.
>
> But creation is not merely something which has already happened. It is not a doctrine about past events. It is a doctrine of the present.
>
> (Birch 1975, 84)

Just as a biological orthodoxy that adheres to the metaphor of mechanism must be challenged because of the facts of the case, so a theological orthodoxy that can speak only of an *intervening* God must be questioned. Birch's theological suggestion is fascinating. From his point of view, the long-standing emphasis upon the God who *intervenes* in the affairs of humanity makes the same error that biological orthodoxy does. Such metaphors now have a mechanistic ring that robs them of the power they once possessed. This suggestion merits prolonged consideration, but one thing is now beyond question. They have now become profoundly misleading. In the midst of a major address to which I will return presently, Birch sharply focused the issue at hand:

> One might have expected Christian theology to resist the mechanistic interpretation of the world and all that is in it. On the contrary. Indeed, mechanism's most famous metaphor of the universe as a clockwork with God as the clockmaker was given it by a bishop, the Frenchman Nicole Oresme in the 14th century. Theology found it easy to accommodate itself to the mechanical conception of the world with the human being curiously detached from the rest of nature and with a clockwork God outside it as a *deus ex machina*.
>
> (Birch 1979, 260)

If humanity is indeed part of the evolutionary process in the manner Teilhard de Chardin and Charles Birch insist to be so, then only a *participating* God can be heard within that same process. This is how that ultimate presence effects the persuasiveness of inexhaustible love. For only so can this presence speak. The deus ex machina is speechless.

Toward this metaphoric horizon theology is driven if the theologically informed biologists among the faithful are given the attention that is their due. A pronounced urgency attends the advent of this possibility, for it is not an option but a necessity if the issues are truly grasped. Birch gave one of the most significant of the addresses at the Conference on Faith, Science and the Future, held in Cambridge, Massachusetts, in 1979, under the auspices of the World Council of Churches (indeed, he was one of the guiding spirits in the planning of this consultation). His address, entitled "Nature, Humanity and God in Ecological Perspective," explored eight theses. The final two of these are as follows:

> 7. The new partnership of faith and science that is emerging acknowledges the unity of the creation, that is the oneness of

nature, humanity and God. It takes seriously both the insights of science and the special characteristics of the human.
8. This ecological view of nature, humanity and God implies
a life-ethic which embraces all life as well as all humanity in
an infinite responsibility to all life. This new ethic and the
new vision provides a foundation on which to build the ecologically sustainable and socially just global society.

(Birch 1980, 62)

The summons to building the ecologically sustainable world is
thus equated with the struggle for a socially just global society. This is
the urgent yield of the theologically profound and genuinely incisive
biologist Charles Birch. He is not the only such figure that insists on
considering nature, humanity, and God together. Precisely this same
passion informs the work of Arthur Peacocke. As I turn to his insights,
the final words of Birch's address ring in my ears:

> We have been warned as Noah was warned. Sceptics
> laughed and ridiculed then as they do now. . . . But this time
> the ark cannot be built of wood and caulking. Its foundations
> will be a new awareness of the meaning of life, of the life of
> all creatures, both great and small. . . . We do not have to be
> the victims of circumstances. In the ecological view the future
> is not predetermined. It is radically open. Through its open-
> ness to the lure of God the self becomes freed from total pre-
> occupation with itself. Its concern becomes the world. That is
> still possible for each one of us.

(Birch 1980, 72–73)

Arthur Peacocke

The issues that emerge from listening to Teilhard de Chardin and
Charles Birch are intensified when the work of Arthur Peacocke is taken
fully into account. His 1986 volume, *God and the New Biology*, carries
further reflections begun in earlier essays and developed in his well-
known *Creation and the World of Science* (1979). Peacocke's specialty
takes shape in the midst of the very center of creativity in today's advances in the field of biology, where physical chemistry and biochemis-
try intersect in the study of "biological macro-molecules (e.g. DNA) and
genetic function" (Peacocke 1986, 1). In his view, a decisive controversy
has been generated by the advent of molecular biology—its seemingly
inexorable gravitation toward reductionism. This focuses on the conten-

tion that "biological organisms are 'nothing but' atoms and molecules," which in turn implies that "a physicochemical account of their atomic and molecular processes is all there is to be said . . . " (Peacocke 1986, 13). Peacocke is convinced that this will not suffice. The reductionism in question is in fact a matter of explanation. Accordingly, it must deal with "a consideration of the 'something more' that has to be said over and beyond purely physicochemical accounts of living organisms" (Peacocke 1986, 13).

Peacocke's "something more" resonates with Teilhard's "the within of things," and it converges with all that is central in the concerns of Charles Birch. Like Birch, he states his affinity with Dobzhansky (see Peacocke 1986, 32–33). But he must go further than this, probably simply because he knows the world of molecular biology as a specialist. That is to say, "holistic" though he is, Peacocke knows that the reductionists have a point that must be taken seriously. For our purposes, the most telling of the many ways in which he states this turns on his understanding of why, and where, we must move beyond Teilhard de Chardin. Teilhard could speak of the "connection between 'complexity' and consciousness" as a decisive implication of "the broad sweep of evolution," but he could do so only in the imprecise terms of a sweeping generalization. Peacocke may or may not be correct in noting that this was informed by Teilhard's "pan-psychic assumptions," but there can be no doubting his contention that the critical issue is this: Can we *quantify* Teilhard's notion of complexity?

Peacocke is convinced that we can, for he knows how this needed quantification must be understood. This involves what has come to be known as the central dogma of molecular biology. Those who are not professionally involved in the study of biology need to know that, along with the theory of organic evolution, this ranks as one of the two major breakthroughs in biology in the postmodern era (see Peacocke 1986, 171). With the discovery, in 1953, of the structure of DNA by Watson and Crick, it came to dominate molecular biology for at least a decade. Peacocke delineates the central dogma as follows:

> DNA replicates its unique sequence of units (nucleotides) autocatalytically by copying one of its two intertwined chains and also acts as a template for single RNA chains, which then control the synthesis and amino acid sequences of proteins.
> (Peacocke 1986, 58)

The theologically significant word in this formulation is the word "autocatalytically." Ponder then what it means for a theologically adept biologist to wrestle with the fact that the creative process leading to the production of protein is intrinsic to the DNA structure itself and that it functions on its own. That is, no external principle of explanation is needed to understand this process. To grasp this is to cross the threshold into the depths of what must already fire the imagination open to listening to Peacocke, having first heard Teilhard de Chardin and Birch:

> The "gaps" for any intervening god to be inserted go on diminishing. For we see a world in process that is continuously capable, through its own inherent properties and natural character, of producing new living forms— matter is now seen to be self-organizing.
>
> (Peacocke 1986, 53–54; italics mine)

The gaps are really gone! We have been thinking this for some time, so much so that to bring the matter up now is *déjà vu* in the extreme. But is it? The real impact of the new biology on theology has to do with the fact that the death of the God-of-the-gaps is even more undeniable than we had thought. The seemingly bizarre dream of the computer age that artificial intelligence can indeed be produced pales in comparison to the fact that we know, and know that we know, that molecular creativity is, in a profound sense, intrinsically automatic. Now the real frontier comes into view. With whom is Peacocke going to argue, having quantified Teilhard's deep hunch in terms now available? He takes on none other than the celebrated F. H. C. Crick himself. At the very outset of *God and the New Biology*, Peacocke notes that Crick has been very emphatic in contending that physics and chemistry suffice for the explanation of all biology, and this epitomizes the reductionism Peacocke combats (see Peacocke 1986, 1).

It would be a mistake to say that the truly polemical dimension of our effort is now unavoidably before us. This is true, and the issue would be even more clear if we stopped to deal with the fact that it is the sociobiologists who carry biological reductionism to it extreme conclusion (see Peacocke 1986, 108–115). Nevertheless, the polemical issue is superficial when compared with the deep point at hand. For us, this has to do with discerning the arena into which theological creativity is now irresistibly drawn. Does the emergence of molecular biology spell the death of all holistic interpretations? An affirmative answer is the only possible one, given Crick's thought, *if* one accepts his identification of "belief in God with vitalism." Vitalism is "the view that living organisms have some special added entity or force over and beyond non-living matter," and such a view is no longer tenable:

> As Crick saw it, molecular biology had triumphantly demon-strated the *molecular* basis of the most distinctive feature of living organisms, their ability to reproduce, and thereby ren-dered all such proposals of vitalism null and void.
>
> (Peacocke 1986, 59–60)

How does a theologically adept holistic biologist, one who gives reductionism its due without selling out to it, deal with the specifically theological issue now before us? Peacocke rejects the equation of theism with vitalism. But he notes that Christian apologists are vulnerable at this point since they "have an unfortunately had . . . a tendency to at-tempt to insert 'God' into the gaps of biological explanation" (Peacocke 1986, 60).

With this formulation, the depths of the theological yield of Peacocke's work come into view. Note carefully that he is as holistic in his theological thinking as he is in his biological research. This is the root of his rejection of the de facto equation in Crick's reflections. Vital-ism does not equal theism for Peacocke because vitalism does not ex-haust the understanding of ultimacy. For him the name for ultimacy is not "vitality" but "God." The basic reason that this is the case for Peacocke manifests his affinity with the thought of the celebrated Anglican prelate William Temple (whom he explicitly cites later in his discussion [see Peacocke 1986, 84]), for he is equally insistent on the view that nature, humanity, and God must be understood together.

All three of these terms must be understood as comprehensively as possible. It is an open question, for Peacocke, as to whether biology has been reduced to physics and chemistry or whether physics and chemistry have been taken up into biology (see Peacocke 1986, 27). This in turn raises the question as to whether such an expansion can ever be arrested until ultimacy itself is encountered. This leads him to a striking claim:

> We can, I would argue, go further. I refer to that most com-plex and all-embracing of the levels in the hierarchies of "systems," namely the complex of nature-man-and-God. For when human beings are exercising themselves in their God-directed and worshipping activities they are operating at a level in the hierarchy of complexity which is more intricate

> and cross-related than any of those that arise in the natural
> and social sciences which are in the province of the humani-
> ties. For in his "religious," i.e., God-related, activities man
> utilises every facet of his total being. . . . For religion is about
> the ultimate meaning that a person finds in his or her relation
> to all-that-is.
>
> (Peacocke 1986, 30)

Precisely because Peacocke is as *holistic* in his theology as he is in his biology, there is not a trace of the God-of-the-gaps here. No intrusions of ultimacy are necessary. For *ultimacy* is the term that denotes the human involvement in "all-that-is." It is thus already within the context of human reflection. Moreover, this involvement in the all-that-is is liturgically and confessionally ordered. It is not a matter of intellectual speculation. It may not be reduced to an equation of any sort. Vitalism does not equal theism, because "God" is neither the result of a syllogism nor the minuscule particle at the end of a reduction. *God* is the focusing term for this sense of ultimacy; *theology* is reflection upon this.

> "Religion is a relation to the ultimate" and that ultimate is usu-
> ally denoted, in English, by the word "God." . . . Theology is
> concerned with the conceptual and theoretical articulation
> of the processes and characteristics of this subtle unity-in-
> diversity and diversity-in-unity which we call "religion." It
> therefore refers to the most integrated level or dimension we
> know in the hierarchy of relations.
>
> (Peacocke 1986, 30)

Clearly, theology, as Peacocke understands it, has to do with reflection on the presence of God *within* the context that has evoked human existence. Its subject matter, that is, transcends that which is immanent within the created realm. Here there is a necessary progression in his thought, since to move the other direction, from transcendence to immanence, inexorably falls into the trap of at least sounding like a God-of-the-gaps maneuver, and that he will not countenance.

Emerging Insights

The line from Teilhard de Chardin through Charles Birch to Arthur Peacocke commands attention simply because, as we have noted, in each of the figures we have remarkably cogent demonstrations of the kind of dual competence upon which we must be reliant in thinking of believing in the creating God. The conclusions that begin to take shape in the light of their work raise questions that cannot be settled simply on the ground of the intersection of biology and theology, but they are so cogent that they cannot be turned aside.

First, our contention at the outset of this section should now be beyond dispute. *Creatio continua* is the only option after the emergence of the new biology. The prevailing consensus regarding evolution is non-negotiable among serious biologists today. We know this, and know that we know it. Intrinsic to this consensus is the assumption that the evolutionary process continues. The sole sense, then, in which we may confess "I believe in God the Father Almighty, Creator of Heaven and Earth" affirms that the creative process itself is still under way. Never ever again will we be able to deny this.

Second, theological inquiry subsequent to the rise of the new biology will invariably move *from* immanence *to* transcendence. Only so will it avoid landing in the cul-de-sac of sounding as though it serves the deus ex machina. This may well prove to be one of the most evident and decisive characteristics of theology as it now must move. Not only the robust tradition of *creatio ex nihilo* is in trouble; also in question is the even more vigorous contention that the transcending God has actually come into our midst in Jesus the Christ. Though this is good news indeed, it begins to have the ring of a cryptic deism. The irony is that what has been the birthright of many now at work on the theological front is being transmuted into a liability. That the reality we know in the relating and liberating God transcends our limitations remains intact. We know this reality *within* the world of which we are a part. But all that we know, and know that we know, concerning this world increasingly renders uncertain all assumptions concerning some other world from which revelation comes to us. The living God in the midst of us is ill served by those who regard the real domicile of ultimacy to be in some remote realm beyond our ken. The only case for transcendence must be made in terms of the immanence of the ultimacy we seek.

Third, the line from Teilhard de Chardin through Birch and Peacocke relentlessly leans on how this immanent transcendence is to be understood, or rather, how it is *not* to be understood. Interventionist metaphors may have spoken in the past, even in the very recent past that has spawned the theological curiosity of most of those now at work on these issues. But they speak no longer. The deus ex machina is mute. A voiceless ultimacy cannot be heard. A voiceless ultimacy probably does not hear. This is the negative side of the powerfully positive point that follows, but before proceeding to that elaboration there is a crucial qualification of the point at hand.

The problem of what we are calling "interventionist metaphors" stems from the irresistible logic of Birch's observations. Here we must be very precise, for this is really the choice yield of listening closely to theologically literate biologists. However, these "interventionist metaphors" are not to be confused with the dimension of *confrontation* that is so central to the biblical witness as a whole. One of the truly abiding themes of the Bible is the intertwining of the judgment of God with the mercy of God. This is so central that it will never lose cogency. Remove the dimension of judgment and the biblical witness as a whole will be misunderstood simply because the dimension of mercy will be sentimentalized. The redeeming love of God has nothing to do with sentimentality. Neither the Law nor the Prophets of the Old Testament can be understood this way, and the justification by faith through grace of which Saul-become-Paul spoke cost the cross and the risk of affirming the resurrection. So God's confrontation of the creature remains.

We have become so accustomed to blending this note of confrontation with the assumption of the intervention of divine power into the affairs of humanity and the workings of the cosmos that we cannot have the one without the other. It is this blending that yields the deistic overtone to our understanding of God, and it is this that cannot abide the scrutiny of those whose theology willingly reckons with the insights of those of the faithful whose dedication to biology has yielded knowledge that cannot be denied. The creating God is not the God of the deists. The confrontation of humanity unfolds at the hand of the God who is in the midst of the context within which humanity struggles to believe. This God is on the same side of an unfolding future that we are.

These three findings represent emerging conclusions that are rooted in the attempt to understand the ontic realm of which we are intrinsically a part. Theologically literate scientists and scientifically literate theologians are now generating a line of reflection that is as compelling in its findings as is that of the theologians of liberation. That these converge should be no surprise, given the dynamics of the contextualization of theology that we have already examined at length. What is genuinely surprising is that the noetic implications of the work of these theologically alert scientists bear so productively on the frontiers of reflection the theologians of liberation can no longer avoid. The God we know to be relating/liberating in character demands that our response manifest a creativity like that of the relating/liberating/creating ultimacy in the midst of us.

DISCOVERY AND INTERPRETATION

The noetic dimension of postmodern science emerged with great forcefulness in the realm of physics in a fashion that is completely complementary with what we have already seen in discussing theology and biology. What happened, to use quite deliberately a hoary theological metaphor, was that physicists stopped thinking in terms of graven images. They really had no choice, given what they were pondering, for their models were useful only if they could be interpreted as clues to the reality being considered. Frederick Ferré was one of the first theologians to wrestle with the portent of this development. Commenting on Erwin Schrödinger's contention that whereas all "irrelevant details" should be eliminated from the "substantive models of science," this need not result in the lack of any "visualizable scheme of the physical universe," he noted that one of the specified irrelevancies would include any attempt to conceive of the color of electrons. Ferré sharply focuses the question this raises:

> Can the electron be "visualized" as colorless? We can hardly understand the question and still answer affirmatively, but if our answer is negative we shall be forced to admit that at least some substantive models defy our *imagining* if not (*pace* Berkeley) our *conceiving*.
>
> (Ferré 1969, 62–63)

If some of the models we must employ can be conceived but not imagined, even that which can be pictured must be *interpreted* in connection with that which cannot. So it is that science has inexorably moved into the domain of hermeneutics.

As we have already seen in our initial consideration of the emergence of postmodern science, the work of Heisenberg and others in developing quantum theory shifted the direction of physics away from all attempts to visualize the subatomic world. This change necessitated the effort to develop a new language, one adequate for dealing with what cannot be seen but even so is known to be present and functioning. Heisenberg himself gave eloquent expression to the formidable difficulties intrinsic to this development. In a lecture entitled "Tradition in

Science," he noted that the history of science entails not only "discoveries and observations" but also "a history of concepts." He then specified the difficulty at hand:

> The state of a system in quantum mechanics can be characterized mathematically by a vector in a space of many dimensions, and this vector implies statements concerning the statistical behavior of the system under given conditions of observation. An objective description of the system in the traditional sense is impossible.
>
> (Heisenberg 1983, 14)

In the light of this, Heisenberg formulated an insight that applied not only to his own immediate experience but to scientific inquiry as a whole:

> When we speak about our investigations, about the phenomena we are going to study, we need a language, we need words, and the words are the verbal expressions of concepts. In the beginning of our investigations, there can be no avoiding the fact, that the words are connected with the old concepts, since the new ones don't yet exist.
>
> (Heisenberg 1983, 15)

Where the problem is that of old words breaking under the pressure of new ideas, the issue turns on interpretation. Thus science inexorably encounters hermeneutics.

Heisenberg's celebrated older contemporary, Niels Bohr, whose role in the development of quantum theory was as crucial as his own, carried the point even further. Heinz Pagels describes this as follows:

> Bohr wondered how we could even talk about the atomic world—it was so far removed from human experience. He struggled with this problem—how can we use ordinary language developed to cope with everyday events and objects to describe atomic events? Perhaps the logic inherent in our grammar was inadequate for this task. So Bohr focused on the problem of language in his interpretation of quantum mechanics. As he remarked, "It is wrong to think that the task of physics is to find out how Nature *is*. Physics concerns what we can say about Nature."
>
> (Pagels 1983, 73)

Obviously, a physics that is concerned with what we can say

about nature has much in common with a theology that is concerned with what we can say about God. This is neither to champion an evasive agnosticism about either subject of reflection, nor is it to equate them. It is to insist that the move beyond what we can say, to what either could, or must, now be said, is indelibly marked by that imaginative interpretation that discerns what is going on when the usefulness of accepted words break down. The central dynamic of the contextualization of theology is here in operation. Prior clarities are transcended by the compelling necessity of a new and undeniable problematic.

This new problematic is one of the decisive yields of postmodern science. *Heuristics* has to do with discovery; *hermeneutics*, with interpretation. To speak of "heuristic hermeneutics" has an immediately exciting portent for theological reflection. But to speak of "hermeneutical heuristics" focuses the real depths of what this entails. To explore this juxtaposition is to move into the overlapping intersection between discovery and interpretation. We can best understand what this involves by giving close attention to the work of two extremely significant figures. The first of these, Michael Polanyi, is decisive for coming to terms with heuristics; the second, Paul Ricoeur, is pivotal for any contemporary theological reflection on hermeneutics.

Michael Polanyi—Heuristics

Michael Polanyi (1891–1976) began his career as a physician; he later became a recognized scientist in the field of physical chemistry. In 1930, outraged over Hitler's policies, he resigned his post at the Kaiser Wilhelm Institute to accept an appointment at the University of Manchester. His interests intertwined his scientific pursuits with philosophical, ethical, and theological concerns, and by the late 1940s his writings manifested an immense range of insights. This turns on what he called the "logic of tacit thought" (Polanyi 1967, 4).

For Polanyi, the movement from one level or layer of thought to the next defies any simplistic explanation, for this movement is silent and imaginative in character. Of the several illustrations that he gives, the most succinct, and perhaps the most revealing, concerns learning how to play chess:

> The playing of the game of chess is an entity controlled by
> principles which rely on the observance of the rules of chess;
> but the principles controlling the game cannot be derived

from the rules of chess. The two terms of tacit knowing, the proximal, which includes the particulars, and the distal, which is their comprehensive meaning, would then be seen as two levels of reality, controlled by distinctive principles.

(Polanyi 1967, 34)

Anyone who has attempted to teach this game knows that the decisive moment comes when the novice makes the leap from preoccupation with how the pieces move to fascination with the whole board, and close attention to the spaces on which pieces have not yet been placed. There is no way to move from one level to the next other than participation in the struggle of the game itself. This participation is intrinsic to discovering what the game is all about, and the movement into the depths of this understanding is tacit in character. Polanyi formulated his central maxim as follows: "I shall reconsider human knowledge by starting from the fact that *we can know more than we can tell*" (Polanyi 1967, 4). It is in terms of this maxim that he clarified the nagging curiosity that forces the imagination beyond the frontiers of what is known in search of what has not yet been discerned. The crucial point has to do with the fact that each move into that "beyond" is also marked by the operation of the maxim just formulated. We will never be in a situation in which it is not the case that we can know more than we can tell. In other words, discovery always leads to new discoveries, for it will always discern unrecognized horizons.

In the brief epitomizing volume entitled *The Tacit Dimension*, the maxim at hand informs Polanyi's insistence that the methodology of science "is not detachment but involvement" (Polanyi 1967, 63). Our imaginations are continually irritated by the fact that there is yet more, and then even more, to say. This involvement is intensely personal in character, as indeed is the knowledge it yields, which is why Polanyi's major work carries the title *Personal Knowledge* (1962). Two decisive passages from this discussion give the meaning Polanyi ascribes to the term "heuristic." The first of these is his memorable delineation of heuristic passion:

> Scientists—that is, creative scientists—spend their lives in trying to guess right. They are sustained and guided therein by their heuristic passion. We call their work creative because it changes the world as we see it, by deepening our understanding of it. The change is irrevocable. A problem that I have solved can no longer puzzle me; I cannot guess what I already know. Having made a discovery, I shall never see the

world again as before. My eyes have become different; I have made myself into a person seeing and thinking differently. I have crossed a gap, the heuristic gap, which lies between problem and discovery.

(Polanyi 1962, 143)

Because discovery changes the interpretative framework within which knowledge is discussed, "it is logically impossible to arrive at these [discoveries] by the continued application of our previous interpretative framework." Thus "discovery is creative, in the sense that it is not to be achieved by the diligent performance of any previously known and specifiable procedure" (Polanyi 1962, 143).

Heuristic passion is rooted in fascination with a genuine problem. As Polanyi would say in *The Tacit Dimension*, "To see a problem is to see something hidden. It is to have an intimation of the coherence of hitherto not comprehended particulars" (Polanyi 1967, 21). The second of our decisive passages from *Personal Knowledge* probes this in the light of a memorable insight from the celebrated mathematician George Polya:

> "Look at the unknown!—says Polya—"Look at the end. Remember your aim. Do not lose sight of what is required. Keep in mind what you are working for. *Look at the unknown. Look at the conclusion.*" No advice could be more emphatic.
>
> (Polanyi 1962, 127)

For Polanyi, this forces into the open both a key question and a decisive answer. The question is this: "How can we concentrate our attention on something we don't know?" (Polanyi 1962, 127). The answer contains one of Polanyi's deepest insights:

> The admonition to look at the unknown really means that we should *look at the known data, but not in themselves, rather as clues to the unknown; as pointers to it and parts of it.* We should strive persistently to feel our way towards an understanding of the manner in which these known particulars hang together, both mutually and with the unknown. By such intimations do we make sure that the unknown is really there.
>
> (Polanyi 1962, 127–128)

Thus the operation of the tacit dimension—the reason we are always in the position of knowing more than we can tell—discloses the presence of a genuine unknown. Heuristics has to do with the discovery of those hitherto undiscerned coherences that lead to the solution of the imaginatively formulated problem at hand. As such, the movement of heuristic passion is both cumulative and irreversible. This contention is the choicest yield of combining the two passages before us. In that I cannot guess at a problem I have already solved, it follows that once the clues to the unknown are verified, the unknown is no longer unknown and takes its place as a new set of clues to a now newly forming hunch concerning a newly discerned problem about which we can know more than we can tell.

The operation of this heuristic capacity is not only cumulative and irreversible; it is also communal in character. For Polanyi, this would have to be the case because he was a scientist and from that vantage point knew that plausibility is intrinsic to the disciplining of heuristics. In one of his last writings, he put the matter sharply:

> All empirical observation rests ultimately on the integration of subsidiaries to a focal center. All such integrations—from perception to creative discoveries—are impelled by the imagination and controlled by plausibility, which in turn depends upon our general view of the nature of things.
> (Polanyi and Prosch 1975, 144)

Now precisely how is it that imagination and plausibility combine in the service of Polanyi's view of the general nature of things? In *The Tacit Dimension* there is an incisive delineation of the answer to this question. It entails his "principle of mutual control" (Polanyi 1967, 72). He argues "that scientists keep watch over each other. Each scientist is both subject to criticism by all others and encouraged by their appreciation of him" (Polanyi 1967, 72). This critical challenge and support defies the capacities of any single person, for no one knows everything, or even enough about a great deal, to supply it alone:

> It is clear that only fellow scientists working in closely related fields are competent to exercise direct authority over each other; but their personal fields will form *chains of overlapping neighborhoods* extending over the entire range of science. It is enough that the standards of plausibility and worthwhileness be equal around every single point to keep them equal over all the sciences.
> (Polanyi 1967, 72)

This is how what he calls "a mediated consensus between scientists even if they cannot understand more than a vague outline of each other's subjects" takes shape (Polanyi 1967, 73). The community of this mediated consensus is what Polanyi called "a society of explorers" (Polanyi 1967, 83).

For such a society, the explorations are never over. There are no final boundaries; there is always more to be understood, for it is always the case that we can know more than we can tell. Personal commitment to the search for unknown truths is central to the transmission of scientific curiosity, and it is precisely this curiosity itself, rather than a fixed set of findings or insights, that is transmitted. The capacity for self-renewal in any living tradition correlates directly with respect for the unknown character of what is yet to be discerned:

> Scientific tradition derives its capacity for self-renewal from its belief in the presence of a hidden reality, of which current science is one aspect, while other aspects of it are to be revealed by future discoveries. Any tradition fostering the progress of thought must have this intention: to teach its current ideas as stages leading on to unknown truths which, when discovered, might dissent from the very teachings which engendered them.
>
> (Polanyi 1967, 82)

To be open to the inexorability of the fact that one day one's own conclusions might be contradicted by those who build on them is to take the idea of heuristics to its furthermost implications. More than that, it is to reach into the depths of the nature of thought itself. There is something at once ancient and yet radically new in his insight. Ever since Socrates, it has been known that any serious answer to any searching question leads to a deeper question. Polanyi's version of this ancient insight comes to us after the establishment of the assumption that science has rigid objectivity as its most basic characteristic. Polanyi sought to counter this view, which he understood to be rooted in the thought of Kant. This is why he gave *Personal Knowledge* the subtitle "Towards a Post-Critical Philosophy." As has been noted, for him involvement, not detachment, is the secret of creativity. So it is that for Polanyi the subject-object split is overcome:

> Insofar as the personal submits to requirements acknowledged by itself as independent of itself, it is not subjective; but insofar as it is an action guided by individual passions, it

is not objective either. It transcends the disjunction between subjective and objective.

(Polanyi 1962, 300)

Any incisive grasp of heuristics depends upon this insistence concerning the involvement of the observer in the observed. This is the most basic component in Polanyi's understanding of the term. And it accounts for the fact that when we ponder both Ferré's recollection of Schrödinger's marvelous remark, and Heisenberg's acknowledgment of the urgency of our search for new words adequate for the tasks we now undertake, we are at a deeper level than we are when we think of these points by themselves. With Polanyi, there can be no doubt concerning the vectoral character of heuristic creativity. Almost as important as his maxim "We can know more than we can tell" is his insistence that "I cannot guess at what I already know" (Polanyi 1962, 143). Passionate preoccupation with a genuine problem has the solution of that problem as the only goal with which it can live. Given the nature of heuristics, all pretense is exposed. There is no creativity where one feigns wrestling with a problem already solved. Thus I now do know that I can know more than I can tell, but I also know that the telling of this intimates new horizons of reflection—irreversibly and irrevocably. Polanyi makes us think new thoughts about telling as well as about knowing, and so it is that we encounter the hermeneutical character of heuristics. That life-long attempt to "guess right" that characterizes creative scientists is done with *words*. After Polanyi's breakthrough, heuristics and hermeneutics cannot be thought about separately.

Paul Ricoeur—Hermeneutics

To think about juxtaposing the words "heuristic" and "hermeneutic" is inevitably to ponder the work of Paul Ricoeur. In his work, interpretation and discovery go together. His writing abounds with maxims that mesh with Polanyi's "We can know more than we can tell." Two of these immediately spring to mind in our present line of reflection: "The symbol gives rise to thought" and "The sense of the text is not behind the text, but in front of it." Unpacking the meaning of these maxims of Ricoeur is no small task, but at the outset of the attempt note what happens when they are combined with Polanyi's insight: On this side of the text, where the symbol gives rise to thought, it is always the case that we can know more than we can tell. Such facile combination is obviously vulnerable to the charge of oversimplification. However, we will see that it is not only true to the depths of Ricoeur's thought; it is a sharply demanding epitomization of the creativity we must achieve if we are to serve the creating God whose relating and liberating of our lives evoke the utmost efforts of the faithfully freed imagination.

The range of Paul Ricoeur's reflections has overwhelmed entire generations of students and colleagues. Central for our concerns is his understanding of *metaphor*, which emerged from his long preoccupation with clarifying the meaning of *symbol*.

Ricoeur's understanding of symbol turns on the distinction between "symbol" and "sign." A symbol is like a sign. It points beyond itself to something else. But unlike a sign, a symbol does its pointing in a way that is not transparent. Technical signs, as distinct from symbols, are transparent; they are not good signs if they are cloudy, blurred, or opaque, for then they yield only confusion. Symbol, on the other hand, thrives on the fact that it conceals within itself what Ricoeur calls "a double intentionality" (Ricoeur 1967, 15). Symbol always entails a double layer of meaning. This idea pervades Ricoeur's writings. One of its most precise formulations follows:

> I define "symbol" as any structure of signification in which a direct, primary, literal meaning designates in addition, another meaning which is indirect, secondary, and figurative and which can be apprehended only through the first.
>
> (Ricoeur 1974, 12–13)

Intrinsic to this idea of the double layer of meaning is the insight into the power of the symbolic it generates:

> By living in the first meaning I am drawn by it beyond itself: *the symbolic meaning is constituted in and through the literal meaning, which brings about the analogy by giving the analogue.* Unlike a comparison that we *look at* from the outside, symbol is the very movement of this primary meaning that makes us share in the latent meaning and thereby assimilates us to the symbolized, without our being able intellectually to dominate the similarity. This is the sense in which the symbol "gives"; it gives because it is a primary intentionality that gives the second meaning.
>
> (Ricoeur 1974, 290)

The power of the symbolic receives a memorable demonstration in Ricoeur's widely discussed *The Symbolism of Evil* (1967). In this work, he develops a comprehensive and profound grasp of the biblical symbolism that illuminates the human predicament. He sees this focused in the Adamic myth—myths being for him "a species of symbol . . . symbols developed in the form of narration" (Ricoeur 1967, 18). Juxtaposing the Adamic myth with all other options shows how it includes and transcends their insights. This enables Ricoeur to set out the manner in which the symbol of original sin defies being restricted to a manageable formula and thus calls into question any literalistic attempt to control it. Moreover, he insists that the point to the biblical symbolism of evil is intensely positive in that it discloses the depths of the possibility of redemption. In the epitomizing conclusion of this book, he gives detailed attention to the maxim pervading the argument, namely, "the symbol gives rise to thought" (see Ricoeur 1967, 347–357). Symbol brings to the surface insights that cannot take shape in any other way.

Subsequent reflection convinced Ricoeur that his point had to be revised—revised in such a way that the understanding of metaphor intrinsic to it could be explicated. Only by so doing could he deal with the semantic component involved in all the layers of meaning symbols entail. "The symbol," he now argued, " . . . only gives rise to thought if it first gives rise to speech. Metaphor is the appropriate reagent to bring to light this aspect of symbols that has an affinity for language" (Ricoeur 1976, 52–53).

Caution must inform the manner in which we proceed at this point. "Symbol" does not mean for Ricoeur what it does by and large for the scientists, even including Polanyi. For them the distinction between symbol and sign is not nearly as pronounced. The symbols of symbolic logic, for example, function algorithmically, that is to say, automatically. There is hardly anything automatic about the functioning of symbols for Ricoeur! He has Rudolf Otto and Mircea Eliade in mind, not the mathematicians, when he uses the term (in spite of the fact that his understanding of symbol resonates at profound levels with that of Charles Saunders Peirce). Thus he thinks of symbols as "being bound to the cosmos" in such a way that they "plunge their roots into the durable constellation of life, feeling, and the universe" (Ricoeur 1976, 61, 64). This is what informs his basic differentiation between symbol and metaphor: "The symbol is bound in a way that the metaphor is not.

Symbols have roots. . . . Metaphors are just the linguistic surface of symbols" (Ricoeur 1976, 69).

Ricoeur's understanding of metaphor bears incisively on clarifying the function of language in the heuristic enterprise. This reaches a sharp focus in his *Interpretation Theory: Discourse and the Surplus of Meaning* (1976). Here he aligns himself with those who hold that the semantics of the sentence precedes the semantics of the word (see Ricoeur 1976, 49). He is therefore convinced that in the operation of metaphors a tension, not a substitution, is in operation. "When," he writes, "the poet speaks of a 'blue angelus' or a 'mantle of sorrow,' he puts two terms . . . in tension." Moreover, he continues, "The angelus is not blue, if blue is a color; sorrow is not a mantle, if a mantle is a garment made of cloth. Thus a metaphor does not exist in itself, but in and through interpretation" (Ricoeur 1976, 50). This leads to a decisive conclusion:

> A metaphor is not an ornament of discourse. It has more than an emotive value because it offers new information. A metaphor, in short, tells us something new about reality.
>
> (Ricoeur 1976, 52–53)

To think of metaphor as that which "tells us something new about reality" obviously intersects with reflecting on Polanyi's maxim "We can know more than we can tell." It is the metaphoric imagination that makes this maxim operational. But there is even more at stake—even more far-reaching a claim to be made. Closely associated with the passage just noted—indeed the idea that informs its cogency—is Ricoeur's discussion of "iconicity." He speaks of the "optic alphabet" of the painters, especially the Dutch artists, whose "invention of oil painting . . . enhances the contrasts, gives colors back their resonance, and lets appear the luminosity within which things shine." For these masters, "Painting . . . was neither the reproduction nor the production of the universe, but its metamorphosis." With this in place, Ricoeur then speaks of abstract art and notes that here "painting is close to science in that it challenges perceptual forms by relating them to non-perceptual structures" (Ricoeur 1976, 41). What this entails is nothing less than a process of "aesthetic augmentation" in which "the re-writing of reality" is under way. From the work of the Dutch masters to abstract art, in search of the clarification of iconicity—this is the route to one of Ricoeur's most incisive formulations:

Constructivism is only the boundary case of a process of augmentation where the apparent denial of reality is the condition for the glorification of the non-figurative essence of things. Iconicity, then, means the revelation of a real more real than ordinary reality.

(Ricoeur 1976, 42)

Thus Ricoeur's reflections yield powerful instrumentalities for dealing with the linguistic frontier sighted by Polanyi's investigations. The crossing of the heuristic gap is hermeneutically achieved. It is by way of metaphor, and the iconic augmentation in which we wrestle with "a reality more real than ordinary reality" that the maxim "We can know more than we can tell" manifests the constant durability of its operation. For in this arduous effort we are actually discerning the operation of unknowns that we know are really there. The hermeneutical crossing of the heuristic gap will be recognizable in theological reflection when we face creativities with the intent of extrapolating what they have done. As has been indicated before, this transcends the work of recapitulation and extension, for past efforts must be interpreted in such a way that we discover layers of meaning that could not have been recognized when they were first articulated. Once one sees that discovery and interpretation go hand in hand, the insight cannot be restricted to the initial arena of discourse. The context expands. Revelation proceeds. For the faithful can only risk the belief that ultimacy not only attends our efforts; it initiates them.

This claim is substantiated when we note the operation of the theological dimension in the work of each of the two figures before us. They do not hesitate to indicate this. They do so in a way that suggests the possibility of heuristic theology, and this alone can meet the demands of reflecting on the creating God.

HEURISTIC THEOLOGY

Our two figures are among the best examples of heuristic theological reflection in action.[2] A genuine sense of searching for real unknowns pervades their theological suggestions as surely as it does everything else in their writings. This is why they are fascinating for theologians of the same mood and devastating to those who think that all we need to do in the present is apply the insights of the past.

It is as a philosopher that Ricoeur works, but his philosophy is so embedded within a theological matrix that it is an open question as to whether his philosophy makes sense without it. An early indication of the presence of this component emerges in the juxtaposition of key remarks in the essays comprising the collection entitled *History and Truth* (1965). Two passages from the 1951 essay "Christianity and the Meaning of History" focus his theological perspective:

> The Christian meaning of history is not exhausted by notions of decisions and crises, of greatness and guilt mingled together. In the first place, sin is not the center of the Christian Credo: it is not even an article of the Christian faith. We do not *believe* in sin, but in salvation.
>
> (Ricoeur 1965, 93)

This profoundly affirmative note is echoed later in the same essay, with the eschatological dimension now emphasized:

> Hope speaks from the depths of the absurd, it takes hold of the ambiguity and manifest incertitude of history and says to me: look for a meaning, try to understand! It is here that Christianity branches off from existentialism. Ambiguity is the last word for existentialism; for Christianity it is real, it is lived, but it is the next to the last word. This is why the Christian, in the very name of this confidence in a hidden meaning, is encouraged by his faith to *attempt* to construct comprehensive schemata, to embrace the terms of a philosophy of history at least as an hypothesis.
>
> (Ricoeur 1965, 95)

Thus there is a negative note to be sounded, but its purpose is the service of the profound affirmation that it presupposes.

This theological perspective resonates with the depths of the philosophical concerns that have dominated Ricoeur's reflections throughout the entirety of his career. An epitomization of this labor occurs in a 1956 essay entitled "Negativity and Primary Affirmation," in the same collection. Here the basic question with which he has always been concerned is sharply delineated: "Does being have priority over the nothingness within the very core of man, that is, this being which manifests itself by a singular power of negation?" (Ricoeur 1965, 305). To put the question this way evokes a confrontation with Sartre, which culminates as follows:

The benefit of a meditation on negation is not to lead us to a
philosophy of nothingness, but rather to carry our idea of
being beyond a phenomenology of the thing or a metaphys-
ics of essence up to this act of existing of which it may be
equally said that it is without essence or that all its essence is
to exist. But is this affirmation a *necessary* one?

Philosophy was born with the pre-Socratics in the
great discovery that *"to think"* is to think being, and that to
think *being* is to think ἀρχή in the double sense of the beginning and the foundation of all that we can establish and dis-
establish, believe and put into doubt.

(Ricoeur 1965, 325)

So it is that Ricoeur contends, both in this essay and throughout his
work as a whole, that "we become *aware of our finitude by going beyond
it*" (Ricoeur 1965, 306).

The Philosopher

One of the very best examples of this process of becoming aware of our
finitude by going beyond it occurs in *The Symbolism of Evil* (1967).
Though Ricoeur as theologian does not pay a great deal of attention to
the work of Karl Barth, there is a remarkable convergence between the
two in Ricoeur's formulation of a point central to Barth's entire perspective, namely, the contention that the Christ is the clue to Adam, not the
reverse:

In the New Testament Jesus himself never refers to the Adamic
story. . . . It was St. Paul who roused the Adamic theme from
its lethargy: by means of the *contrast* between the "old man"
and the "new man," he set up the figure of Adam as the in-
verse of that of Christ, called the second Adam (I Cor. 15:21–
22, 45–49; Rom. 5:12–21). . . . From this, two conclusions
must be drawn: that it was Christology that consolidated
Adamology, and that the demythologization of the Adamic
figure, as an individualized personage from whom all mankind
would be descended physically, does not imply any conclusion
concerning the figure of Christ, which was not constructed
with reference to the figure of Adam but which, on the contrary, gave individuality to the latter by retroaction.

(Ricoeur 1967, 238–239)

The use to which Ricoeur puts the Pauline doctrine of Christ as the
second Adam is uniquely his own. For him there is nothing quite so

tragic as the manner in which the doctrine of original sin took shape on the presupposition of a literalizing of the Adamic myth:

> The harm that has been done to souls, during the centuries of Christianity, first by the literal interpretation of the story of Adam, and then by the confusion of this myth, treated as history, with later speculations, principally Augustinian, about original sin, will never be adequately told. In asking the faithful to confess belief in this mythico-speculative mass and to accept it as a self-sufficient explanation, the theologians have unduly required a *sacrificium intellectus* where what was needed was to awaken believers to a symbolic superintelligence of their actual condition.
>
> (Ricoeur 1967, 239)

It is by way of the symbolism of evil that the possibility of redemption unfolds. The possibility of contrition is the new thought aroused by this symbolism. In theological perspective, this is the zenith of that process by which we become aware of our finitude by going beyond it. Such an awakening of the "symbolic superintelligence" is the function of grace, and this is completely in accord with Ricoeur's understanding of the nature and task of theology. Again, though his references to the thought of Barth are indeed infrequent, there is complete and explicit convergence with him as regards this understanding. One of the clearest indications of this is in the essay entitled "The Demythization of Accusation." Part II of this essay is concerned with "The Kerygmatic Core of Ethics," and early on in this section Ricoeur insists that "the kerygma . . . is accessible only as *witness*" (Ricoeur 1974, 343). Building on this contention, he then sets out his understanding of the distinction between philosophy and theology:

> Theology deals with relations of intelligibility in the domain of witness. It is a logic of the Christological interpretation of salvation events. In saying this, I am remaining basically Anselmian and Barthian. Theology is *intellectus fidei*. The philosophy of faith and religion is something else. What theology organizes in terms of the Christological basis of witness the philosophy of religion organizes[3] in terms of man's desire to be. And here I do not hesitate to say that I return to the Kantian analyses in *Religion within the Limits of Reason Alone*, to the degree that they diverge from a formalism.
>
> (Ricoeur 1974, 343–344)

The reference to Kant is more important than it may seem. Theologians in particular must not be swept away by the clarity of Ricoeur's theological perspective. It is as a *philosopher* that he makes his *theological* points. Indeed, it could be maintained that the relationship between philosophy and theology in his thought is uniquely exemplary of the synergistic relationship between these two realms of reflection that has pervaded the history of Christian thought. What is crucial here is the fact that the manner in which this informs Ricoeur's thought is the decisive clue to the significance of his work as exemplary of what we are calling "heuristic theology." This can be stated succinctly. Ricoeur knew, with the conclusion of *The Symbolism of Evil*, that he could proceed no further with the development of his broad argument without coming to terms with Freud, and not only him, but Nietzsche and Marx as well. For in Freud's work, as well as that of the other two, the same understanding of symbol as his own operates.

It was with his profound investigation of Freud's thought that Ricoeur discovered the depths of his own hermeneutic.[4] This set in motion what has proved to be a permanent interruption in the formal production of the philosophical system of which *The Symbolism of Evil* was a part. The collection of essays entitled *The Conflict of Interpretations*, unfolding after his study of Freud, is absolutely indispensable for discerning the operation of the theological vector of his thought. Were one to leave Ricoeur's thought with only the former treatise in mind, as all too many in the theological camp are prone to do, then the point to understanding the functioning of the symbolic would be simply the reconstruction of the kerygma. Taking into account Freud, Nietzsche, and Marx, the point to understanding how symbols work is the deciphering of all that is deliberately distorted. Hence the *conflict* of interpretations! The usefulness of insight into the symbolic depends on the purpose for which it is being employed. Ricoeur passionately insisted on this:

> [Any] discussion which treats my double interpretation of religious symbolism as an isolated theme necessarily retrogresses to a philosophy of compromise from which the incentive for struggle has been withdrawn. In this terrible battle for meaning, nothing and no one comes out unscathed.
>
> (Ricoeur 1974, 175–176)

This is not to say that Ricoeur has no interest in the continual reconstruction of the kerygma. It is to say that this interest, and the only responsible theological use to which it can be put, presupposes the permanence of the arena of conflict within which it lives. The fact is that "the terrible battle for meaning" will never end. This forces conclusions initially encountered in *The Symbolism of Evil* into even deeper levels in *The Conflict of Interpretations*. Consider, for example, his idea of the "second naïveté":

> I believe that being can still speak to me, no longer indeed in the precritical form of immediate belief but as the second immediacy that hermeneutics aims at. It may be that this second naïveté is the postcritical equivalent of the precritical hierophany.
>
> (Ricoeur 1974, 298)

Leading into this delineation is the remarkable formulation "we can believe only by interpreting," an insight that Ricoeur elaborates as follows:

> The second immediacy, the second naïveté that we are after, is accessible only in hermeneutics; we can believe only by interpreting. This is the "modern" modality of belief in symbols. . . . [H]ermeneutics proceeds from the preunderstanding of the very matter which through interpretation it is trying to understand. . . . I can today still communicate with the Sacred by explicating the preunderstanding which animates the interpretation. Hermeneutics, child of "modernity," is one of the ways in which this "modernity" overcomes its own forgetfulness of the Sacred.
>
> (Ricoeur 1974, 298)

The Prophetic Preacher

This same insight, in virtually these same terms, is present in the conclusion of *The Symbolism of Evil* (see Ricoeur 1967, 352). However, its impact is fully realized only when the issue is not simply that of the double interpretation of religious symbolism, but rather that of the terrible battle for meaning from which no one emerges unscathed. One of the most significant essays included in *The Conflict of Interpretations* is entitled "Religion, Atheism and Faith." It contains a memorable delineation of the "prophetic preacher," one who "with the power and the freedom of Nietzsche's Zarathustra would be able to make a radical return to the origins of Jewish and Christian faith and, at the same time, make of this return an event which speaks to our own time" (Ricoeur

172

1974, 447–448). This is the preacher for whom the philosopher (Ricoeur himself, of course) longs:

> He dreams of the prophet who would speak only of freedom but would never utter a word of prohibition or condemnation, who would preach the Cross and the Resurrection of Christ as the beginning of a creative life, and who would elaborate the contemporary significance of the Pauline antinomy between the Gospel and the Law. In terms of this antinomy, sin itself would appear less as the transgression of a prohibition than as the opposite of a law ruled by grace.
> (Ricoeur 1974, 448)

There are three reasons, Ricoeur argues, that "the philosopher is not this prophetic preacher." (1) Utilizing Nietzsche's phrase, "the philosopher belongs to a time of dryness and thirst in which Christianity, insofar as it is a cultural institution, still remains 'a Platonism for the people,' a kind of law in Saint Paul's sense of the word." (2) Deeper than this, though, is the profound demand of a time in which nihilism has not yet run its course, so that "the period of mourning for the gods who have died is not yet over, and it is in this intermediate time that the philosopher does his thinking." (3) The demands of thinking in such a context are too drastic to permit such a philosopher to escape too readily into the task of the prophetic preacher, for such a philosopher

> remains suspended between atheism and faith. . . . The philosopher's responsibility is to think, that is to dig beneath the surface of the present antinomy until he has discovered the level of questioning that makes possible a mediation between religion and faith by way of atheism.
> (Ricoeur 1974, 448)

Despite his disclaimer that the philosopher is not the prophetic preacher he so memorably describes, Ricoeur himself reaches this pinnacle on those comparatively rare occasions when he preaches. We might well expect this, for only one who preaches can describe the prophetic preacher as vividly as he does. One of his sermons manifests the operation of his incisive grasp of the relationship between metaphor and reality, and this epitomizes how the idea of the "surplus of meaning" functions for theology. This is the sermon "Listening to the Parables of Jesus." The understanding of parable central to this sermon indicates why the kind of creativity he countenances can never reach final conclusions:

> The Gospel says nothing about the Kingdom of Heaven, except that it is *like* . . . It does not say what it *is*, but what it *looks like*. This is hard to hear. Because all our scientific training tends to use images only as provisory devices and to replace *images* by *concepts*. We are invited here to proceed the other way. And to think according to a mode of thought which is not metaphorical for the sake of rhetoric, but for the sake of what it has to say. . . . No translation in abstract language is offered, only the violence of a language which, from the beginning to the end, *thinks through* the Metaphor and never *beyond*. The power of this language is that it abides to the end *within* the tension created by the images.
> (Reagan and Stewart 1978, 242 [Ricoeur's ellipses])[5]

At Ricoeur's hand, overstatement of the power of the parabolic is virtually impossible. The parables, taken together, "say more than any rational theology. " This is so because "there is more to think about in the answer said in a parabolic way than any kind of theory." The most formidable obstruction to discerning the realm of the more-to-think-about is the long-standing propensity to trivialize this parabolic capacity:

> I fear that a too-zealous attempt to draw immediate application from the Parables for private ethics or for political morality must necessarily miss the target. We immediately surmise that such an indiscreet zeal quickly transposes the Parables into trivial advice, into moral platitudes. And we kill them more surely by trivial moralizing than by transcendent theologizing.
> (Reagan and Stewart 1978, 243)

Ricoeur's deepest concerns surface in the fact that he cannot state what is going on in parabolic thought without reaching for the idea of poetics, because each of these pivots on the unleashing of the imagination. This discloses the sense in which imagination is at the heart of the theological process. In "Listening to the Parables of Jesus," having indicated trivialization as the chief enemy of the insights at hand, Ricoeur pressed forward to a conclusion that may prove to be one of his most significant contributions to theological reflection:

> Let me draw the conclusion which seems to emerge from this surprising strategy of discourse used by Jesus when he told

the Parables to the disciples and to the mob. To listen to the Parables of Jesus, it seems to me, is to let one's imagination be opened to the new possibilities disclosed by the extravagance of these short dramas. If we look at the Parables as at a word addressed first to our imagination rather than to our will, we shall not be tempted to reduce them to mere didactic devices, to moralizing allegories. We will let their poetic power display itself within us. . . . Poetic means more than poetry as a literary genre. Poetic means creative. And it is in the heart of our imagination that we let the Event happen, before we may convert our heart and tighten our will.

(Reagan and Stewart 1978, 245)

A heuristic theology is one that functions in terms of a parabolic imagination that is always outrunning its capacity for theoretical coherences. This is the sense in which any theology worth its salt will continually be in the predicament of reaching beyond its conclusions. The parabolic imagination generates issues that demand a system-transcending inquiry. It is here that our phrase "heuristic theology" gains its meaning. Theological reflection discovers new avenues of meaning as its parabolic imagination functions. Only such a theology working with its genuine unknowns can grasp and be grasped by the full import of the second of the two maxims from Ricoeur with which we began listening to him:

The sense of the text is not behind the text, but in front of it. It is not something hidden, but something disclosed. What has to be understood is not the initial situation of discourse, but what points towards a possible world. . . . The text speaks of a possible world and of a possible way of orienting oneself within it.

(Ricoeur 1976, 87, 88)

The Parabolic Imagination

So to live on this side of the text is to know that there is far more to tell and understand than we have yet discovered. The Spirit, whose internal testimony alone authenticates the past for our present risks, still speaks and always will. This liberating relationship evokes such risky creativity, for the creating God shares the discoveries yet to be made.

By now it is clear that relating Ricoeur's maxims to Polanyi's is not a sleight-of-hand maneuver. Is the reverse of this the case? Does

Polanyi's theological dimension resonate with Ricoeur's on Polanyi's own terms? It most surely does.

We need not speculate about either the contours or the content of theological reflection as it emerges from the thought of one who insisted that we must "reconsider human knowledge by starting from the fact that *we can know more than we can tell*" (Polanyi 1967, 4). In the midst of his central work, *Personal Knowledge,* he was willing to say, "An era of great religious discoveries may lie before us" (Polanyi 1962, 285). A decisive clue to the depths of his insight is to be found in lectures he gave at the end of his career. Polanyi never did advance a case for religion. He rather suggested its possibility:

> The religious hypothesis, if it does indeed hold that the world is meaningful rather than absurd, is . . . a viable hypothesis for us. There is no scientific reason why we cannot believe it. But to find no scientific reason why we cannot believe it is not to believe it.
>
> (Polanyi and Prosch 1975, 179)

The reasons behind this assertion are set out with admirable precision:

> Religious meaning . . . is a transnatural integration of incompatible clues and is achieved through our dwelling in various rituals and ceremonies informed by myths. These must, of course, be specific rites and myths—not just rites and myths in general. There are no such things. Religion "in general" is thus not religion, just as language "in general" is not language. To be religious we must have *a* religion.
>
> (Polanyi and Prosch 1975, 179)

This conviction and precision combine to indicate the fact that Polanyi's theological suggestions are profoundly confessional in character. Thus, in the context of his last lectures, he could say:

> This present work is not directed toward effecting conversions to any religion. At the most, it is directed toward unstopping our ears so that we may hear a liturgical summons should one ever come our way.
>
> (Polanyi and Prosch 1975, 180)

In *Personal Knowledge* we have a striking indication of the liturgical summons Polanyi has heard, and which he issues himself. This turns on what, to my knowledge, is a genuinely unprecedented understanding of the gospel. We have already noted Polanyi's fascination with his notion of the problem. It is in terms of this concern that he develops his understanding of the crossing of heuristic gaps that is the central dynamic of scientific reflection. As we have seen, he adduced Polya's maxim "Look at the unknown" as the clue to the recognition of genuine unknowns, for our task is to "look at the known data, but not in themselves, rather as clues to the unknown; as pointers to it and parts of it" (Polanyi 1962, 127–128; see also p. 160 in this volume).

Now it is precisely this passion for involvement with the problem *and* what it can disclose—namely, the unknown—that shapes Polanyi's version of the gospel. Here we encounter his fascinating claim that Christian faith is nourished by an inexhaustible problematic that functions as the central clue to God:

> Christian worship sustains, as it were, an eternal, never to be consummated hunch, a heuristic vision which is accepted for the sake of its unresolvable tension. It is like an obsession with a problem known to be insoluble, which yet follows, against reason, unswervingly, the heuristic command: "Look at the unknown!" Christianity sedulously fosters, and in a sense permanently satisfies, man's craving for mental dissatisfaction by offering him the comfort of a crucified God.
>
> (Polanyi 1962, 199)

I am convinced that what we encounter in this postmodern formulation is a new insight into the depths of Luther's phrase.[6] The gospel according to Polanyi has to do with a "never to be consummated hunch," one that is sustained by liturgy so that the "unresolvable tension" intrinsic to that "craving for mental dissatisfaction" characterizing human intelligence is always confronted with "the comfort of a crucified God." One would be hard-pressed indeed to find a metaphor more in accordance with Ricoeur's insights than this last one. To speak of the *comfort* of a crucified God stretches the idea of category confusions to its outer limit. Even deeper, this hints at a haunting, intriguing thought. Clearly enough, Polanyi could never have said this had he not already been the scientist he was. Is the reverse the case? Is his contention that all human inquiry is informed by the maxim "We can know more than we can tell" itself theologically informed?

This question can neither be settled easily nor ignored. What can be argued is that with Polanyi the christological imagination is itself understood as the synergistic partner of liturgy. Is it also the root of the eschatological dimension without which Christian theology is impoverished? The answer to this question is Yes! But with Polanyi's thought before us, even this affirmation receives a new and compelling understanding. The problems with which he was initially concerned were scientific, and the epistemology for which he contended was ontic, so that the version of the gospel he proclaims carries with it the overtones of the natural. It is covered over with the indelible marks of inquiry into the only world we know—the *natural* world, which faith *confesses* to be *created*. As is the case with any scientist worth her or his salt, for Polanyi the question of evolution is beyond debate; but, he argues, it has been misconstrued: "Darwinism has diverted attention for a century from the descent of man by investigating the *conditions* of evolution and overlooking its *action*. Evolution can be understood only as a feat of emergence" (Polanyi 1962, 390). With this in mind, we can discern how deeply intertwined are science and faith in the work of this remarkable man. The closing paragraph of *Personal Knowledge* is a memorable example, par excellence, of heuristic theology at work:

> So far as we know, the tiny fragments of the universe embodied in man are the only centres of thought and responsibility in the visible world. If that be so, the appearance of the human mind has been so far the ultimate stage in the awakening of the world; and all that has gone before, the strivings of a myriad centres that have taken the risks of living and believing, seem to have all been pursuing, along rival lines, the aim now achieved by us up to this point. They are all akin to us. For all these centres—those which led up to our own existence and the far more numerous others which produced different lines of which many are extinct—may be seen engaged in the same endeavour towards *ultimate liberation*. We envisage then a cosmic field which called forth all these centres by offering them a short-lived, limited, hazardous opportunity for making some progress of their own towards an unthinkable consummation. And that is also, I believe, how a Christian is placed when worshipping God.
> (Polanyi 1962, 405; italics mine)

The constant struggle toward the "ultimate liberation" is at the heart of worship. Thus we arrive at the same point encountered in Ricoeur's incisive moves. The parable, so Ricoeur, is a metaphor that reverses our prevalent passion to replace images with concepts by insisting that we move in the opposite direction by thinking "according to a mode of thought which is not metaphorical for the sake of rhetoric, but for the sake of what it has to say" (Reagan and Stewart 1978, 242). Recall now that this led Ricoeur to contend that in the parables of Jesus

> no translation in abstract language is offered, only the violence of a language which, from the beginning to the end, *thinks through* the Metaphor and never *beyond*. The power of this language is that it abides to the end *within* the tension created by the images.
>
> (Reagan and Stewart 1978, 242)

As we have seen, in the light of Ricoeur's work it is virtually impossible to overstate the power of the parabolic. This underlies the fact that for him the parables, taken together, "say more than any rational theology." More can be said "in a parabolic way" than can be uttered in terms of "any kind of theory" (Reagan and Stewart 1978, 243). Such a passion will always be theologically restive until it encounters the faithfully ordered insight that a yearning for an "unthinkable consummation" characterizes the mood of a Christian worshiping God (Polanyi 1962, 405). Even then the restiveness will not disappear; it will be sanctified and challenged. What, in short, Ricoeur discerns in terms of metaphor and symbol Polanyi understands on a cosmic scale. Their discussions resonate so deeply that intertwining them is not only possible; it is necessary. In a mathematical sense, the thoughts of each can be "mapped" onto the insights of the other. When this happens, we arrive at the very nerve center of heuristic theology. For we know, and know that we know, that we will always know more than we can tell, on this side of the text, where the symbol gives rise to thought, having first given rise to speech.

NEW CONTEXTS, NEW WORDS

We live and work theologically in the era in which hermeneutics and heuristics intersect, demanding a creativity that knows that there is no interpretation worth our attention that is not open to discoveries that move beyond the very clarities evoking the interpretation itself, even possibly to the point of shattering them. This, now, is the real force of hearing Ricoeur's claim that we do our believing by interpreting. Believing is always on the move. Otherwise, it freezes into that orthodoxy that orthopraxis struggles to transcend.

New contexts evoke new words. This is the precondition of preaching, as every preacher worth her or his salt knows. This is why Troeltsch's demand that we must think thoughts never thought before does not fall on deaf ears if one seeks to listen to the summons of the relating/liberating/creating God. What happens when we search out new words in the name of the Christ of the contexts, whom we call the Christ, as Sittler said, because he was not centered on himself at all?

Metaphorical Theology

A truly remarkable figure in our midst has given us a set of works that show what happens when questions such as ours are taken with the utmost seriousness. Sallie McFague's *Speaking in Parables* (1975) manifested a promise that was fulfilled in her *Metaphorical Theology* (1982). It is with this work in mind that we must face the fact that the confession of what has always been known as the first article of the creed, "I believe in God the Father Almighty, maker of heaven and earth," is in trouble on two fronts, not just one. We now know that the latter half of this confessional affirmation, "maker of heaven and earth," can make sense only in terms of the phrase *creatio continua*. Creation is still under way. So far, so good. But what it has taken the struggle caught up in the women's liberation movement to show us is that the problem with the phrase "God the Father" is not a *simple* linguistic problem. Far more is at stake in the relentless demand for gender-inclusive language in speaking of the creating God than a mere changing of words. McFague sharply focuses this: "What is not named is not thought; symbol and concept go together and hence the form of the naming dictates the nature of the thought" (McFague 1982, 217–218 n. 31).

Again we encounter the central issue confronting us throughout the entirety of our discussion. It takes a *metaphorical* theology to unmask the idolatry intrinsic to freezing creativity in yesterday's insights. Only if our grasp of the struggle after ultimacy is growing and expanding can the oppressive restrictions of absolutizing yesterday as the only arena of imaginative insight be overcome. More than that, the world in which "the form of the naming dictates the nature of the thought" must recognize that *if the form of naming is fixed, there can be no thought about the unexpected, the genuinely new*. Any line of theological reflection that is open to this insight assumes that there is more to be understood *in the gospel itself* than has been understood so far.

The major breakthrough in McFague's thought is her insistence that we may no longer confine our understanding of the God of whom the gospel speaks to a single, regnant root-metaphor. Her use of this concept, derived from the thought of its originator, Stephen Pepper, leads her to assert that "the root-metaphor of Christianity is not God the father but the kingdom or rule of God, a relationship between the divine and the human that *no* model can encompass" (McFague 1982, 146). There is no single key concept in terms of which the gospel is to be grasped. This is the threshold across which lies the insight into the deci- sive issue at stake in the women's liberation movement. The problem may not be restricted to the metaphor, God the father, for it lies, rather, in the regnant insistence that absolutizes this metaphor in theological reflection. She is open to the fact that this judgment must pertain to her own suggestions. Though she develops a compelling case for thinking of God as friend, and thus overcoming the limits of parental models of either gender, she is equally compelling in claiming that she is not offer- ing a new root-metaphor. The nature of theological reflection inheres not in its *roots*, but in its *dynamisms*. Thus many metaphors come to mind, and all are valid as long as none is absolutized:

> The root-metaphor of Christianity is not *any one* model but a relationship that occurs between God and human beings. Many models are needed to intimate what that relationship is like; none can capture it.
>
> (McFague 1982, 190)

McFague's subsequent work has carried this insight into genuinely new realms of reflection. Her *Models of God: Theology for an Ecological, Nuclear Age* (1987) manifests even more powerfully than does *Meta- phorical Theology* the fact that her insights combine liberation concerns with those from theology on this side of the emergence of postmodern science. The most striking yield of this combination in her thought reaches sharp focus in an article epitomizing the 1987 volume, under the title "Models of God for an Ecological, Evolutionary Era: God as Mother of the Universe."

The subtitle of this remarkable article already alerts us to the sug- gestion McFague is now making. This, however, will not be truly as co- gent as in fact it is apart from a crucial clarification informing her thought. This is the delineation of the relationship between *metaphors* and *models*, and the risk that attends theological reflection that is knowl- edgeable concerning this relationship. McFague argues that metaphor "always has the character of 'is' and 'is not' '" because it entails an "asser-tion" that is "a likely account rather than a definition." Thus:

> To say "God is mother" is not to define God as mother, not to assert identity between the terms "God" and "mother," but to suggest that we consider what we do not know how to talk about—relating to God—through the metaphor of mother. The point that metaphor underscores is that in certain mat-ters there can be no direct description.
>
> (McFague 1988, 252–253)

This, as McFague contends, is precisely the juncture at which the exchanges between science and theology under way in these latter years have produced such suggestive leads for grasping the kind of creativity we now must attempt. These turn on the fact that "the use of meta-phors and models in natural and social sciences has widened the scope of metaphorical thinking considerably and linked science and theology methodologically in ways inconceivable twenty years ago" (McFague 1988, 253). In the light of this, McFague sets out the key differentiation:

> The difference between a metaphor and a model can be ex-pressed in a number of ways, but most simply, a model is a metaphor with "staying power," that is, a model is a meta-phor that has gained sufficient stability and scope so as to present a pattern for relatively comprehensive and coherent explanation. The metaphor of God the father is an excellent example of this. In becoming a model, it has engendered a wide-ranging interpretation of the relationship between God and human beings: if God is seen as father, human beings become children, sin can be seen as rebellious behavior, and redemption can be thought of as restoration to the status of favored offspring.
>
> (McFague 1988, 253)

The true persuasiveness of McFague's insight inheres in the risk being run in suggesting it. What is this risk? In a brief but telling refer-ence to Jacques Derrida, McFague takes on his insistence that "meta-phor lies somewhere between 'nonsense' and 'truth' '" by conceding that "a theology based on metaphor will be open to the charge that it is closer to the first than the second." Why this concession? McFague's answer is unequivocal: "This is, I believe, a risk theology in our time must be willing to run" (McFague 1988, 253).

A Risk Theology

The risk is demanded by the new context of the intersection of the theologies of liberation with theological reflection that comes after the rise of postmodern science. That it is a risk echoes the reasoning of Ricoeur. In the great struggle for meaning, he warned, no one goes unscathed. What shows up, though, in the midst of this struggle for meaning when one listens to the suggestions of McFague? "The 'wager' of this essay," she argues, "is the belief that to be a Christian is to be persuaded that there is a personal, gracious power who is on the side of life and its fulfillment, a power whom the paradigmatic figure Jesus of Nazareth expresses and illuminates" (McFague 1988, 254). This wager involves a massive claim indeed. Moreover, it manifests what she calls "a functional, pragmatic view of truth," one that can be tested only by "functional, rather than metaphysical criteria" and that awaits the verification of the church, "which in its wisdom must judge whether novel models are in continuity with the deepest beliefs that characterize the Christian faith" (McFague 1988, 254).

The wager McFague sets out is the wager caught up in the subtitle of the article. What are we suggesting when we think of God as Mother of the universe?

> In the Judaeo-Christian tradition, creation has been imaginatively pictured as an intellectual, aesthetic "act" of God, accomplished through God's word and wrought by God's "hands," much as a painting is created by an artist or a form by a sculptor. But the model of God as mother suggests a very different kind of creation, one which underscores the radical dependence of all things on God, but in an internal rather than an external fashion. Thus, if we wish to understand the world as in some fashion "in" God rather than God as in some fashion "in" the world, it is clearly the parent *as mother* that is the stronger candidate for an understanding of creation as bodied forth from the divine being. For it is the imagery of gestation, giving birth, and lactation that creates an imaginative picture of creation as profoundly dependent on and cared for by divine life.
>
> (McFague 1988, 256–257)

Note well that by now McFague has moved beyond her earlier suggestion regarding thinking of God as friend, and in so doing she has returned to thinking of God as parent, but in an entirely new mode. She does so on the ground that "there simply is no other imagery available to us that has this power for expressing the interdependence and inter-relatedness of all life with its ground" (McFague 1988, 257). In advocating this way of thinking, of imagining, McFague remains true to her abiding theme. No single metaphor, even this one, can be final. The suggestive character of authentically theological metaphors will always elaborate in their own way the maxim we learned from Polanyi. In saying what we can now say, we will encounter the fact that here, too, we can know more than we can tell. The received tradition is confronted with a new possibility, evoked by the new contexts within which we now know our own becoming. This "alternative imaginative picture" can be neither denied nor contained:

> The kind of creation that fits with this model is creation not as an intellectual act but as a physical event: the universe is bodied forth from God, it is expressive of God's very being: it could, therefore, be seen as God's "body." It is not something alien to God but is from the "womb" of God, formed through "gestation." There are some implications of this picture we need to follow out, but first we must remind ourselves once again that this is a picture—but then so is the artistic model. We are not claiming that God creates by giving birth to the world as her body; what we are suggesting is that the birth metaphor is both closer to the Christian faith and to a contemporary evolutionary, ecological context than the alternative craftsman model.
>
> (McFague 1988, 259)

The power of McFague's model is immense. We are now able to express the fact that "the universe and God are neither totally distant nor totally different" (McFague 1988, 259). We are also in possession of a way of expressing our faith in the creating God in a way that transcends the dualisms of past modes of thought, those of "body and mind, flesh and spirit, nature and humanity." Here McFague is particularly persuasive:

> God's body, that which supports life, is not matter or spirit but the matrix out of which everything evolves. In this picture, God is not spirit over against a universe of matter, with human beings dangling in between, chained to their bodies but eager to escape to the world of spirit. The universe, from God's being, is properly body (as well as spirit) because in some sense God is physical (as well as beyond the physical). This shocking idea—that God is physical—is one of the most

important implications of the model of creation by God the mother. It is an explicit rejection of Christianity's long, oppressive, and dangerous alliance with spirit against body, an alliance out of step with a holistic, evolutionary sensibility as well as with Christianity's Hebraic background.

(McFague 1988, 260)

Moreover, McFague's model yields a powerfully significant understanding of God's judgment upon our present involvement, and all others. Accordingly, there is in this way of speaking a new "clue to the nature of sin," one that theology in the mode of orthopraxis both needs and can put into action with great forcefulness as it begins to function in this mode. In the picture of "God as artist," the anger of God is rooted in the fact that "his good, pleasing creation is spoiled by what upsets its balance and harmony, or because what he molded rebels against the intended design," but in the picture of God as mother a quite different insight is at hand, for now:

God is angry because what comes from her being and belongs to her lacks the food and other necessities to grow and flourish. The mother-God as creator is necessarily judge, at the very basic level of condemning as the primary (though not the only) sin the inequitable distribution of basic necessities for the continuation of life in its many forms. In this view, sin is not "against God," the pride and rebellion of an inferior against a superior, but "against the body," the refusal to be part of an ecological whole whose continued existence and success depend upon a recognition of the interdependence and interrelatedness of all species.

(McFague 1988, 262)

McFague's sense of the limitations of her suggestion is as powerful as the suggestive character of her proposal, for as she claims, "We flesh out these metaphors and models sufficiently to see their implications and the case that can be made for them. Hence, although this theology 'says much,' it 'claims little' " (McFague 1988, 262). This is entirely in order, but one wonders even so whether it may prove to be the case that something irresistibly central in the faith has here received a holistic expression that will defy being forgotten. Polanyi is echoed once again. We cannot guess at a problem we have already solved. Given McFague's work, we no longer need to search for ways of saying that the creating God is on the same side of an expanding future that we are.

We now know how to express this. She is with us as a mother is with her child, for her child is bone of her bone, flesh of her flesh, with a body that originates as part of her own.

New contexts, new words. The relating/liberating/creating God shows us the liberation of relating creatively to the unfolding creativity in our midst. Revelation proceeds. We know, and know that we know, what we did not know before. An inexhaustible future awaits us too, then, for we shall know, even as we are known.

EPILOGUE

We are beyond the far horizon that was visible when we began. Attempting to respond to Troeltsch's challenge that we must think thoughts that have never been thought has forced us into altering the way we think. To understand revelation in processive terms is to alter the nature of theological reflection itself. For the theological assertion of the processive character of revelation is not only a theological statement; it is a statement about theological statements. To think theologically about theology is to encounter the risk of meta-theology. We began with the necessity of dealing with the contextual character of theology. But the context itself expands, and the dynamics intrinsic to the expansion manifest a fluidity all their own.

In the light of Troeltsch alone, we could say that the locus of theological creativity is discerned at those points where the ethic theology generates forces grappling with issues not yet confronted by theology itself. Now we must see that more than simply the ethical nature of theological reflection is at stake. What is involved is the contextual nature of ultimacy itself. The way ahead must always demand the expansion of the theological enterprise, but we must now understand this far more radically than ever before.

There is nothing new about the claim that any serious theological treatise points beyond itself to further reflection. We have always known this. But our times and places now demand that we see more clearly what we always should have known. The proleptic dimension of theology is not simplistically contextual; it is rooted, rather, in the nature of the God who is alive. We follow her into a future that has the ring of ultimacy, because ultimacy itself summons us into its own becoming. The biblical promise of this primordial companionship must say more to us now. The future is open to God as well as to ourselves. Our destiny is the sharing of God's own becoming. The relating God is liberating us into the possibility of participating in her creating work—now. This is the one who is always ahead of us, saying, "I am with you always, to the close of the age."

NOTES

CHAPTER 1.
THE DYNAMICS OF CONTEXTUAL THEOLOGY

1. In the preface of this remarkable book, Niebuhr notes that Ernst Troeltsch and Karl Barth have been his teachers, "though only through their writings." He then remarks: "I have tried to combine their main interests, for it appears to me that the critical thought of the former and the constructive work of the latter belong together. If I have failed the cause does not lie in the impossibility of the task. It is work that needs to be done" (Niebuhr 1941, x). I share this perspective to the letter, though I was able to study Barth in the flesh during a sabbatic leave in Basel in 1963–64. It will be clear that at countless points these two figures have influenced my work heavily. Accordingly, I know from the inside why Niebuhr included his disclaimer. I share this too. The task is indeed formidable, though not impossible. If anything, it demands attention now even more urgently than it did when Niebuhr wrote his incisive essay.

2. See Niebuhr 1941, 132ff., and Troeltsch 1925, 40ff.

3. For my own detailed discussion of these particular developments, see my *Theology in Red, White, and Black* (1975).

4. This distortion of Harnack's own title obscures completely the fact that Troeltsch's response to it—in which he relates his own understanding of the history of Christianity, as this emerged in his massive *The Social Teaching of the Christian Churches* (Troeltsch 1931), to Harnack's—pivoted on the understanding of this phrase.

5. This article is now available in English translation. Robert Morgan and Michael Pye include it in their very useful collection, *Ernst Troeltsch: Writings on Theology and Religion* (1977, 124ff.). Pye does the translation of this particular item. Equally good fortune had them include an extensive and incisive note by Stephen Sykes, delineating the many changes that set in between the original publication of the article and its final form in the *Gesammelte Schriften*, II, in 1913. See Morgan and Pye 1977, 180–181, for Sykes's note. In this connection,

notice should also be indicated concerning Sykes's very significant discussion, *The Identity of Christianity*, which appeared in 1984; the issue at hand plays a central role in his argument (see Sykes 1984, esp. 152ff.). It will become evident that I resonate deeply with his discussion.

6. For my understanding of this, Troeltsch's first major work, see my *Toward a Theology of Involvement* (1966, 25ff. and 90ff.).

7. This article first appeared in English in *The American Journal of Theology* 17, no. 1 (January 1913): 1–21, because it was requested by the editors of this journal. The translation does not appear to have been Troeltsch's own, though no translator is indicated. The German text was included in the second volume of the *Gesammelte Schriften*, and my own translation is of a passage on p. 511 of that volume.

8. So Lehmann told me. This was inscribed on his copy of Bonhoeffer's *Akt und Sein*.

9. Bethge himself indicates this in his "Paul Lehmann's Initiative," in the issue of the *Union Seminary Quarterly Review* devoted to articles in celebration of Lehmann's work (vol. 29, nos. 3 and 4 [Spring and Summer 1974]: 151–152). This issue contains my own discussion of Lehmann's work under the title "The Context of Contextual Theology" (pp. 153–167).

10. For my treatment of Bonhoeffer's thought as a whole, see my *The Promise of Bonhoeffer* (1969).

11. See Polanyi 1962, 11. Polanyi is quoting (and translating) Einstein's 1905 article "Zur Elektrodynamik bewegter Körper."

CHAPTER 2.
THE RELATING GOD

1. All references to the *Institutes* will be given in terms of the standard notation: capital Roman number for the book, lowercase Roman number for the chapter, and Arabic number for the paragraph. Added in brackets is the page number for the definitive English translation of the *Institutes*. This is the edition in the Library of Christian Classics, edited by John T. McNeill and translated by Ford Lewis Battles (McNeill and Battles 1960).

2. For a more comprehensive analysis of Calvin's thought in this regard, see my *A Reading of Calvin's Institutes* (1991).

3. At the same time, let it be noted that Calvin's thought will be misunderstood unless one takes into account that he was a Renaissance thinker as well as a reformer. The best recent treatment of this is the incisive discussion by William Bouwsma in his *John Calvin: A Sixteenth-Century Portrait* (Bouwsma 1988).

4. See Dowey 1952, 8. Dowey's *The Knowledge of God in Calvin's Theology* joins Bouwsma's discussion as one of the key books for my understanding Calvin's thought. McNeill indicates that Dowey "provided the materials that have been incorporated in numerous theological notes in Books I and II [of the McNeill-Battles translation of the *Institutes*]" (McNeill and Battles 1960, xx).

5. References to Barth's *Church Dogmatics*, II/2, are from the English translation (Barth 1957), and will be indicated by *CD*, followed by the page number.

References to the original German text (Barth 1942) will be indicated by *KD*, followed by the page number.

6. It is also the case that Barth was closer to Schleiermacher than he was willing to admit (though he maintained a lifelong fascination with Schleiermacher's thought). This is remarkably germane to the argument developed here. Barth's insistence on the asymmetric relationship between the Yes and No of the gospel turns on his view that the doctrine of sin can be understood only in terms of the doctrine of grace. This leads to his celebrated discussion of The Nothing (*Das Nichtige*) in *Church Dogmatics*, III/3. Here he insists that The Nothing can only be understood in terms of the grace of God. In the most incisive treatment of Schleiermacher to be found in his writings (Barth 1960, 324ff.), he notes that Schleiermacher had understood this too. This mystified Barth (see Barth 1960, 326); I for one am convinced that his mystification would have either deepened or disappeared had he lived to develop a discussion of his doctrine of redemption, the proposed subject matter for the unwritten Volume V of the *KD*. I am even bold enough to think that what I am saying in this chapter bears some resemblance to what that discussion might have entailed.

7. *The Book of Confessions* of the Presbyterian Church (U.S.A.) contains the confessional documents normative for that church. References to these documents are not given by page numbers, but by the number of the document and the number(s) of the paragraph(s) being cited. The number preceding the decimal point indicates the document; the number(s) following the decimal point, the paragraph(s). It should be noted that the Confession of 1967 was heavily influenced by the theology of Karl Barth. This makes the citations here considered all the more remarkable.

CHAPTER 3.
THE LIBERATING GOD

1. I concur with Eberhard Bethge's suggestion that this is indeed a new christological title. Bethge so argues in his "Bonhoeffer's Christology and his 'Religionless Christianity' " (Bethge 1968, 56–57).

2. One often encounters the contention that this is not the case, particularly in students who enter serious theological study by way of the works of the liberation theologians. The claim that we need new action, not new concepts, is not only a half-truth; it is potentially a deadly error. As has been contended throughout the present discussion, ours is a time that demands thoughts that have never been thought before. What is now clear is that only a genuine orthopraxis, involving action and reflection in synergistic interrelationship, will yield such thoughts, accompanying, informing, and being generated by the actions now evoked by the contexts in which we know our own becoming.

3. The central contention informing Whitehead's thought as a whole receives its most succinct formulation in the work that is the real key to the full range of his philosophical writings, *Science and the Modern World* (1925). He spoke of a "provisional realism," which at that point was all that he wished to clarify. This

is at least ironic, because this "provisional realism" becomes the central pivot of all that he had to say:

> We can be content with a provisional realism in which nature is conceived as a complex of prehensive unifications. Space and time exhibit the general scheme of interlocked relations of these prehensions. You cannot tear any one of them out of its context. Yet each one of them within its context has all the reality that attaches to the whole complex. Conversely, the totality has the same reality as each prehension; for each prehension unifies the modalities to be ascribed, from its standpoint, to every part of the whole. A prehension is a process of unifying. Accordingly, nature is a process of expansive development, necessarily transitional from prehension to prehension. What is achieved is thereby passed beyond, but it is also retained as having aspects of itself present to prehensions which lie beyond it.
>
> (Whitehead 1925, 72)

Note well in this complex but epitomizing passage the relational understanding of reality is what engenders the understanding of development. Thus *process* thought emerges as the result of the claim that nothing can be understood in itself. Or, to put it positively, everything must be understood in terms of the dynamic context of which it is a part. Given this, the way is prepared for the central syllogism informing the entire range of Whitehead's philosophical writings, and these lines follow immediately the ones just cited: "Thus nature is a structure of evolving processes. The reality is the process" (Whitehead 1925, 72).

4. So Robert Morgan translates the title of Troeltsch's work in the collection he and Michael Pye brought out in 1977 (see Morgan and Pye 1977, 182ff.). Troeltsch's actual title was *Die Bedeutung der Geschichtlichkeit Jesu für den Glauben* (Troeltsch 1911). I question the translation of "Geschichtlichkeit" by the phrase "Historical Existence." I would much prefer the translation of the title to read "The Significance of the Historicity of Jesus for Faith." Morgan's rendering reads too much existentialism into Troeltsch, as far as I am concerned, even though I am delighted that he and Pye have worked out the collection of translated articles with this as one of their selections.

5. I concur completely with the remarkably incisive study of Troeltsch's thoughts concerning Christology by Sarah Coakley, *Christ Without Absolutes* (1988).

6. I find the work of Stephen Sykes particularly illuminating in this connection. His careful delineation of the development of Troeltsch's reflections on the essence of Christianity (see Sykes 1976) is epitomized in his note appended to the translation of "What Does 'Essence of Christianity' Mean?" in the Morgan and Pye collection (Morgan and Pye 1977, 180–181). Sykes develops his own constructive suggestions in this connection in his incisive discussion of *The Identity of Christianity: Theologians and the Essence of Christianity from Schleiermacher*

to Barth (Sykes 1984). I sense a deep resonance between his reflections and the conclusions I am reaching here.

7. The text of the Theological Declaration of Barmen may be found in *The Book of Confessions* of the Presbyterian Church (U.S.A.); it is confessional document 8 (Theological Declaration of Barmen 1934). It is one of the formally adopted confessional documents of this church and accordingly has confessional status in this communion. See *The Constitution of the Presbyterian Church (U.S.A.), Part I, The Book of Confessions,* published by the Office of the General Assembly of the Presbyterian Church (U.S.A.), Louisville, Kentucky.

CHAPTER 4.
THE CREATING GOD

1. In December 1987, the Task Force on Theology and Cosmology of the Presbyterian Church (U.S.A.) conducted a consultation on "The Church and Contemporary Cosmology: Implications of Science for Christian Life and Thought." I was one of the participants, and the paper I prepared, under the title for this section, is slightly adapted for inclusion here. It was originally published in 1990 as part of the proceedings of this consultation and was entitled *The Church and Contemporary Society,* edited by James B. Miller and Kenneth E. McCall.

2. My understanding of heuristic theology is closely related to that delineated by Sallie McFague (see McFague 1987, xi and 192–193 n. 37; and McFague 1988, 250–252). There are, however, differences, and they are significant. Her distinction between heuristic theology, on the one hand, and hermeneutical and constructive theology, on the other (see McFague, 1987, 36), is one I do not share. I think that heuristic theology has to do with the doctrine of God, not just with our metaphoric imaginations concerning the doctrine of God, intrinsic though these are to understanding the processive character of revelation. Even so, I quite agree with McFague's insistence that our advances on these fronts are at best "small" (McFague 1987, xi), and certainly she is helpful in clarifying so incisively the fact that literalization of our metaphors can only lead us into the fundamentalist cul-de-sac. When I speak of the becoming of God as the real source of the heuristic character of our reflection on the relationship between God and the world, I am surely as metaphorical in what I say as McFague is. It may prove instructive, however, that my attempts lean more in the direction of coming to terms with the activity of God than does McFague's brilliant discussion of God as the Mother of the universe, and the universe as God's body. Clearly, I find McFague's work indispensable for what I am trying to say, but I am convinced that her insights are more significant than she seems to think, given the distinction she presses. There is a vectorial character to our advances on the metaphorical front. Once new insights are seen, they cannot be forgotten. As Polanyi has shown us, we cannot guess at problems we have already solved. We are beyond the struggle that led to these new formulations. McFague's work as a whole is exemplary of the interlinking of heuristics and hermeneutics. Discovery and interpretation go hand in hand as her creativity unfolds. This is heuristic theology par excellence.

3. Not "What philosophy organizes . . . ," as the English translation has it; cf. *Le Conflit des Interprétations*, p. 338: "Ce que la théologie ordonne au foyer christologique du témoignage, la philosophie de la religion l'ordonne au désir d'être de l'homme."

4. In the summer of 1977, just as my own detailed and comprehensive study of Ricoeur's thought was getting under way, I had the good fortune to make the acquaintance of Beatriz Melano Couch. She had by then completed her dissertation on Ricoeur's theory of interpretation for the Protestant faculty of the University of Strasbourg. Melano Couch helped me to see that Ricoeur's hermeneutic turns on his study of Freud, and that this informs his grasp of the *conflict* of interpretations. Thus I had the advantage of knowing this as I proceeded into the study, among other things, of the collection Ricoeur brought out under this title.

5. "Listening to the Parables of Jesus" was published in *Criterion* 13 (1974): 18–22 [Reagan and Stewart 1978, 214]. Charles E. Reagan and David Stewart included it in their *The Philosophy of Paul Ricoeur: An Anthology of His Work* in 1978; this is the source of the citation.

6. Jürgen Moltmann, in his memorable and incisive *The Crucified God*, notes this same passage (see Moltmann 1974, 77 n. 20). It is an open question, however, as to whether he realizes that his study exemplifies Polanyi's insight, rather than the reverse. On this side of Polanyi's work, no treatment of the crucified God, even one so instructive as Moltmann's, can be final.

WORKS CITED

Barbour, Ian
1966   *Issues in Science and Religion.* San Francisco: Harper Torchbooks, 1971. (Originally published by Prentice-Hall, Englewood Cliffs, N.J., 1966.)
1968   *Science and Religion: New Perspectives on the Dialogue.* New York: Harper & Row.
1974   *Myths, Models and Paradigms: A Comparative Study in Science and Religion.* San Francisco: Harper & Row.

Barth, Karl
1942   *Die kirchliche Dogmatik,* II/2. Zollikon-Zürich: Evangelischer Verlag A.G.
1949   *Dogmatics in Outline.* Translated by G. T. Thomson. New York: Philosophical Library. (Originally published in German in 1947 as *Dogmatik im Grundriss* by Christian Kaiser Verlag und Evangelischer Verlag.)
1957   *Church Dogmatics,* II/2. Translated by G. W. Bromiley, J. C. Campbell, Iain Wilson, J. Strathearn McNab, Harold Knight, and R. A. Stewart. Edinburgh: T. & T. Clark.
1960   *Church Dogmatics,* III/3. Translated by G. W. Bromiley and R. J. Ehrlich. Edinburgh: T. & T. Clark. (Originally published in German in 1950 by Evangelischer Verlag A. G., Zollikon-Zürich.)
1963   *Evangelical Theology: An Introduction.* Translated by Grover Foley. New York: Holt, Rinehart & Winston.

Bethge, Eberhard
1967   *Dietrich Bonhoeffer: Theologe, Christ, Zeitgenosse.* Munich: Chr. Kaiser Verlag.
1968   "Bonhoeffer's Christology and his 'Religionless Christianity.'" In *Bonhoeffer in a World Come of Age,* edited by Peter Vorkink II, 46–72. Philadelphia: Fortress Press.
1974   "Paul Lehmann's Initiative." *Union Seminary Quarterly Review* 29, nos. 3 and 4 (Spring and Summer 1974): 151–152.

Birch, Charles
1975   "What Does God Do in the World?" *Union Seminary Quarterly Review*
        30, nos. 2–4 (Winter–Summer 1975): 76–84.
1977   "Can Evolution Be Accounted for Solely in Terms of Mechanical Cau-
        sation?" In *Mind and Nature*, edited by John B. Cobb, Jr., and David
        Ray Griffin, 13–18. Washington, D.C.: University Press of America.
1979   "Nature, God and Humanity in Ecological Perspective." *Christianity &*
        Crisis 39, no. 16 (October 29, 1979): 259–266.
1980   "Nature, Humanity and God in Ecological Perspective." In *Faith and*
        Science in an Unjust World. Report of the World Council of Churches'
        Conference on Faith, Science and the Future, Massachusetts Institute
        of Technology, Cambridge, December 12–24, 1979. Vol. 1, *Plenary*
        Presentations. Edited by Roger L. Shinn. Philadelphia: Fortress Press.
        An adapted epitomization of this address was published in *Christianity*
        & Crisis 39, no. 16 (October 19, 1979) under the title "Yahweh Ques-
        tions a Modern Job."

Birch, Charles and John B. Cobb, Jr.
1981   *The Liberation of Life: From the Cell to the Community*. Cambridge: Cam-
        bridge University Press.

Bohm, David
1980   *Wholeness and the Implicate Order*. London: Routledge & Kegan Paul.

Bonhoeffer, Dietrich
1955   *Schöpfung und Fall*. In *Theologische Auslegung von Genesis 1 bis 3*. 3d ed.
        Munich: Chr. Kaiser Verlag. Translated by John C. Fletcher. New York:
        Macmillan Co., 1959. Paperback ed., 1965 (includes Temptation).
1963   *The Cost of Discipleship*. Translated with a memoir by G. Leibholz.
        New York: Macmillan Co. First ed., abr., 1948. 2d ed., unabr. and rev.,
        1959. Paperback ed., 1963. Translation of Nachfolge, 1937.
1965   *Ethics*. Edited by Eberhard Bethge. Translated by Neville Horton
        Smith. New York: Macmillan Co., 1955. Paperback ed. (following the
        order of the 6th German ed.), 1965.
1967   *Letters and Papers from Prison*. Edited by Eberhard Bethge. Translated
        by Reginald H. Fuller. London: SCM Press. 1st ed., 1953. 2d ed., rev.,
        1956. American ed. entitled *Prisoner for God*. New York: Macmillan
        Co., 1954. Paperback ed. entitled *Letters and Papers from Prison*, 1962.
        3d ed., rev. and enlarged. New York: Macmillan Co., 1967. Paperback
        ed., 1967. Translation of Wiederstand and Ergebung.

Bouwsma, William J.
1988   *John Calvin: A Sixteenth-Century Portrait*. New York and Oxford: Ox-
        ford University Press.

Brown, Delwin
1981   *To Set at Liberty: Christian Faith and Human Freedom*. Maryknoll, N.Y.:
        Orbis Books.

Brunner, Emil
1952   *The Christian Doctrine of Creation and Redemption.* Vol. 2 of *Dogmatics.* Translated by Olive Wyon. Philadelphia: Westminster Press. Preface to German original dated August 1949.

Coakley, Sarah
1988   *Christ Without Absolutes: A Study of the Christology of Ernst Troeltsch.* Oxford: Clarendon Press.

Confession of 1967, The
        Document 9 in *The Book of Confessions of the Presbyterian Church (U.S.A.).* Louisville, Ky.: The Office of the General Assembly of the Presbyterian Church (U.S.A.).

Dowey, Edward A., Jr.
1952   *The Knowledge of God in Calvin's Theology.* New York: Columbia University Press.

Ferré, Frederick
1969   "Mapping the Logic of Models in Science and Theology." In *New Essays on Religious Language,* edited by Dallas M. High, 54–96. New York: Oxford University Press. Reprinted from *The Christian Scholar* 46 (1963).

Freire, Paulo
1972   *Pedagogy of the Oppressed.* Translated by Myra Berggman Ramos. New York: Herder & Herder. (Originally published in Portuguese, 1968.)

Heisenberg, Werner
1983   *Tradition in Science.* New York: Seabury Press.

Herzog, Frederick
1972   *Liberation Theology: Liberation in the Light of the Fourth Gospel.* New York: Seabury Press.

Hofstadter, Douglas R.
1980   *Gödel, Escher, Bach: An Eternal Golden Braid.* New York: Random House, Vintage Books. (Originally published by Basic Books, New York, 1979.)

Lehmann, Paul
1953   "The Foundation and Pattern of Christian Behaviour." In *Christian Faith and Social Action,* edited by John A. Hutchison, 93–116. New York: Charles Scribner's Sons.
1963   *Ethics in a Christian Context.* New York and Evanston: Harper & Row.
1972   "Contextual Theology." *Theology Today* 29, no. 1 (April 1972): 3–8.

1975   *The Transfiguration of Politics.* New York: Evanston, San Francisco, London: Harper & Row.

McFague, Sallie
1975   *Speaking in Parables: A Study in Metaphor and Theology.* Philadelphia: Fortress Press.
1982   *Metaphorical Theology: Models of God in Religious Language.* Philadelphia: Fortress Press.
1987   *Models of God: Theology for an Ecological, Nuclear Age.* Philadelphia: Fortress Press.
1988   "Models of God for an Ecological, Evolutionary Era: God as Mother of the Universe." In *Physics, Philosophy, and Theology: A Common Quest for Understanding,* edited by Robert J. Russell, William R. Stoeger, S.J., and George V. Coyne, S.J., 249–271. Vatican City State: Vatican Observatory.

McNeill, John T., and Ford Lewis Battles
1960   *John Calvin: Institutes of the Christian Religion.* Edited by John T. McNeill. Translated by Ford Lewis Battles. Philadelphia: Westminster Press. (Vols. 20 and 21 of The Library of Christian Classics.)

Moltmann, Jürgen
1974   *The Crucified God.* New York, Evanston, San Francisco, London: Harper & Row.

Morgan, Robert, and Michael Pye
1977   *Ernst Troeltsch: Writings on Theology and Religion.* Atlanta: John Knox Press. Paperback ed. by Westminster/John Knox Press, Louisville, Ky., 1990.

Nagel, Ernest, and James R. Newman
1956   "Gödel's Proof." In *The World of Mathematics,* vol. 3. Edited, with commentaries and notes, by James R. Newman, 1668–1695. New York: Simon & Schuster.

Niebuhr, H. Richard
1941   *The Meaning of Revelation.* New York: Macmillan Co.

Pagels, Heinz
1983   *The Cosmic Code: Quantum Physics as the Language of Nature.* New York: Bantam Books. (Originally published by Simon & Schuster, 1982.)

Peacocke, Arthur
1979   *Creation and the World of Science.* Oxford: Clarendon Press.
1986   *God and the New Biology.* San Francisco: Harper & Row.

Polanyi, Michael
1962   *Personal Knowledge: Towards a Post-Critical Philosophy.* Chicago: University of Chicago Press. Corrected ed., 1962. (Originally published, 1958.)
1967   *The Tacit Dimension.* Garden City, N.Y.: Doubleday Anchor Books. (Originally published, 1966.)

Polanyi, Michael, and Harry Prosch
1975   *Meaning.* Chicago: University of Chicago Press.

Reagan, Charles E., and David Stewart
1978   *The Philosophy of Paul Ricoeur: An Anthology of His Work.* Boston: Beacon Press.

Reist, Benjamin A.
1966   *Toward a Theology of Involvement: The Thought of Ernst Troeltsch.* Philadelphia: Westminster Press.
1969   *The Promise of Bonhoeffer.* Philadelphia: J. B. Lippincott.
1974   "The Context of Contextual Theology." *Union Seminary Quarterly Review* 29, nos. 3 and 4 (Spring and Summer 1974): 153–167.
1975   *Theology in Red, White, and Black.* Philadelphia: Westminster Press.
1983   "Faith and the Natural Sciences: Focus on the Thought of Michael Polanyi." *Pacific Theological Review* 16, no. 3 (Spring 1983): 3–11.
1983   "Ricoeur for Preachers." *Homiletic* 8, no. 2 (1983): 1–6.
1985   "New Theological Horizons in the Light of Postmodern Science." *Pacific Theological Review* 18, no. 3 (Spring 1985): 4–15.
1986   "Dogmatics in Process." *Pacific Theological Review* 19, no. 3 (Spring 1986): 4–21.
1990   "Theology and Biology." In *The Church and Contemporary Cosmology: Proceedings of a Consultation of the Presbyterian Church (U.S.A.),* edited by James B. Miller and Kenneth E. McCall, 271–295. Pittsburgh: Carnegie Mellon University Press.
1991   *A Reading of Calvin's "Institutes."* Louisville, Ky.: Westminster/John Knox Press.

Ricoeur, Paul
1965   *History and Truth.* Translated with an introduction by Charles Kelbey. Evanston, Ill.: Northwestern University Press. (Originally published as *Histoire et vérité,* 1955 and 1964.)
1967   *The Symbolism of Evil.* Translated by Emerson Buchanan. New York: Harper & Row; and Boston: Beacon Press, 1969. (Originally published as *La Symbolique du mal,* 1960.)
1974   *The Conflict of Interpretations: Essays in Hermeneutics.* Edited by Don Ihde. Evanston, Ill.: Northwestern University Press. (Originally published as *Le Conflit des Interprétations: Essais d'herméneutique,* 1969.)
1976   *Interpretation Theory: Discourse and the Surplus of Meaning.* Fort Worth: Texas Christian University Press.

Russell, Letty
1974   *Human Liberation in a Feminist Perspective: A Theology.* Philadelphia: Westminster Press.

Schilling, Harold K.
1973   *The New Consciousness in Science and Religion.* Philadelphia: United Church Press. (A Pilgrim Press Book.)

Segundo, Juan Luis, S.J.
1976   *The Liberation of Theology.* Translated by John Drury. Maryknoll, N.Y.: Orbis Books.

Sittler, Joseph
1972   *Essays on Nature and Grace.* Philadelphia: Fortress Press.

Sykes, Stephen
1976   "Ernst Troeltsch and Christianity's Essence." In *Ernst Troeltsch and the Future of Theology,* edited by John Powell Clayton, 139–171. Cambridge: Cambridge University Press.
1984   *The Identity of Christianity: Theologians and the Essence of Christianity from Schleiermacher to Barth.* Philadelphia: Fortress Press.

Teilhard de Chardin, Pierre
1955   *The Phenomenon of Man.* Translated by Bernard Wall, with an introduction by Julian Huxley. London: William Collins Sons; and New York: Harper & Row, 1959. Harper Torchbook ed., 1961. (The title of the French original is *Le Phénomene Humain.*)
1959   *The Future of Man.* Translated by Norman Denny. New York and Evanston: Harper & Row.

Theological Declaration of Barmen, The
1934   Document 8 in *The Book of Confessions of the Presbyterian Church (U.S.A.).* Louisville, Ky.: The Office of the General Assembly of the Presbyterian Church (U.S.A.).

Troeltsch, Ernst
1903   "Was heisst 'Wesen des Christentums'?" In *Gesammelte Schriften,* II, pp. 386–451. Tübingen: J. C. B. Mohr (Paul Siebeck).
1911   *Die Bedeutung der Geschichtlichkeit Jesu für den Glauben.* Tübingen: J. C. B. Mohr (Paul Siebeck). Translated by Robert Morgan as "The Significance of the Historical Existence of Jesus for Faith." In *Ernst Troeltsch: Writings on Theology and Religion,* translated and edited by Robert Morgan and Michael Pye, 182ff. Atlanta: John Knox Press, 1977.
1912   *Die Soziallehren der christlichen Kirchen und Gruppen.* Published as *Gesammelte Schriften,* I. Tübingen: J. C. B. Mohr (Paul Siebeck).
1913   "The Dogmatics of the *'religionsgeschichtliche Schule.'"* *The American*

Journal of Theology 27, no. 1 (January 1913): 1–21. (German text: *Gesammelte Schriften*, II, pp. 500–524.)

1922   *Der Historismus und seine Probleme*. Published as *Gesammelte Schriften*, III. Tübingen: J. C. B. Mohr (Paul Siebeck).

1925   *Glaubenslehre: Nach Heidelberger Vorlesungen aus den Jahren 1911 und 1912, mit einem Vorwort von Marta Troeltsch*. Munich and Leipzig: Duncker & Humblot. (From the notes of Gertrud von le Fort.)

1931   *The Social Teaching of the Christian Churches*. Translated by Olive Wyon. London: George Allen & Unwin.

Whitehead, Alfred North

1925   *Science and the Modern World*. New York: The Free Press, a division of Macmillan Co., 1967. (Originally published by Macmillan Co., 1925.)

1929   *Process and Reality: An Essay in Cosmology*. Corrected ed. Edited by David Ray Griffin and Donald W. Sherburne. New York: The Free Press, a division of Macmillan Co., 1978. (Originally published by Macmillan Co., 1929.)

INDEX